The joy of discovering our rich literary legacy is greatly enhanced whenever we have the gift of wise guides to steer us clear of the many hazards pointing us toward the grand vistas of delight. Elizabeth McCallum Marlow is just such a guide, and this latest book of hers is just such a gift. This is a book for teachers, for parents, for writers—really, for all readers who desire to grow in their appreciation and understanding of the written word.

> George Grant, MA, D.Litt, PhD, D.Hum, D.Min.Cand.
> Pastor, Parish Presbyterian Church, Franklin, TN
> Director, King's Meadow Study Center
> Founder, Franklin Classical School and New College
> Franklin

By creating *How to Teach Literature: Introductory Course*, Elizabeth Marlow has given students and teachers of 9th grade literature a treasure. Her work is firmly founded on a deep love of literature, a hard-earned knowledge of the subject, a Christian understanding of the philosophies and issues of literature, and thirty-five years' experience teaching literature to high school and college students. Her knowledge, experience, and discernment have led her to select an excellent content for this invaluable teaching resource. Here is sage advice for teachers on dealing with authors' creations and students' attitudes, and here are intensely practical teaching tools like reading lists, assignments, class activities, and handouts. This is *the* work for the teacher of 9th grade literature—in the home school, Christian school, public school, and college—to have, ponder, and use. Experienced or not, you will find this book delightful, wise, and powerfully useful. Your students will receive immense practical and lasting benefits from your use of Elizabeth's teaching guide.

> Archie P. Jones, PhD
> University professor and author of
> *The Gateway to Liberty: The Constitutional Power of the Tenth Amendment*
> *The Influence of Historic Christianity on Early America*
> and other works on Christianity and the US
> Constitution

If you feel as if you are facing Everest as you contemplate teaching literature, Elizabeth's book provides the wisdom and experience of a teacher who knows every step of the journey whom you can trust to lead you safely to the summit. Elizabeth is passionate about teaching and has a heartfelt love for literature. She has written a series of textbooks detailing techniques she has used over the years. These books are the fruit of thirty–five years of experience in the classroom. They provide a well-traveled path for teachers who want to inspire their students with an appreciation for the breadth and depth of literary works. Elizabeth's writing style is clear and practical; she provides guidance for understanding literature through teaching techniques that make us feel like "anyone can teach." Elizabeth equips teachers with ways to spark a deep love for literature.

> Matthew Bullard, BA, MA
> Director of Christian Education
> Parkway Presbyterian Church, Cumming, GA

Elizabeth McCallum Marlow has developed a quality comprehensive guide for the teaching community based on her thirty-five years of experience and her passion for literature. Teaching professionals will find her tried and true practices to be invaluable.

> Johnathan Arnold, MBA, M.Ed, D.Ed.Min
> Headmaster
> Covenant Christian Academy
> Cumming, GA

How to Teach Literature: Introductory Course by Elizabeth McCallum Marlow is a thorough, traditional approach to teaching classic literature. The author's emphases on reading and writing will aid teachers, novices, and veterans to build a solid curriculum. This volume includes many supplemental resources and student-centered activities. The guide is a valuable tool for teachers.

> Jane Ferguson, M.Ed, Ed.S
> High School English Teacher and College English
> Instructor
> Truett McConnell College, GA
> University of Georgia, Athens, GA

Inspiring high school students to gaze across the landscape of literature is not only part of the legacy of Elizabeth Marlow's thirty–five years as an English teacher but one of her greatest passions and a source of joy. In these pages, she welcomes us into her library of literature to sit down for tea, teacher to teacher, and stay a while as she generously pours out cup after cup of her wealth of knowledge and teaching experience.

> Kathy Bailey, BA, MA
> Head of School, Clapham School, Wheaton, IL

I was thrilled to learn of Elizabeth Marlow's new 9th grade *How to Teach Literature: Introductory Course*. It is a wonderful resource for the homeschooling parent that is well-balanced, thorough, and insightful. Especially appreciated is the chapter organization according to literary device—brilliant! Mrs. Marlow shares her years of experience and wisdom about carefully selected content and teaching techniques. I highly recommend this wonderful textbook to any and all homeschool parents and other teachers of freshman high school students.

Melanie Anderson, BS
Veteran homeschool mom

Also by Elizabeth McCallum Marlow

How to Teach British Literature: A Practical Teaching Guide

Westbow Press, Copyright 2017.

How to Teach British Literature: Student Review Questions and Tests

Westbow Press, Copyright 2018.

How to Teach American Literature: A Practical Teaching Guide

Westbow Press, Copyright 2017.

How to Teach American Literature: Student Review Questions and Tests

Westbow Press, Copyright 2018.

How to Teach World Literature: A Practical Teaching Guide

Westbow Press, Copyright 2018.

How to Teach World Literature: Student Review Questions and Tests

Westbow Press, Copyright 2018.

Co-authored by Elizabeth McCallum Marlow

The Book Tree: A Christian Reference for Children's Literature,

Canon Press, Copyright 2001, 2008 second edition.

HOW TO TEACH
LITERATURE

INTRODUCTORY COURSE

ELIZABETH MCCALLUM MARLOW

WESTBOW
PRESS®
A DIVISION OF THOMAS NELSON
& ZONDERVAN

The author and publisher gratefully acknowledge permission to reprint material from the following:
Peter J. Leithart, *Heroes of the City of Man: A Christian Guide to Select Ancient Literature* (Moscow, ID: Canon Press, 1999) by permission.
Leland Ryken, *Homer's The Odyssey* (Wheaton, IL: Crossway, 2013) by permission.
Leland Ryken, *Realms of Gold: The Classics in Christian Perspective* (Wheaton, IL: Harold Shaw, 1991) by permission.

Scripture taken from the New King James Version®. Copyright © 1982 by Thomas Nelson. Used by permission. All rights reserved.

WestBow Press books may be ordered through booksellers or by contacting:

WestBow Press
A Division of Thomas Nelson & Zondervan
1663 Liberty Drive
Bloomington, IN 47403
www.westbowpress.com
1 (866) 928-1240

ISBN: 978-1-9736-4847-5 (sc)
ISBN: 978-1-9736-4848-2 (e)

Library of Congress Control Number: 2018914676

Print information available on the last page.

WestBow Press rev. date: 01/23/2019

This book is dedicated to my dearest husband,

Bill Marlow.

Without his constant encouragement and advice,

as well as technical and editing skills,

these teaching guides would not have been written.

English teachers everywhere

are my inspiration for this series of teaching guides.

I have written these books for you.

Contents

How to Teach Literature: A Practical Teaching Guide

Preface

Teaching literature is a joyful thing. It offers the teacher an opportunity to open up new worlds for young people—cultures, time periods, problems and circumstances they have never thought about before. The study of great literary works allows teenagers to vicariously experience new ways of looking at life and to ponder decisions people make, emotions they yield to, hardships they suffer. Via reading, they learn how to relate to others in their own lives and how to cope with their own conflicting impulses. Reading great literature matures them into thoughtful, compassionate human beings and instills in them the joy of reading. Teaching the subject is challenging, but it yields delightful benefits for both teacher and students.

Antoine de Saint-Exupéry once commented, "If you want to build a ship, don't drum up people to collect wood and don't assign them tasks and work, but rather teach them to long for the endless immensity of the sea."[1] Instead of telling students that many works they are about to read are esoteric pieces they will have to stumble through, the wise teacher talks about the benefits they will gain from the literature they read and the sheer fun of literary study. After all, God made human beings to want to learn. Teachers should do their best to ensure that young people learn to the best of their ability.

Inevitably, I've learned to avoid some teaching pitfalls and to use methods that usually work. I've learned a lot about teenagers. Most of them love the subject, get the reading bug, and thrive. Some of them, subconsciously at any rate, realize they must acquire a high school diploma but want to do so with as little exertion and inconvenience as possible. A few arrive at English class never having read through a book longer than one hundred pages.[2] Students in this group are addicted to XYZNotes. When you show them a short movie clip of a literary work, they beg you to let them watch the whole thing, and watching the movie, in their minds, equals reading the book. Ignore this mindset. Stick to your agenda. And press forward. A few

---

[1] Antoine de Saint-Exupéry, *Citadelle* LXXV, (Paris, France: Gallimard, 1948), 687.

[2] According to a recent survey, most children and teenagers spend many of their leisure hours communicating with one another via electronic devices, playing video games, or watching television. They rarely spend time reading for pleasure.

students may complain that a book is too long or too difficult. Include methods during class that test their reading and always keep in mind the goal of making literature *enjoyable*.

I began teaching English accidentally. A few days before the beginning of the school year in 1978, the headmaster of the private school my five children attended called me into his office, told me his English teacher had resigned, and asked me to take her classes. Although I was significantly under qualified and unprepared, he was adamant. He pointed out that I am British and would therefore be an *English* English teacher. Somewhat daunted, I took classes at graduate school in the evenings and taught high school students during the day launching my teaching career with much trepidation and keeping one page ahead of the students. My children have vivid memories of their mother hunched over piles of books at the dining room table studying for next day's classes. I had no access to the previous teacher's lesson plans, no job description. I simply showed up each day, taught as well as I could, and in the process became an ardent lover of literature and of teaching the subject. I would not wish any other teacher to be placed in such an invidious position. I have therefore written a series of literature guides for teachers that cover the high school courses I've taught, from 9th grade through 12th grade. The sequence is as follows:

9th grade: Introduction to Literature
10th grade: World Literature
11th grade: American Literature
12th grade: British Literature

All four teaching guides give teachers and parents a detailed methodology for teaching high school literature that I have developed over the years and have found to be effective in the high school classroom. They are designed for teachers to use as they work through a literature anthology.

The need for a teacher's guide

I've taught for many decades, and now I want to give back what I have learned. I've thought for a long time that teachers need a detailed guide for teaching the discipline of high school literature. During my thirty-five years of teaching literature, many students who come into my classes have told me that they've never understood the point of reading literature and they rarely understood what a piece of literature is about. They appreciate the value of learning mathematics (everyone must balance a checkbook and figure out taxes) or science (we have to understand how the body works and how to cure disease) or history (we need to know something about our past), but they fail to understand why they're required to read poems, plays, and novels written centuries ago about people and situations that they regard as irrelevant to life today and often written in a language that's abstruse. Of course, they don't share these objections in such detail with their English teachers; most of them don't even know they harbor them, but deep down inside they feel this way when they enter the literature classroom. What a challenge for the English teacher. Fundamentally, teachers want two things: They want students to like them and to like the subject. Forget the first part. Just teach and keep the bar high. Insist that your students perform to the best of their ability. If your standards are high, even exacting, they will respect you and flourish in your classroom. Years later, they will thank you.

I hope my guides will serve as useful references for traditional teachers, homeschool parents or any parents who want to assist their children in the learning process, and perhaps students who are looking for clarification and fairly in-depth analyses of literature. I restrict myself entirely to literature, which includes writing about different works in order to facilitate comprehension. I do not discuss how to write; therefore, I don't discuss grammar, mechanics, or vocabulary. I don't deal with other aspects of the English curriculum. Those are subjects for future books. At the end of each book in the series, you will find a glossary of literary terms, an index, handouts I've used in the classroom, and tests.

Books for teachers

When preparing literature courses, teachers need books written by scholars to guide and inspire them. There are, of course, countless scholarly books from which to choose. I will mention a few that I have found indispensable. Among many books that have shaped my thinking about literature, I have found the analyses of Christian critics Leland Ryken and Peter J. Leithart to be invaluable. I have also much appreciated *Invitation to the Classics* by Louise Cowan and Os Guinness and *Reading Between the Lines: A Christian Guide to Literature* by Gene Edward Veith, Jr. Another fascinating resource is titled *The Atlas of Literature* edited by Malcolm Bradbury, which explores the places in which writers set their works, both real and fictitious. The book contains gorgeous illustrated maps, paintings, and photographs of iconic literary locations such as Shakespeare's Stratford, the Romantics' Lake District, and Hardy's Wessex.

I must mention Harold Bloom, reputed to be one of the most prestigious literary scholars alive today. Sterling Professor of Humanities at Yale, Bloom has written volumes about every great writer, every literary genre and period. Go to any library or bookstore, and you will find hundreds of essay collections that Bloom has compiled. These collections, published by Chelsea

House, fall into two main groups—*Modern Critical Interpretations*, a series that provides what Bloom considers to be the best critical essays currently available on specific literary works, and *Modern Critical Views* that includes his selection of the best critical essays of a specific writer's works or a group of specific writers' works (such as Victorian poets). I cannot list all Bloom's books that I have found essential to my research; I found two were indispensable: *Shakespeare: The Invention of the Human*, in which Bloom analyzes all Shakespeare's plays, and *The Western Canon*, in which he surveys the most representative works of the western world including works by Shakespeare at the center of the canon, Milton, Wordsworth, Dickens, Whitman, Dickinson, and many others.

The finest editions of many literary texts are the Norton Critical Editions. If a Norton edition is available for the works I include in the curriculum, I use it as my teaching text. These volumes include an authoritative edition of the literary work itself and scores of essays by the finest scholars of that work. The Norton volumes are like holding a library in one's hands. I also recommend Twayne's British Author Series, American Author Series, and World Author Series published by G. K. Hall.

The need for a student's guide

Although my primary objective in writing these books is to suggest a methodology for literature teachers, there are occasions when students themselves develop an interest in certain literature beyond the classroom and wish to know more about a particular work or writer. They may be inspired to learn more than a teacher with a full class load or a homeschool parent can provide. One of my objectives in writing this book is to furnish serious literature students with a supplemental resource.

Students' disinterest in reading

We are living in a post-literary world. Few people read for pleasure any more. Many young people adopt the habits of their parents and read books they are assigned for school or college courses. Although some teenagers enjoy reading, the vast majority of them do not. As Allan Bloom pointed out decades ago, there has been a drastic decline in young people's reading habits.[3] Bookstore employees and librarians tell me the same story. Most teens look for two genres of fiction—lurid fantasy and horror. They don't usually read classic literature unless a teacher requires them to do so. And they're more likely to read a book if it's been made into a movie. They love graphic novels. Apparently, publishers of children's books clamor for diverse books on questionable subjects so that children can read about these issues in an allegedly safe

---

[3] Allan Bloom, *The Closing of the American Mind* (New York: Simon and Schuster, 1987), 62.

environment. (What's happened to parental supervision?) It is a sad state of affairs. Today's teens and young adults are engrossed in their electronic gadgets. They also struggle with issues such as peer pressure (reading is boring) or hormones or challenges at home or school (girls especially can be unkind). Their lives are so busy that reading has been crowded out.[4]

Cultivating good reading habits

I do all I can to introduce students to a life-long love of reading good literature. I tell young people that good books contain beauty and wisdom. They are not flashy or vulgar or trite. I remind the young that fiction helps us to mature into useful adults, to reflect on difficult situations, to grapple with unfamiliar ideas, to understand other people. We read stories about people very different from ourselves, and we learn about their customs; we vicariously experience their trials and their joys; we applaud or condemn decisions them make. Good books retain their value forever. I introduce students to books that relate to their lives. Some of them enjoy non-fiction especially if they're interested in science or history. I suggest that they listen to audio tapes of novels on a long drive to a vacation spot or grandma's house. I list some of the genres—science fiction, romance, mysteries—and I share with them what I'm reading and how much I'm enjoying a current book. A few of them agree with Harper Lee: "Now…in an abundant society where people have laptops, cell phones, iPods, and minds like empty rooms, I still plod along with books."[5]

To increase students' interest in reading, I tell them that research has proved that readers live longer than non-readers (which may not impress them) and that readers earn a higher income than non-readers (which may get their attention). I persistently encourage young people to read good books so that they develop a natural love for reading and learning. To this end, I assign regular book reports. Early in the school year, I distribute a reading list of books I recommend for a particular grade. I do this to ensure that students read good books. A vast amount of appalling reading material written for teenagers is widely available, so a reliable guide is essential. Students pick one book from the list every six weeks or so, read it, and three weeks later write an in-class book report about it. I suggest various ways to write these essays and allow them a few days to make their book selection. On the next class day, they sign a sheet giving the author and title of the book they have chosen; this strategy avoids endless

---

[4] Here are Benjamin Franklin's thoughts on reading: "Reading feeds the brain. It is evident that most minds are starving to death." Franklin was describing the situation over 200 years ago. The nineteenth-century American educator, historian, and writer William Thayer asserted that "The habit of reading established early in life cannot fail to develop young people into intelligent, useful citizens." *Gaining Favor with God and Man.*

[5] Harper Lee in a letter for Oprah Winfrey's magazine. Qtd. by Marja Mills, *The Mockingbird Next Door* (New York: Penguin, 2014), 80.

procrastination. They get the message: They really do have to read a book then write about it to prove they've done so.

What about those students who claim to hate reading? I remember once handing out a reading list early in the school year to a 9ᵗʰ grade class. I noticed that one student's expression remained absorbed in my remarks—the class was asked to choose a book from the reading list and make an interesting poster with material found on line. He looked cooperative. Then his expression changed radically as an appalling detail dawned on him—he was required to read an entire book, the whole thing! To combat students' apathy about reading, I find out their interests, take them to the school library, and pull books off the shelves for them to look at; eventually they usually find something (a slim volume) that looks all right. I call it match making. To ensure completion, I ask students to write out and sign a statement at the end of their report that they have completed the book. In almost all cases, this procedure compels compliance. At the end of each teaching guide, I include book report handouts that provide some ideas about my handling of this type of essay. Students are not allowed to summarize the plot, and they may not include material from internet sources.

Students read out-of-class novels from a reading list for their grade level; at the end of each academic year, I give all students except seniors a summer reading list and require them to read two or three novels during the summer. During the first week of school, students write short in-class reports on the novels they've read on the plane or at the beach. How do teachers handle all this grading? I assign a holistic grade for these brief (one-page) essays whenever possible. After all, one is simply verifying that students have completed their assignment and read some books during the summer. In terms of reading assignments for the course, students generally come to class having read a short story or a novel. We read lyric poetry, epic poetry, drama, and non-fiction together in class.

A book about books for students
In order to help teenagers choose books they genuinely enjoy, you may want to consult the reading guide I wrote with my daughter Jane Scott entitled *The Book Tree: A Christian Reference for Children's Literature*, which is a reference book for children's literature written for young people themselves rather than adults. The second edition was published by Canon Press in 2008. Jane and I read and selected the best books written for young people from pre-school through high school; we attempted to say enough about each book to convey its contents in order that young people can refer to our guide and choose a book they'll enjoy. We added

various indexes including a subject index so that readers can find books on favorite topics or genres—fairy tales, science fiction, biography, historical fiction, and so on.[6]

Rewritten and abridged books

I am disturbed about a current trend—the plethora of rewritten or abridged books. Even young children's books—*Alice in Wonderland, A Little Princess, Black Beauty, Pollyanna*—are now published in retold editions that diminish the beauty of the original story. God has allowed the great books of past centuries to be preserved, and young people simply must be taught to relish and learn from the wisdom of great writers. Frequently, retold and abridged editions do not stay true to the original story. They represent an altered version and tend to change so-called politically incorrect content. If one buys a rewritten or abridged classic, it's like buying a ring with a synthetic stone rather than a genuine diamond.

eBooks

I'm also dismayed about the potential demise of literature in hard copy format. We live in a world of laptops, smart phones, and eBooks that supplement or replace traditional books. I don't own an eBook, although I realize that eBooks have advantages in terms of their convenience, portability, and cost. I prefer traditional books as an educational tool. There's an aesthetic value to holding a traditional book in one's hand, even more so if that book is beautifully bound and illustrated. Traditional books engage a reader's visual, tactile, and olfactory senses. I was heartened recently when I read a survey of eBooks that reported college students prefer to read traditional books. Apparently, many young adults complain of eyestrain and headaches when they read eBooks, and they relish the feel and smell of a physical book. Although I love traditional books, I realize that a teacher's main concern is to encourage the young to enjoy reading so that they pass on that love to their children and grandchildren, and future generations will experience the joys of reading Austen or Dickens or Shakespeare—via an electronic book or a traditional book that may be old and battered and well-loved.

Inappropriate language

Literary works often include language that one does not want young people to cultivate. Literature mirrors life in all its variety, both its beauty and its ugliness. If a great writer includes dialogue, he concerns himself with comments that sound authentic and natural for that particular speaker; comments expressed by corrupt people will necessarily include a poor choice of words. In any case, if one were to adopt an extreme position and decide to avoid all

---

[6] *The Book Tree* is available at various internet sites including www.amazon.com, www.barnesandnoble.com, and www.christianbook.com.

literature that contains inappropriate language, one would have few great works from which to choose. (I'm reminded of Dr. Bowdler who thought Shakespeare's plays were unwholesome reading for women and children and published an expurgated edition in 1818 that omitted all coarse language. I expect it was a rather slim volume.) How then should a conscientious teacher handle the issue? When selecting books for young people to read, it is important to consider whether the inappropriate words are gratuitous and whether they are pervasive throughout the book. If one finds that either or both of these situations exist, the book is unsuitable for young people. At all times, the teacher should apply God's Word to book selections: "Finally, brethren, whatever things are true, whatever things are noble, whatever things are just, whatever things are pure, whatever things are lovely, whatever things are of good report, if there is any virtue and if there is anything praiseworthy—meditate on these things."[7]

Choosing literary works

When designing a one-year literature course, one has to be extremely selective. In addition to a basic textbook for both teacher and students, every literature teacher should choose pieces that supplement the works in the textbook. In all four of my teaching guides, I chose literary works that I think are most representative of their time periods and are most excellent. I've also chosen pieces that students enjoy. I'm certain to have omitted some of your favorite authors or literary works, but bear in mind the seemingly limitless choice any literature teacher faces. You may decide to tailor your course quite differently and make other selections than many of mine. In any case, I recommend that as you read my comments, you have the literary work I am discussing in front of you.

Cultivating a love for literature

How does one cultivate in young people a genuine love for literature? You will go a long way towards accomplishing this goal if you do the following:

1. Assign poetry memorization.
2. Show movie clips of plays and novels and DVDs of authors' lives.
3. Schedule time for acting key scenes of drama.
4. Enhance literature with artwork, maps, music, and tapes.
5. Ensure that students talk about the literary works they study.
6. Encourage them to study diligently.

I know I've said a mouthful with this list, so let's break it down.

---

[7] Phil. 4:8. All Bible references are from the New King James Version (New York: Thomas Nelson, 1982).

1. **Poetry memorization**

Poetry is the oldest form of literature and was memorized and recited long before it was written down. Poetry is memorable; its rhythm, rhyme, and syntax make it easy to learn. If young people memorize beautiful lyrics, they will take a quantum leap in their understanding of a particular poem as well as poetry in general. It is well proved that they will also increase their intelligence quotient.

2. **Movie clips and DVDs**

In order to bring a novel or play off the page, show important scenes from a good movie production. Ask the class questions about casting, atmosphere, or interpretation, and discuss the extent to which the movie enhanced the writer's meaning. Include questions about movie clips on tests. As time allows, I show students DVDs about authors such as the Famous Authors Series by Kultur Video. This series, which may be purchased on line, provides fascinating information about authors' lives as well as the historical background to their writing and increases student interest in literary works. Titles in the series include British authors Shakespeare, Austen, the Brontës, Dickens, Hardy, Wordsworth and American authors Hemingway, Steinbeck, Twain, as well as many others.

3. **Acting key scenes of drama**

Drama differs from other literary genres because it is written to be performed not read; therefore, it makes special demands on the reader. Allow your class to act the final scene of a play such as *Macbeth* or the assassination scene in *Julius Caesar,* complete with simple costumes and props. (Shakespeare's plays lend themselves to this activity more readily than other dramas because there are so many characters to assign to a class.)

4. **Artwork, maps, music, and tapes**

Art and music are affective; they appeal to our emotions. Language is cognitive; it appeals to our intellect. Therefore, artwork and music enhance the impact of a piece of literature on the mind of the student. Students enjoy looking at writers' portraits or photographs. It's also a good idea to bring in artwork from the internet or literature books to increase enjoyment of a literary piece. Another useful resource is a time line. Time lines are invaluable for keeping students chronologically in sync, especially for survey courses that cover many centuries of literature. I remember that my older daughter graduated from high school with no idea that Shakespeare was writing his plays shortly before the Puritans landed at Cape Cod. Most textbooks include time lines of each literary period that one can refer to in order to keep students chronologically in sync. I display maps on classroom walls such as the following:

- Kingdom of Camelot[8]
- National Geographic Society map of Shakespeare's Britain
- Globe Playhouse conjectural chart by C. Walter Hodges[9]
- Thomas Hardy's Wessex[10]

Students enjoy listening to poetry recitations accompanied by music. Play Debussy's *Claire de Lune* or Beethoven's *Moonlight Sonata* when reading romantic poetry with classroom lights turned off. Dvořák's *Largo* is an appropriately mournful accompaniment for the final lines of *Beowulf*. Audio cassettes enhance students' enjoyment of poetry or drama. One can listen to an entire Shakespearean comedy or tragedy on a Caedmon or Arkangel audio cassette tape while reading the play during class. I play the tape for a page or two as students read along in their books then stop the tape for questions. Caedmon and Arkangel have recorded all of Shakespeare's plays unabridged and dramatized by fine actors. Caedmon tapes of poetry are also available.

5. **Discussion of literary works**

Students should be willing to voice their opinions during literature class. To encourage them to speak up, I conduct *graded discussions* for 9th and 10th grade classes. I discuss this procedure in the course material for those grades. Older students have, one hopes, learned to exchange opinions fairly readily. As students mature, I assign *student presentations*; for example, I ask different students to teach a poem to the class. They must read and thoroughly understand the piece then take notes on salient points. Having talked over difficulties with me and mastered the poem fairly well, they complete a handout of important points to distribute to the class on the day of their presentation. I rely increasingly on this type of assignment in upper high school classes.

6. **Literary study**

Most students benefit from studying in small groups. Although some prefer to study on their own, most of them refine their understanding as they exchange ideas about the literature they have read. This is an excellent strategy to adopt before semester exams. They congregate at Starbucks and discuss the material over an overpriced latte.

---

[8] available at www.pinterest.com

[9] available at www.folger.edu

[10] available at www.bl.uk/collection-items and www.dorsetcountymuseum.org

Review questions

Each book in this series of teaching guides includes review questions after discussion of a major literary work or unit. Review questions provide an opportunity for students to assess their knowledge of a specific work or era; we review their answers during class before they take a unit test.

Literature tests

In high school classes, I generally avoid quizzes. They take up valuable time and are not as effective cognitively as tests, which are more rigorous. Literature tests should be challenging. I generally avoid true-false, fill-in-the-blank, multiple-choice tests and compose some questions that require paragraph responses. When composing tests, one should bear in mind that questions should vary in scope and difficulty and should target different aspects of a person's understanding. Benjamin Bloom's taxonomy helps here; the taxonomy lists the types of questions one should ask in order to correctly ascertain students' grasp of a subject.[11]

One type of literature test popular among students is the quotation format. I reproduce key passages from a novel or play—usually from the beginning, middle, and end of the work—and ask them to supply the speaker, context, and significance of each passage. This type of question can be adapted for all literature you teach. As I grade tests, I note down names of students who give excellent answers; I review the graded tests in class asking different students to read their responses. This strategy accomplishes several things: It discourages flagging attention spans, it implicitly rewards good answers, and it allows students to learn from one another. Throughout these teaching guides, I provide suggested responses in brackets for all review questions and test questions.[12]

Essays

It's essential that students write about literature covered in class. They should be required to respond to many pieces they read, more or less, in essay form. An essay by definition is an organized, well-developed discussion of one subject dealt with at some length. I remind them of a good essay's structure or organization:

1. Brief opening paragraph with a clear central idea or thesis statement usually at the end of the paragraph.

---

[11] Detailed discussion of Bloom's taxonomy is available on several websites including cft.vanderbilt.edu.

[12] Student booklets are available for the 9th through 12th grade teaching guides. The booklets include review questions and test questions with suggested responses omitted.

2. Several half-page body paragraphs each of which includes a topic sentence that introduces one aspect of the thesis.

3. Brief concluding paragraph that gives closure to the essay but does not restate the thesis.

In addition to these organizational criteria, essays should include transitional devices that link paragraphs and contain minimal grammatical or mechanical errors. 11th and 12th grade students should support their opinions with close references to the literary work being discussed and quotations that support their remarks. Before writing an essay, students should organize their ideas by taking notes and developing an outline of key ideas. Although most essays are written out of class, a few are written in class so that I can regularly assess each student's writing ability. My procedure for essay writing is to assign the topic, discuss it with the class, and clarify misconceptions. Students always ask about length. As a homework assignment, they organize their ideas in note form then write a minimum of five paragraphs including introduction, body, and conclusion, and proofread their work. (Yes, it's challenging to get them to do this last part). Out-of-class essays are 2 to 2 ½ pages double spaced and typed in Times New Roman twelve-point font. I grade essays based on a rubric such as this: 40% organization, 40% development, and 20% grammar and mechanics. I do not correct mistakes but add marginal abbreviations—*cs, frag, pron/ref, wordy*, and so on—to indicate errors.

Essay grading

How does a teacher constantly assign essays throughout the year and manage the grading? Grading essays is not like grading math tests since it is extremely subjective. One also has to bear in mind that poor grammar or poor penmanship can affect a teacher's response to an essay, and after an hour's reading, the teacher gets tired. In order to be fair to each student, this is my procedure: I quickly read a set of essays, assign a temporary grade, and place the set into piles—*A* essays, *B* essays, and so on. I then reread each essay more carefully, note errors in the margin for students to correct, and make sure that all essays in each category—*A, B*, etc.—are of the same caliber.

When graded essays are returned with my marginal notes, students correct mistakes, and I review the work again for completion. I do not pick up the essays to reread at home but review corrections during class. If students don't complete their corrections, points are deducted from the original grade. *Never correct their mistakes.* If you do, they will glance at the grade and endlessly repeat their errors. During the first weeks of the year, I hand out essay guidelines together with a list of my abbreviations; that way, I'm less likely to be asked 101½ times what *cs* means. A list of abbreviations that I use when correcting essays is included in the handouts. In each teaching guide, I have included specific essay topics for many literary works.

Training good writers

In order to reward good writing, I display a set of well-written essays on the wall of a hallway where other students, faculty, and visitors can admire the work. Students' names are prominently displayed on each essay. Young people usually react negatively to essay writing, but I've never had a college student return to tell me I assigned too many essays. Young people usually recognize the value of such training. However, an obvious question arises: What does one do about parents who are dissatisfied with their son or daughter's essay grades? I meet with them and the student and show them sample essays. They look at average and excellent student essays, with names deleted, so that they can compare their son or daughter's writing with other students' work. The strategy is effective. I also arrange to meet regularly with the student in order to help improve his or her writing skills. I do not assign an *F* for a poorly written essay but require a student to rewrite the essay after we have met to discuss methods of improvement. If students fail to do so, they receive a zero for the essay assignment. This technique usually ensures compliance.

Attributions

Before moving to the literature, I should inform the reader about my attributions. Because of copyright law, I do not generally cite from specific editions, although I know that would be helpful to the reader. In the footnotes, I supply references to sections or chapters in a given work. In the bibliography, I include recommended editions of specific novels, plays, non-fiction, and long poems in addition to books that have profoundly impacted my studies and books that may be useful for English teachers. My bibliography does not include specific editions of short stories or poems since these are readily available in literature anthologies or the internet. I quote almost exclusively from works in the public domain because I want my reader to easily follow my comments about the literature. If a work or a translation of a work is not in the public domain, I comment on the work and avoid quotations or restrict myself to a few brief passages.

****

I have thoroughly enjoyed compiling this series of books. It's been therapeutic work for me because I retired a few years ago, and I miss teaching and my students. Writing these guides has been like being in the classroom—without the interruptions. I hope you find some ideas that work for your particular situation. If any of my suggestions help a few teachers on their way, my time has been well spent. Teaching is a great privilege and a great responsibility. A teacher exerts tremendous influence on the minds and hearts of future generations. Over the years, I have derived deep satisfaction from teaching the young. I'm genuinely fond of many of my students, some of whom I chat with at church, a few come by my home to bring their home-grown vegetables, and some bump into me at a store astonished that I actually buy groceries like a normal person.

I hope God will richly reward teachers who take their calling seriously each day and work hard, year in and year out, to inculcate in their students a love of learning and a love for great literature. Then future generations will experience the joys of reading Austen or Dickens or the immortal Bard of Avon.[13]

If you would like to contact me, email me at eamarlow0103@gmail.com.

The only people who achieve much are those who want knowledge so badly
that they seek it while the conditions are still unfavourable.
Favourable conditions never come.

C. S. Lewis, The Weight of Glory

---

[13] As Harold Bloom has observed, these authors seem to be the only ones who have survived today's handling of literary works on the silver screen and television. *How to Read and Why* (New York: Simon & Schuster, 2001), 117. In other words, people still continue to read these authors in spite of the endless stream of visual productions of their works.

How to Teach Literature:
Introductory Course
Introduction

Sherlock Holmes

This book is the fourth in a series of teaching guides for high school literature teachers and homeschool parents.[14] Since this guide is an introduction to literature for students entering high school, I want to make brief mention of teaching as a profession. I recently reread a dated but invaluable book for teachers by renowned author, literary critic, and teacher, Gilbert Highet, entitled *The Art of Teaching*.[15] The title speaks volumes. Highet talks about the requirements for the good teacher. He contends that an effective teacher loves his subject, that the teacher constantly learns about that subject and likes young people.[16] He points out that students have all kinds of vague ideas and that the teacher's task is to shape their thinking so

---

[14] As mentioned in the preface, the other three guides for 10th, 11th, and 12th grades cover world, American, and British literature.

[15] Gilbert Highet, *The Art of Teaching* (New York: Vintage Books, 1958). Highet (1906–1978) was an American academic originally from Scotland and a professor at Oxford and Columbia universities. He was a brilliant scholar and a superb teacher who was committed to life-long learning.

[16] Highet, *The Art of Teaching*, 18, 25.

that they can reason cogently.[17] What a privilege and responsibility. Highet comments that young people are going to oppose the teacher and it is natural for them to do so.[18] I find that insight immensely reassuring. One must rid oneself of the assumption that students will find literature or any other subject as endlessly fascinating as the teacher does. That rarely happens. On the other hand, one doesn't want a class of robots, young people who gaze unblinkingly at one and regurgitate facts.

In a healthy classroom, it is vital to generate thinking and questioning. The classroom should be a place for a stimulating exchange of ideas, the teacher in control and the class respectful. The climate should be such that students feel comfortable about respectfully questioning information as it is given or adding their perceptions. It is incumbent on the teacher to respect young people's arguments and be willing to admit a faulty explanation if that is warranted. It is a given that *a teacher's main task is to equip young people to learn for themselves*. That is true education. Highet makes another point that I feel is crucial to the classroom environment: A teacher should use humor, which he says connects the teacher to his students.[19] I thoroughly concur. Have a good laugh with your class regularly. Laughter tears down barriers between teens and teacher. There's nothing in life more enjoyable than shared amusement.

Highet provides an astute methodology for teaching. He lists three criteria:

- The teacher must prepare his material thoroughly.
- He should communicate it clearly.
- He should ensure that the class learns it.[20]

Any teacher would agree with these principles, but I want to elaborate on Highet's insights.

1. **Preparation**
In terms of preparation, a teacher should review and amend course material every year. One should strive as far as possible to be unpredictable. That takes planning. Young people, all of us are bored by monotonous routine, so one should plan different methods of teaching the material. Obviously, basic principles must be reviewed, often repeatedly, but a good teacher varies his or her technique. Ideally, a literature teacher attempts to vary literary selections as much as possible in order to avoid monotonous instruction. In my literature guides, I

---

[17] Ibid., 10.

[18] Ibid., 11.

[19] Ibid., 55.

[20] Ibid., 66.

intentionally include more literary works than can be covered in one year to give teachers a variety of selections from which to choose. How else does one accomplish variety in one's instruction? By reading new literary works and new scholarship and keeping current with new trends in criticism, although one may not agree with those trends. Young people should realize that teaching is a learning process, that teachers never stop growing intellectually. The teacher needs to cover much of the same material year after year but vary the way it is taught in order to adapt it to a particular group of students. As far as possible, one should avoid monotonous predictability and keep students guessing about what will happen next.

2. Communication

A teacher must communicate information lucidly. This means that one should enunciate well and stop when frowns appear. It's essential to allow interruptions for questions and to adopt a leisurely pace. New literary terms should be defined on the dry erase board. The unfamiliar should be explained in terms of the familiar. The class should be able to follow the teacher's train of thought. One should ensure that everyone is taking notes on the material as the teacher lectures.[21] A good teacher communicates information in several ways such as lecture, questioning, graded discussion, and breaking the class into groups to compare ideas. These methods are discussed below.

3. Comprehension

The teacher must ensure comprehension. To make sure that students are learning the material, it is essential to ask frequent questions. As Highet points out, the most important reason for questioning is not to discover whether students have completed their homework but to ascertain whether they understand the material.[22] One should schedule regular reviews and testing over manageable amounts of information. An essay assignment is an invaluable way to gage understanding. It's the teacher's responsibility to determine students' grasp of the subject, and that can only be accomplished by frequent questioning and testing. One should always schedule time for review before major tests or exams. As mentioned in the preface to these teaching guides, I discuss graded tests and mid-term exams with the class and ask individual students to read effective responses. This technique accomplishes two things: Diligent students are rewarded for good work; other students learn to recognize appropriate responses and to refine their understanding.

---

[21] I am adamantly opposed to the practice of handing out notes that students merely glance at and stuff in their book bags. They must learn to take their own notes. Like any other skill, efficient note taking takes constant practice.

[22] *The Art of Teaching*, 125.

One point to emphasize for literature teachers is this: Young people tend to judge fictional characters according to their own attitudes and customs; for example, one can't fault Juliet's parents for arranging a marriage for their thirteen-year-old daughter because this was the custom in Renaissance Europe. How does one teach teenagers to evaluate fiction appropriately? By constantly reminding them to put aside their ways of thinking about life and to bear in mind the customs of the period in which a piece of literature is written.

Refining students' taste in books

Before leaving the topic of education per se, I must mention a book by a superlative theologian, educator, and writer, C. S. Lewis. *The Abolition of Man* is a work that contains Lewis's reflections on education. Lewis draws on Aristotle who said that *"the aim of education is to make the pupil like and dislike what he ought* [italics added]."[23] That seems to me to be the teacher's ultimate goal. A teacher should develop a young person's mind but also his or her taste and moral sense. One effective way to accomplish this goal is to ensure that students read and discuss good literature. If they are exposed to writing that is noble and wholesome, they will develop a taste for it and will be less likely to be drawn to writing that is sordid and worthless or misleading. To resort again to the ancient Greek philosopher, Aristotle defined literature as an "imitation of life." Students should understand this principle. Works of literature offer us pictures of life's experiences that we can evaluate and that help us mature.

The freshman classroom

Middle school students in general have coasted through school because, well, that's where they have to go on weekdays until the blissful sound of the three o'clock bell. High school is a different matter. They've been warned by parents, teachers, older siblings, and the rest of the world that high school is vital—grades are cast in cement and the GPA is the entry ticket to college and a decent career. They file into Freshman English on the first day of class terrified, eyes down, willing to do anything to stay out of trouble. They scramble for the back row hoping they won't be noticed if they keep quiet and don't mess with the teacher. The teacher's job, of course, is to disabuse them of these notions. I want students to talk—a lot. That's the last thing 9th grade students want to do. They would rather die than call attention to themselves. I make a seating chart of their names and begin to call on individual students. Desperately hoping for semi-permanent anonymity, they are horrified that I seem to know them already.

---

[23] C. S. Lewis, *The Abolition of Man* (New York: HarperCollins, 2001), 16. Lewis is quoting from Aristotle's *Nicomachean Ethics*, II.3.

I mention a few other issues: Write essays in ink, check spelling of all written work in a personal dictionary, write assignments in a dedicated notebook, keep handouts, take copious notes, and constantly ask questions. (This list goes on the wall for me to point to throughout the year.) A week or two into the school year, I give students various instructions for writing an essay. (See handouts.) I tell them that I dislike pop quizzes, but I will resort to them if I suspect that they haven't finished their reading assignments.[24] No one's eyes are on the clock now. Some are nervously digging into smart new book bags and huge purses to find a notebook and pen.

Literary works

I don't include as many literary works in the introductory course as I do in other high school courses. This textbook is primarily intended for teachers of 9th grade students, and one must make time for subjects such as grammar, composition, and vocabulary, all of which reduce time available for literary study. I select literature that is based on the needs and, to some degree, the interests of a particular freshman class. I also do much more lecturing in this course. Freshman students are generally unwilling to participate or unable to do so as capably as upper-class students. They need instruction in many areas of literature before they can discuss the subject with their peers. I assign group work that trains students to exchange ideas with one another, but I don't expect 9th graders to prepare the presentations that I assign for older students. I want to make certain that freshman students develop the skills they will need in later literature courses. Freshman English prepares students to analyze the various genres and elements of literature.

Textbook

Any anthology of 9th grade literature is fine as your main textbook as long as you add other selections. No anthology includes everything you're familiar with or want to teach, so you should supplement the main textbook with other literary works. This teaching guide is designed to be a detailed resource that supplements and enhances material found in a 9th grade literature anthology. It includes benefits not found in most textbooks such as the following:

- detailed analyses of each literary work
- teaching techniques
- essay topics
- review questions
- tests that cover major works or units
- classroom handouts

---

[24] Failing quiz grades prompt most students to complete their work in future.

- audio-visual aids
- out-of-class reading list

Scope of the course

In other high school literature courses, I adopt a chronological method, but the genre approach to literary study is preferable for freshmen students since it allows the teacher to focus on basic elements that relate to each genre. I start the year with the short story, followed by the novel, drama, epic, and end with lyric poetry.

Textbook questions

Many literature textbooks include questions of varying caliber and usefulness. I do not routinely require students to answer all questions, especially factual questions, but assign some of the interpretive and critical response questions included in many literature textbooks. I inspect students' work and record zeroes for incomplete answers. One has to recognize that the only motivation for many students is the grade book.

Reading assignments

To reiterate comments made in the preface to this series of teaching guides, students generally come to class having read a short story or a novel. We read poetry and plays together in class. During the first week of class, students write in-class essays on two books they've read over the summer. When I've graded and returned these, I distribute a reading list (see handouts) from which they select books that appeal to them, read the book, and write an in-class report approximately every six weeks or so throughout the year.[25] They write in-class essays on a novel or a book of short stories that they have selected.

Writing assignments

As also mentioned in the preface, essays are usually a minimum of two typed, double spaced pages in Times New Roman twelve-point font. Students must take notes in order to organize their ideas and attach the notes to the back of their essays. I give them two or three days to complete an out-of-class essay and often base the grade on three criteria—clear organization, adequate development, sound grammar and mechanics—with a rubric of 40%, 40%, and 20% respectively. I do *not* read students' essays as if I'm determined to find every error and deduct a point for each one. I require students to correct spelling mistakes and other errors, but I take a holistic approach and grade mainly on content and logical flow of ideas. I assign

---

[25] I distribute a reading list to safeguard against students choosing books from the copious amount of inappropriate YA fiction written for today's teens.

a few essays, such as book reports, in class so that I can regularly familiarize myself with the caliber of each student's writing. Some instructions about essay writing are included in the handouts at the back of this book. You may want to refer to the paragraph in the preface entitled "Essay grading" in order to read my suggestion about handling this time-consuming task throughout the year.

Teaching techniques

Here's a list of teaching techniques that I frequently use for 9th grade:[26]

- **Brainstorming a topic**. I raise an issue, and students share their ideas as I write them on the board.
- **Brainstorming an essay assignment**. After assigning an essay topic, I talk with the class about different ideas for a thesis statement, sub-topics, and supporting details and write them on the board.
- **Plot diagram**. Students sometimes create a plot diagram for drama or other genres. I discuss this technique during discussion of the short story entitled "Through the Tunnel." Students also create a diagram of the plot of *Romeo and Juliet*. A template of a plot diagram is included in the handouts.
- **Note taking**. See below.
- **Unannounced quizzes**. See below.
- **Review questions**. See below.
- **Graded discussion**. See below.
- **Book reports**. See below.
- **Book report posters**. See below.

Note taking

Students should take detailed notes on the literature we study. However, they should not attempt to turn themselves into human tape recorders and write down everything the teacher says. With constant practice, they learn to write notes on essential information such as definitions of literary terms, characters' personality traits, importance of setting, and so on. How does one ensure they do so? Walk up and down the rows to check the note taking. Students' notes create an invaluable study resource before tests and exams. Young people certainly need to acquire this skill prior to taking college courses. In the 9th grade course, one should take up students' notebooks periodically and assign a holistic grade based on completion.

---

[26] A more comprehensive list of general techniques is included at the end of the book.

Unannounced quizzes

As already indicated, I avoid reading quizzes in the high school literature classroom. They take up valuable time and are not as effective cognitively as tests, which are more rigorous. I prefer other methods such as review questions in addition to tests and semester exams. However, I resort to an unannounced quiz if I find that many students have not completed a reading assignment.

Review questions

As also noted in the preface, I include review questions after each major literary work or unit. Some of these questions could be included in tests or exams. I separate students into small groups to answer the questions. They use their notes and literature books and submit answers for grading on an assigned date.

Graded Discussion[27]

I use the graded discussion technique in the 9th and 10th grade classrooms. It's another way to ensure that homework is completed and to elicit student responses. Here's how it works: The night before class, I write down a list of students' names and a long list of thought-provoking questions about the material. In class the next day, students respond to each question by raising his or her hand, and if it's a reasonable response, I put a check mark by the name. I try to ensure that all students get many opportunities to respond. They can enlarge on a previous response or ask a related question. They may not repeat material we've already covered. That night, I assign grades based on the number of each student's responses. Students like the activity. It tends to become lively, and it ensures that everyone adds to the discussion. And no one gets to snooze in the back row. I schedule graded discussions after we complete a major unit such as a play or a novel.

Book reports

It seems to me that one of an English teacher's primary tasks is to heed Flannery O'Connor's exhortation and "change the face of the best-seller list."[28] What wisdom and what a challenge for literature teachers. At the end of the previous academic year, rising 9th graders are given a summer reading list from which to choose two books to read over the summer.[29] During the first week of the academic year, students write short in-class essays on these two books. When I've graded and returned the reports, I distribute a reading list from which they select books

---

[27] This technique is not usually applicable for a homeschool teacher.

[28] Flannery O'Connor, *Mystery and Manners* (New York: Farrar, Straus & Giroux, 1969), 128.

[29] In my guides that cover 11th and 12th grade literature, I suggest that students read three books during the summer. Almost every student I have ever taught complies with this requirement.

to read throughout the year. I tell students that approximately every six weeks, they'll choose a novel from the list, read it, and write an essay about it. Throughout the school year, I bring a stack of books into the classroom and talk about them in order to generate student interest. I pass the books around the room so that they can get their hands on them and hopefully choose one. (They've sometimes accused me of telling them too much about the plot, which is probably true.) In any case, they select a book that appeals to them and write an in-class essay on a different book about every six weeks. I attempt to compose a list for many types of readers, bearing in mind that reading ability and taste vary widely. The reading list for this class includes some hefty reading material in addition to lighter suggestions and books that some students may have read.[30]

Book report posters

As an alternative to reading novels or short story collections, 9th grade students read two biographies a year. I bring several biographies to class from the school library and talk about them in order to whet students' interest in people who have made enormous sacrifices, even given their lives, for the safety and well-being of others. I give students a few days to make their selections that they record on a list in order to avoid endless procrastination. I then ask them to create a colorful poster about the person they are reading about. I tell them to research information about him or her. They search the internet to find maps, colorful drawings, and other artwork and arrange the materials on a large poster board to make an attractive display of the person's achievements. I show them posters made during previous years. On an assigned day, each student discusses his or her biography in front of the class and explains each item on the poster. If they wish, they can dress up as the person they've read about. Students enjoy this activity, and it develops their ability to speak fluently and informatively in front of a group.

Attributions

Before moving to the literature, I should remind the reader about comments made in the preface regarding my attributions. Because of copyright law, I do not generally quote from specific editions although I know that would be helpful to the reader. In the footnotes, I supply references to sections or chapters in a given work. In the bibliography, I include recommended editions of specific novels, plays, non-fiction, and long poems in addition to books that have profoundly impacted my studies and books that may be useful for English teachers. My bibliography does not include specific editions of short poems or short stories since these are readily available via literature anthologies or the internet. I quote almost exclusively from

---

[30] The 9th grade reading list is included in the handouts. As indicated on the list, students may not select a book they've already read.

works in the public domain because I want my reader to easily follow my comments about the literature. If a work or a translation of a work is not in the public domain, I comment on the work and avoid quotations or restrict myself to a few words.

At the end of each teaching guide in the series, I include a glossary of literary terms, index, bibliography, specific class assignments, as well as handouts such as explanatory material I've used in the classroom, and tests. As an aid for the reader, I italicize the literary terms discussed in order to emphasize techniques that pertain to a specific literary work.

Unit I

Short Story

Freshman English is, in part, a course that covers basic interpretation of literary genres—short story, novel, drama, epic, and lyric poetry. I start the freshman course by analyzing several short stories in terms of the main elements of fiction. Students need to know that authors don't emphasize every literary element but instead focus on several elements depending on their purpose for writing a particular story. We analyze the main elements—plot, setting, characterization, and so on—to see how the author uses those elements in each story we discuss. Students read all short stories before class, and I tell them it's ideal to read each one in a single sitting in order to appreciate the impact of the story that the author wishes to create in the mind of the reader.

The short story genre

Students should know that story telling is an ancient art. People have been telling stories since the world was created. Think about the many stories one finds in the Bible—stories about Noah, Jacob, Jonah, Ruth, and Daniel. Freshmen students should become familiar with the basic criteria that make up a story. It must have certain elements such as plot, conflict, and characters in order to qualify as a story, but you can't really talk about a story in terms of these elements alone. A story must be complete. You can't add or subtract anything—a character, an incident, a piece of dialogue—from a good story. I love the way Flannery O'Connor phrases it: "A story really isn't any good unless it successfully resists paraphrase, unless it hangs on and expands in the mind."[31] That exactly describes the impact of a good story on the perceptive reader.

Apart from specialized genres such as science fiction or fantasy, events in a short story or a novel are controlled by the kind of people that are in the story, and the entire narrative conveys a slice of experience, something that is true to life. Stories help us to see some part of reality via events set forth in the narrative. As we read a story, we experience this slice of reality via our senses. To be less esoteric, the class should also know that a short story usually centers on a single incident, whereas a novel contains many incidents connected together to form a more complex plot.

I attempt to provide the reader with a wide range of choices in the short story unit; I therefore discuss more stories that a teacher will want to include in his or her curriculum for any one year. Individual teachers will select from the stories covered and supplement other favorites. Another point to be made is that I vary the pace at which I review stories with a class. Some stories require a detailed discussion, while others can be handled fairly rapidly. To repeat a

---

[31] O'Connor, *Mystery and Manners*, 108.

previous observation, I strive for variety in the classroom. And two principles for the teacher bear repeating:

> A *teacher's main task is to equip young people to learn for themselves.*
> "*The aim of education is to make the pupil like and dislike what he ought.*"[32]

We begin the short story unit by analyzing that most basic element of fiction—plot.[33]

---

[32] Aristotle. Qtd. by C. S. Lewis, *The Abolition of Man*, 16.
[33] I quote from stories in the public domain.

Plot

"Through the Tunnel"
by
Doris Lessing[34]
1919–2013

The *plot* of a story is its sequence of related events without which there is no story. A plot always involves *conflict* or struggle. I compose and distribute these examples:

> When the king got up in the morning, he couldn't find his royal slippers. He became very annoyed. The queen, however, found them under the bed and placed them on her husband's feet. The king then proceeded with the onerous duty of running his kingdom. ...
>
> (No plot. No conflict.)

> When the king got up in the morning, he heard an ominous noise. Cautiously peering out of his bedroom, he noticed the faint outline of a stranger stealing down the hallway. Looking fearfully over his shoulder, the queen screamed. Suddenly a blood-curdling sound of swords clashing echoed through the palace. A disheveled servant stumbled into the royal bedchamber stammering incoherently. ...
>
> (Plot established. Conflict suggested.)

Without a plot or any conflict, we are disinclined to continue reading a work of fiction. A plot must be established in order to draw us into the story so that we read on. To focus on a story's plot, students read "Through the Tunnel," a coming-of-age story. Freshmen students relate well to the protagonist's conflict that involves a self-imposed quest.

Plot

First, the class should understand the stages or parts of a well-made plot: *exposition, rising action, turning point, climax, falling action,* and *dénouement.* I write down and define these terms on the board as students copy them into their notebooks for future reference:

> **exposition:** information that conveys important facts about the characters and the situation so that the reader understands subsequent events
> **rising action:** events or actions that complicate the basic situation
> **turning point:** the point at which the protagonist's situation worsens so that the outcome for him or her is inevitable
> **climax:** the most intense moment in the story

---

[34] Doris Lessing is an acclaimed British author and Nobel Laureate.

> **falling action**: resolution of conflicts or tensions begins to occur
>
> **dénouement**: all tension is resolved happily or unhappily

Incidentally, freshman students may question the need to write down information when they can look up facts and definitions in their literature books. I tell them that we remember a fraction of what we see, but we remember far more about material we write down. I repeat an old Chinese proverb: "I hear, and I forget; I see, and I remember; I do [or I write], and I understand."[35]

Plot diagram

We discuss the plot developments in Lessing's story. I distribute a plot diagram that students complete. (See "diagram of plot" in the handouts.) Students separate into small groups to discuss the various stages of the plot and add brief notations to their diagrams about each part—exposition, rising action, and so on. They complete their diagrams at home and return them in a day or so for grading. I repeat this assignment throughout the year for different pieces of literature.

Conflict

I use Lessing's story to discuss several other literary elements—conflict, rite of passage, and setting. All stories involve *conflict*, in other words, tension or opposition of some sort. It is a fundamental element of fiction because conflict creates interest in the reader. In fiction as in life, we are interested when things go wrong. Without conflict, there is no story. A story imitates life, and life is full of conflict or struggle. We constantly struggle with situations, with other people, or with ourselves. Because stories are about life and human nature, they inevitably involve conflict.

Students readily agree that we all deal with conflict throughout our lives—conflict with authority figures such as parents or teachers as well as conflict with friends and others. We distinguish among the four main types of conflict:

> **external**: a character's struggle against some aspect of the natural world
>
>   a character's struggle against another character or antagonist
>
>   a character's struggle against a community or society at large
>
> **internal**: a character's struggle within himself or herself

---

[35] The proverb has been attributed, probably erroneously, to Confucius (551 BC– 479 BC).

The class should understand that Jerry struggles with both external and internal conflict. *External conflict* arises between him and his mother over Jerry's activities at the beach. He is drawn to the excitement of the bay where some boys are involved in a fascinating activity, whereas his mother would prefer that Jerry remain with her on the beach. *Internal conflict* involves Jerry's determination to accomplish something dangerous versus his knowledge that the French boys' activity is life-threatening. He wants to prove to himself that he is strong and brave by overcoming an ordeal just as he has witnessed the boys performing a risky feat. He realizes it's dangerous, that it could possibly kill him, but he is determined to conquer his fear and his physical limitations. A second internal conflict involves Jerry's awareness of his widowed mother's loneliness and her concern for him versus his desire to overcome his dependence on her. When he has completed his ordeal, he finds it unnecessary to tell his mother of his conquest. He is also aware that his mother would be overly concerned, even frightened, by his accomplishment. Having conquered his fears, Jerry has survived his self-imposed test and is happy to succumb to his mother's wish to stay with her on her beach.

I suggest that internal conflict can be the most interesting conflict depicted in literature. Although we enjoy watching someone wrestling with an outside force, it's often more interesting to watch a person struggling with his or her conscience or desires. Young teenagers are impacted by and learn from fiction that depicts internal conflict. I tell them they will read other stories in which characters struggle with significant inner conflicts.

Rite of passage

"Through the Tunnel" is a *rite of passage* story. The term needs explanation. A rite of passage is some sort of ceremony or experience that marks an important development or change in someone's life—for instance, graduation from college or marriage. The main character in Lessing's story learns something significant. That's the reason the story resonates well with young teenagers. We talk about rites of passage individual students may have experienced. Some students are disinclined to talk about times of personal growth, but others are willing to share insights they've gained from a memorable feat or challenge.[36] When teaching literature, one should attempt as far as possible to relate the literary piece to students' lives. This technique allows the piece to come alive for them. They begin to grasp a crucial fact: Literature does indeed imitate a slice of life, sometimes a large slice as depicted in a novel, and sometimes small like the glimpse of life we are given in a short story or a poem.

---

[36] The climate in the classroom should be conducive to a healthy exchange of ideas. It is incumbent on the teacher to ensure that young people feel comfortable about expressing their opinions or adding to the discussion.

Students should realize that Jerry experiences a rite of passage. He proves to himself that he can achieve difficult tasks, he gains a new sense of independence from his mother, and he matures as a result. His experience is beneficial to his maturing. Jerry has a close relationship with his mother, but he needs to become independent of her. One must emphasize to freshmen students that the quest is highly dangerous and extremely unwise, in spite of its helping Jerry begin to achieve some independence. The story also allows a teacher to discuss with young teenagers the life-long requirement to respect and love their parents as well as their natural and healthy need to achieve ultimate independence from them. It is right for young people to gradually become independent of their parents, but they should always be sensitive to their parents' preferences and strive to honor their parents' wishes.

Setting

We discuss the way Lessing manipulates the two *settings* to suggest the central conflict. She contrasts the rocky bay with the beach via *connotative diction* and *comparisons*. Negative wording describes the bay; the colors are menacing, and other wording carries sinister implications. In contrast, colors and similes that describe the mother's beach are warm and comforting. I ask the class for specific examples of these points. Students should realize that Lessing's wording suggests the danger of the bay versus the safety of the beach. Before moving on to another story, we review the elements we've studied—in this case, plot, conflict, rite of passage, and setting.

Note taking

At the 9th grade level, it's important to check that everyone is writing notes. While teaching literature, I walk up and down the rows to ensure that everyone is diligently writing. I'm always amused by the freshman who suddenly realizes what I'm doing, straightens up and tries to act as if he has been diligently taking copious notes. I warn students not to write down everything I say but to make notes on key ideas, and I tell them that, like anything else one does, one becomes proficient at note taking with practice. I collect 9th graders' notebooks every quarter, glance through them, and grade them. I base the grade on the thoroughness of each student's notes.[37]

---

[37] One trick many teachers probably use is to grade an excellent note-taker's notes first and use that example as a comparison for other students' notes. This procedure allows one to establish a criterion for the top grades.

Setting
"To Build a Fire"[38]
by
Jack London
1876–1916

The next literary element we focus on is a story's *setting* or the time and place of a literary text. The setting of a story has several possible functions:

- It often provides a background for the story, a place where the characters live.
- It can also evoke a specific mood.
- It may provide conflict; sometimes the characters are in conflict with hostile weather conditions to endure, a stormy sea to navigate, or a mountain to climb.
- Setting can be used to reveal a person's character.

In order to appreciate the importance of setting, we discuss London's well-known story, "To Build a Fire." Many 9th graders have read novels by Jack London such as *The Call of the Wild* and *White Fang* and enjoy "To Build a Fire" mainly due to its fast pace and suspense: Is the man going to survive?

Setting

London set "To Build a Fire" in the Yukon, a mountainous, wild territory in northwestern Canada where gold was discovered in the late nineteenth century and where London himself prospected for gold. I show the class photographs of the area that can be viewed at several websites.[39] Students should note London's continual references to the weather and the time of day so that they can appreciate the man's increasingly dangerous situation. London frequently reminds the reader of the passage of time and the omnipresent, sub-zero cold. These references to time and temperature alert the reader to the man's dilemma. The later it gets, the further the temperature falls. The cold is also depressing and inescapable; there is no glimpse of the sun, and the atmosphere is gloomy. The *setting* conveys the unlikelihood of a happy ending. It suggests that the man is doomed. At this point, the class begins to appreciate the importance of the setting to the overall impact of the story.

---

[38] "To Build a Fire" is discussed in more detail in my teacher's guide to American literature.

[39] One can find spectacular photographs of the Yukon at <u>www.travelyukon.com</u>.

Conflict

This story involves the most basic literary *conflict*: man versus his environment—in this case, the rigors of an Alaskan winter where the temperature drops to seventy-five degrees below zero. Thus, the basic conflict is between *protagonist* and *antagonist* or environment. In this case, the environment wins.

Contrast between dog and man

Students provide details that characterize both the dog and the man as I write their suggestions on the board, and they take notes.[40] It's important that the whole class gets involved in the activity. Here are some points young people often make:

The husky

- The dog's instincts are far more astute than those of the man.
- The husky is apprehensive and depressed about the sub-zero temperature.
- It is nervous about thin ice over pools of water.
- There is a lack of camaraderie between man and dog— "the only caresses it had ever received were the caresses of the whiplash"; the dog has no concern for the man's welfare.
- If the dog had been a devoted companion, it may have run off to the old claim for help from other prospectors, and the man could have survived.
- The dog instinctively shies away when the man attempts to kill it.
- At the end of the story, the dog abandons the dead man to find food and shelter.

The man

- In sharp contrast, the man, a newcomer to the Yukon who lacks imagination and insight, does not share the dog's concerns.
- Although he is constantly aware of the cold, the freezing temperature does not concern him.
- He is not concerned about being without a sled or companions.
- He forgets to build a fire until his extremities are frozen.
- He neglects to watch the ice under his feet and falls into a spring of water hidden under the snow and is soaked to his knees.

---

[40] This procedure is a good way to get everyone involved. Students readily call out ideas and like to see them displayed for everyone else to admire.

- He builds a fire beneath a tree laden with snowy branches; a heavy fall of snow extinguishes his fire— "The man was shocked. It was as though he had just heard his own sentence of death."
- This moment is the story's *climax*.
- The end is now inevitable as the man vainly attempts to rebuild the fire.

I ask the class why London does not name the protagonist. The man represents all mankind pitted against implacable nature. Some 9th graders are reluctant to accept this explanation, but it appears to be the writer's intention.

Finally, I ask students what they would have done differently. Students enjoy sharing their ideas, and as far as possible I ensure that they do so. Here are some typical responses:

- Take a companion along, especially because the man is a newcomer to the area.
- Before setting out, determine the extreme to which the temperature will fall.
- Dress more warmly, especially one's extremities.
- Be more alert to the dropping temperature.
- Stay on the main trail.
- Build a fire in the open.

The whole class agrees that the newcomer to this particular setting in the Yukon was doomed the moment he set out without a companion on circuitous path along a little-used trail in frigid temperatures. And that about sums up this man's lack of common sense.

Essay[41]

Write a 1½ to 2-page essay in which you discuss the reasons for the story's tragic outcome.

Because this is the first essay of the year, I talk to the class about an essay's organization:

- Brief opening paragraph with a clear central idea or thesis statement usually at the end of the paragraph
- Two or three half-page body paragraphs that contain a topic sentence introducing one aspect of the thesis
- Brief concluding paragraph that gives closure to the essay but does not restate the thesis

---

[41] As already noted, some instructions about essay writing are included in the handouts at the back of this book. You may want to refer to the preface in order to read my suggestion about handling essay grading throughout the year.

I tell students they should organize their ideas by taking notes and developing an outline of key points. My procedure for essay writing is to assign the topic, discuss it with the class, and clarify misconceptions. Students always ask about length. As a homework assignment, they organize their ideas in note form then write out an outline consisting of main points. The essay should be at least four paragraphs including the introductory paragraph, body paragraphs, and brief concluding paragraph. I attempt to train students to proofread their essays before submitting them for grading.

After giving an essay assignment, I ask the class to suggest ideas as I write them on the board. Here are some sample notes on this essay:

- the man's personality—unimaginative and impulsive
- his obliviousness to the frigid temperature
- his ignorance about the terrain
- his taking a little-used trail
- his lack of a companion
- his inadequate clothing
- his relationship to the dog
- his walking on a little-known trail
- his inability to build a fire

Students' outlines could center on these topics:

- man's personality and relationship to the dog
- ignorance about temperature and terrain
- inability to build a fire

"Top Man"
by
James Ullman
1907–1971

This is another adventure story with an exciting setting that resonates well with 9th grade students. James Ullman was one of the first Americans to climb Mount Everest and has written several mountaineering novels that students may have read such as *Banner in the Sky* and *The White Tower*. Some of the details in "Top Man" were possibly based on George Mallory's fateful climb up Mount Everest in 1924.[42] We talk about mountaineering expeditions, and I show the class photographs of the Himalayas.[43] The narrator is a geologist named Frank.

Setting

This story's *setting* pits men against mountain thus providing the main *conflict*. Ullman's setting is Kalpurtha, a fictional mountain in the Himalayas in South Asia supposedly known as K3. The class may be impressed to learn that the Himalayan mountain range includes all the summits on earth that are more than five miles high. The peak of Mount Everest reaches five and half miles above sea level and actually touches the jet stream. The mountain, which in this story is explicitly called an *antagonist*, is vividly described in all its majesty and grandeur. It's a formidable opponent.

Topography

The class should understand the topography. Ullman alerts the reader to the exact locations of the six camps, and it is from the sixth camp that only the finest mountaineers in the expedition—the Englishman Nace and the American Osborn—will make the ascent to the summit. We carefully review the group's ascent. When a storm dumps twelve feet of snow on the glacier, the men must wait until the snow freezes tight enough for them to advance safely up the mountain. Nace's superb mountaineering skills are demonstrated early in the story. We note his instant reaction when a porter falls into space. I draw a diagram of that situation on the board to facilitate understanding. Students should understand that all the men owe their lives to Nace's quick thinking. After that ordeal, Nace is keen to move on to the sixth camp for a cup of tea—the ultimate panacea for a Brit!

---

[42] Mallory was a British mountaineer who climbed Everest in the 1920s. During the expedition, he disappeared, and his fate was unknown until his body was discovered in 1999. It is not known whether he reached the summit. Sir Edmund Hillary was the first mountaineer known to have ascended to the summit of Everest in 1953.

[43] One can find photographs of the Himalayas at many websites such as www.freeyork.org.

Mountain versus men

Like "To Build a Fire," this story involves the most basic *conflict*, man pitted against some aspect of nature or the environment, in this case the mountain. K3, the story's *antagonist*, is personified and becomes, as it were, a tangible opponent. It is a brutal enemy against whom the men must pit their strength and expertise in an attempt to conquer it. I ask the class to find examples of K3 as antagonist. Students point out Ullman's graphic references to the treacherous mountain. They question why men would travel thousands of miles, endure such hardships, and risk their lives to tackle such a foe. Mallory's reply is legendary: "Because it's there."

Nace versus Osborn

Even more fascinating than the conflict between men and mountain is the conflict between the two foremost mountaineers. Nace is experienced. He understands the challenge K3 presents better than any of the others. Students should note the reference to Nace's mountaineering friend, John Furness, who fell to his death while climbing Everest. The class should realize that the main disagreement between the Nace and Osborn involves the best route up K3. As the two men continue to climb, their personalities are clearly drawn.

Protagonists' contrasting personalities

I divide the class into small groups, and students make a chart listing the differences between the two men. They note, for example, that Nace is an introvert who is prudent and self-sacrificing, whereas Osborn is an extrovert who is reckless and egotistical.

Climax

Teens enjoy the climactic section that describes Osborn's selfish refusal to submit to Nace's better judgment and return to base. Osborn risks the other men's lives for his own glory. When Nace sets off after him, the geologist insists that he should go with him. (Well, of course. Someone has to tell the rest of the story.) I draw a diagram on the board to help students understand what happens next. They should appreciate Osborn's near fatal predicament as well as Nace's instinctive and immediate reaction. Perhaps Nace fleetingly hopes that Osborn will live to conquer K3.

Symbolism

At this point, we're exhausted! We turn to the epilogue—Osborn's supposedly unsuccessful attempt to reach the summit. We discuss symbols and the *symbolism* of the axe. A symbol is a detail or an item in a literary piece that stands for itself but, more importantly, represents something beyond itself, usually an abstract idea. In other words, a symbol operates at a deeper level than something that is not symbolic. What about the axe in Ullman's story? Various students decide that it represents courage or sacrifice or perhaps gratitude. In any case, it is Paul Osborn's mute tribute to Martin Nace.

Top man

It remains for the class to decide on the "top man." A strong case can be made for either Nace or Osborn. The Englishman embodies experience, leadership skills, loyalty, and a willingness to make the ultimate sacrifice. The American climber exhibits unusual selflessness in giving the honor of conquering K3 to Nace and concealing his own achievement. The issue makes for good discussion, and freshmen students have strong opinions on the issue. Incidentally, if any students have mountaineering knowledge or experience, they will be of invaluable help to others in the class during discussion of this exciting story.

Mount Everest

Essay

Write a 1½ to 2-page essay in which you contrast the personalities of Nace and Osborn. To conclude your essay, state who you think is "top man" and give reasons for your opinion.

"Antaeus"

by

Borden Deal[44]

1922–1985

"Antaeus" is a third story in which *setting* is crucial. The tale includes two settings—the rooftop of a factory in an industrial northern city that is implicitly contrasted with rural Alabama—the setting T.J. remembers. The first point to establish, however, is the *allusion* in the title. When students research the myth, they discover that Antaeus maintained his superhuman strength as long as he remained in contact with the earth. On learning his secret, Hercules lifted the giant off the ground and killed him. I ask the class to write down the connection between Antaeus and T. J.

Setting

We talk about places teenagers like to escape to—a bedroom, a tree, or other hideaways the class remembers from childhood. We all agree that everyone needs a special place, a place one can call one's own. The city boys in this story climb up a fire escape to a flat rooftop above a factory. The rooftop setting becomes the headquarters for their gang. The rooftop is the boys' escape from the rest of the world, a place where they rule undisturbed.

Contrast between T.J. and the city boys

The dialog between the other boys and T.J. reveals the vast differences in attitudes and lifestyles between the city kids and the country boy from Alabama. Students should appreciate T.J.'s self-confidence. I ask the class how they react to new students or new kids in their neighborhoods. They admit they think other teens should be just like them. We all have this problem.[45] The rooftop has an adverse effect on T.J. Again, I ask for examples of T.J.'s attitude to the city boy's hideaway. Then I ask someone to explain why T.J.'s attitude angers the other boys. The class needs to appreciate that the city kids associate things people grow with ornamental things like flowerbeds and grass whereas T.J. immediately thinks of practical things like crops and fruit. The city kids feel defensive about their way of life and object to the country boy's implicit condemnation. Students relate to this viewpoint. Some of them admit to feeling similar hostility to other kids whose backgrounds and attitudes are different from theirs.

---

[44] Borden Deal is an American writer whose family were cotton farmers. He obviously sympathized with the country boy in this story. Deal wrote hundreds of short stories and several novels.

[45] To cite two amusing literary examples of this very human trait, Professor Higgins in *My Fair Lady* declares, "Why can't a woman be more like a man!" And in Harper Lee's *To Kill a Mockingbird*, Jem scolds Scout for becoming more like a girl every day.

T.J.'s leadership qualities

T.J.'s enthusiasm is endearing. He rapidly persuades the other boys to start growing watermelons—on a rooftop! Students recognize that T.J. is a born leader. They break into groups and discuss T.J.'s leadership abilities. Everyone makes a list of his abilities, writes down examples, and fleshes them out with supporting detail.

T.J.'s motivation

Students ponder the next question—Why is T.J. so keen on the project? They realize that he must have land and things to grow in order to thrive. He can't bear hanging out with other kids on a flat roof. That's why the contrast in the two *settings*—industrial city versus rural Alabama—is crucial if we are to understand T.J.'s predicament. We talk about the things students think they must have to be content. I question the class: Do you need a smart phone or an iPad to be happy?

Antagonists

Like the relatives in Truman Capote's story that we read next, the *antagonists* appear abruptly from the adult world. I point out the adjective that defines the businessmen; someone suggests that "plump" belittles the men further in our eyes. Unlike the city kids, T.J. apparently has little experience of adult authority, which is communicated via terse questions. He alone has the confidence to defend his project. His naiveté is poignant. Most teenagers understand T.J.'s distress, his futile objections.

T.J. escapes

Students also understand why this modern Antaeus runs away. Someone asks why he arrived in the city in the first place. That question is beyond the parameters of the story. What most young people don't immediately understand is T.J.'s refusal to allow the businessmen to get rid of the dirt. To him, it's precious. Finally, we talk about the *connotations* of the word "home" in the last paragraph.[46] Everyone agrees that one's home is a place where one is accepted and loved unconditionally.[47] Home for T.J. is the countryside of Alabama, but the city kids have no such safe haven to return to.

---

[46] 9th grade students should recognize the difference between a word's connotation and its denotation. If they don't, we analyze words that illustrate the difference—*skinny* versus *slender* or *nag* versus *steed*, for instance.

[47] I write on the board two opposing definitions of "home" included in Robert Frost's narrative poem "The Death of the Hired Man." Warren: "Home is a place where, when you have to go there, / They have to take you in." Mary: "I should have called it / Something you somehow haven't to deserve." Students invariably agree with Mary.

To close the discussion, I tell the class that it took Borden Deal ten years to get this story published. Since its publication, it has been included in countless anthologies. The author has told his readers that they, like T.J., should persevere in something they believe in, no matter how long it takes to achieve the goal. That's a truth worth learning.

Characterization

"A Christmas Memory"
by
Truman Capote[48]
1924–1984

The next element the class explores is *characterization*. Fiction writers tell stories about people. They explore key moments in people's lives—failure, disappointment, success, temptation, and other aspects of life. We come to know people that exist in fiction, especially main characters, just as we do in real life. Getting to know fictional characters is what makes stories so fascinating.

Characterization

I write on the board methods authors use to convey character as the class writes down definitions of each technique:

direct:	the author tells us directly or explicitly about the character's personality
indirect:	the author allows us to infer personality in several ways:
	actions
	thoughts
	speech
	appearance
	others' reactions to the person

Buddy's friend

"A Christmas Memory" is a good story to discuss in terms of its characterization. Capote uses most methods in his *indirect characterization* of the unnamed woman who is Buddy's distant cousin.[49] Students break into small groups and write notes based on the text that provide examples of each method used to convey the woman's personality. They find examples of

---

[48] Some teenagers are interested to learn that Truman Capote is the author of *Breakfast at Tiffany's,* which was made into a movie starring Audrey Hepburn. Capote also wrote *In Cold Blood,* a chilling account of a mass murder in Kansas. He was a close childhood friend of Harper Lee and the model for Dill in *To Kill a Mockingbird,* a novel that is discussed in my world literature teaching guide.

[49] The old woman calls the boy Buddy although that is not his name. She names him in memory of a childhood friend whose name was Buddy. This detail could be cited as an example of the woman's mental fragility.

her actions, speech, appearance, and others' reactions to Buddy's odd but charming friend. Students should also note Capote's *use of lists* that conveys the woman's naiveté. Whether or not the class is willing to admit it, Buddy's cousin *is* endearing. Immured in our prevailing blasé, been-there-done-that mindset, we would all do well to emulate some of the woman's zest for living and her generosity.

Mr. Haha Jones

Students enjoy the *direct characterization* of Mr. Haha Jones and his wife as well as their café. Talk about atmosphere! Even the dog is terrified. Haha, so named because he's permanently miserable, presents a terrifying appearance, and the atmosphere around his café is nothing short of heart-stopping.

The relatives

The relatives' entrance is managed via short fragments. (Fragments? The class looks at me accusingly. No, you can't write in fragments. You're not a well-known author.) Like the businessmen in "Antaeus," the relatives' brief words convey their meanness.

Fruitcakes for strangers

When discussing the cake-baking episode, young people find it hard to imagine that someone—anyone—would go to all this trouble and expense to bake cakes for strangers. "I don't get it." Well, they may not, but Capote makes sure that the sensitive reader will. I don't allow obstinate students to dismantle my class, but I try to help them see. That, by the way, was Joseph Conrad's purpose as a writer, a purpose that impressed Flannery O'Connor: "My task which I am trying to achieve is, by the power of the written word, to make you hear, to make you feel—it is, before all, to make you *see*. That—and no more, and it is everything."[50] A good story, any piece of good literature, allows the reader to see or understand truths about life or human nature that are captured in it. In this case, Capote surely wants the reader to appreciate the kind, loving spirit of Buddy's friend who bakes fruitcakes for people she hardly knows or will never meet.

Symbolism

Some 9th graders find the ending of "A Christmas Memory" too sentimental; most of them will not admit to finding it moving. We discuss the *symbolism* of the kites. Perhaps they represent the two friends' mutual affection. "How do we know that?" Well, look at the last paragraph.

---

[50] Joseph Conrad, Preface to *The Nigger of the "Narcissus"* (New York, Norton: 1979), vii. Qtd. by Flannery O'Connor, *Mystery and Manners*, 80.

The *diction* suggests the dissolving of a friendship that developed over many years of Buddy's childhood. The last paragraph takes us back to the kites Buddy and the old woman used to make for each other every Christmas—the only present they could afford. The two kites in the final paragraph surely symbolize the affection they always had for each other. Some students won't agree, and I don't press the point. I remind them that a *symbol* stands for itself but also represents something beyond itself, usually an abstract idea.

"Thank you, M'am"

by

Langston Hughes[51]

1902–1967

This story is another fine example of *characterization*. I love this piece by a well-known African-American poet and fiction writer. It's a short story packed with meaning that leaves one's heart full. Before we discuss it, I talk with the class about today's high incidence of juvenile crime and ask for students' opinions of this distressing situation. A few of them cite a lack of communication between teenagers and parents and the high incidence of one-parent, usually fatherless homes. Some young people realize that juvenile criminals have no one in their lives to love them and teach them essential life lessons such as moral values and respect for a good education. They sense that such youngsters don't have a chance to mature into productive, thoughtful human beings. One hopes that the boy in this story learns an indelible lesson and will mature into a sensitive, moral young man. Throughout his arresting story, Langston Hughes uses *indirect characterization*.

Indirect characterization

The first sentence conveys the woman's daunting personality. And if that doesn't do it for us, we get the point with her immediate reaction to the would-be thief. Most people would call the police or take off. Not this lady. After his potential victim grabs him, the boy has one thought in his mind—to put some distance between him and this terrifying old woman, but she's not about to let him get away. This strong young man is no match for Mrs. Luella Bates Washington Jones.

We look for examples of the woman's character conveyed via *speech*. Students find many. What does the class infer from Roger's monosyllabic reply when Mrs. Jones tells him he could have asked her for money to buy the coveted shoes? Young people should realize that he lives in a world where people take rather than ask for things. This tough lady educates him.

Mrs. Jones is also characterized by her generous *actions*. Again, the class looks for examples. Her compassionate nature is further defined by what she does *not* do. She doesn't turn Roger over to the police or haul him off to jail. On the contrary, she tells him that she's done things that she's ashamed of and exhorts him to behave himself in future.

---

[51] Langston Hughes was an African-American writer known primarily for his poetry. He also wrote short stories, an autobiography, and some novels.

The boy's reaction

Students realize that Roger struggles with preconceived notions about other people. His conversation with the old woman is punctuated by long pauses. He's never met anyone like Mrs. Jones who takes him in hand and seems to care about him. He tries to come to grips with this woman who's unlike anyone he's ever known, someone who attempts to reach him respect and decent behavior. He struggles with conflicting emotions. During their brief acquaintance, Roger acquires respect for Mrs. Jones, and students are certain he's learned a lesson he'll never forget. When he leaves, they realize that he wants to say so much more but can only mumble, "Thank you, m'am."

Atmosphere
"The Storm"
by
McKnight Malmar[52]
1903-1985

We turn to the next literary element. The class should understand what is meant by the *atmosphere* of a literary piece. Atmosphere or mood is the emotional setting of a work. It's how we feel when reading it. Charles Dickens, for example, is a prime example of an author who creates a specific, almost tangible mood. In the following passage from one of his best-known novels, Dickens creates a dismal mood:

> It was a rimy morning, and very damp. I had seen the damp lying on the outside of my little window, as if some goblin had been crying there all night, and using the window for a pocket-handkerchief. Now I saw the damp lying on the bare hedges and spare grass, like a coarser sort of spiders' webs; hanging itself from twig to twig and blade to blade. On every rail and gate, wet lay clammy, and the marsh-mist was so thick that the wooden finger on the post directing people to our village—a direction they never accepted, for they never came there—was invisible to me until I was quite close under it. Then as I looked up at it, while it dripped, it seemed to my oppressed conscience like a phantom devoting me to the Hulks [prison ships].[53]

Students tend to confuse *atmosphere* and *tone*. The two literary elements are very different:

- Atmosphere or mood is how the writer makes the reader feels while reading a piece.
- Tone refers to the writer's attitude or approach to the piece he or she is writing.

Before we read the mystery entitled "The Storm," I ask students about times when they've been alone in the dark. If they were walking home on a dark street, did they turn an ordinary sound into something sinister? Did they start to think that someone was creeping up on them? Or did they imagine, to paraphrase Shakespeare, a bush to be a bear?[54] How would they feel if they were at home alone at night during a storm in utter darkness? Then we talk about the increasingly tense *atmosphere* created in Malmar's horror story. From the *personification* in the second sentence, the writer introduces a mood of suspense. The storm pervades the story like a menacing beast. The class breaks into small groups and writes down details that add to

---

[52] McKnight Malmar is a modern American writer of short fiction and several mystery novels.

[53] Charles Dickens, *Great Expectations* (New York: Norton, 1999), 19.

[54] *A Midsummer Night's Dream*, V.i.22.

the suspense. Students should appreciate Janet's terror that steadily increases and seems almost palpable when she finds the horrifying thing in the trunk. The writer intensifies the suspense with every word until the last grisly detail of the ring.

I ask the class about the moment when they first realized, or began to realize, that the husband is a murderer. A bright student mentions the lack of jagged glass shards around the cellar's broken window frame. Apart from the incontrovertible clue of the ring taken from the dead woman's finger, there are several other instances. We then exchange ideas about the wife's shifting attitude to the storm: It terrifies her while she's alone, it becomes increasingly menacing, but at the end it provides welcome relief as she stumbles away from her husband into its "safe, dark shelter."

Surprise ending

Every student is jolted by the ending. The class should be able to outline the husband's actions before Janet returns home. I ask the class about the personalities of both wife and husband and why Ben placed the dead woman's ring on his finger. The writer tells us that Janet is immature and indecisive, and that Ben is frugal, a characteristic that explains his taking the ring. We talk about unanswered questions that remain after the story ends, questions such as these: Why did the murder take place? When did it occur? Did the letters have anything to do with the murder? Above all, will Janet escape? Young people want things to be neatly explained with no loose endings. We hope she gets away, but the writer withholds that information. I ask the class to suggest an ending. They usually describe the girl stumbling into the storm, perhaps falling to the ground terrified with her husband pursuing and killing her. Such an ending is logical. No neighbors live in the area, and no cars would be driving past the house because the roads are flooded. There is probably no one who can help Janet and nowhere she can hide to avoid Ben's finding her.

The story's effect is based on the sinister *atmosphere* that is maintained throughout the events described. Teenagers always agree that this is one suspenseful horror story.

Theme

"The Story-Teller"

by

Saki[55] (H. H. Monro)

1870–1916

Some stories such as "The Storm" are not written to explore a main idea, but many have an underlying *theme* or fundamental insight that the writer wishes to convey. "The Story-Teller" by Saki is such a story. It's a fun, uncomplicated piece to read, but underneath the humor, the writer makes a fundamental point. We talk about stories students read, or had read to them, when they were young, stories that punish bad children and reward good children who live happily ever afterwards. I ask for students' opinions about this type of story. They are quick to point out that the scenario is not true to life. Inequality exists. In this life, bad people commit evil deeds with impunity, while good people are not rewarded for their valiant actions.

In "The Story-Teller," we notice that Saki reverses the model. In other words, his amusing story *satirizes* conventional children's stories. Students look puzzled. I define satire for them: The satirist criticizes some aspect of human nature or life in order to expose and correct weakness, inequality, or inaccuracy of some sort. The satirist often does so via humor. Saki's story disparages the sort of story adults like to read to small children, a story that is good for them like eating spinach. He is also satirizing adults' perceptions about children. He implies that we should not patronize them or encourage them to automatically expect to be rewarded or punished for good or bad behavior. Life isn't like that. Good people's noble deeds are frequently unheeded, and sometimes thugs get away with—well yes, murder.

Frame narrative

"The Story-Teller" is a *frame story.* The class should know that means there's a story within a story; there's an outer framework within which a story or many stories are told. In this case, the outer framework is the train journey. A bachelor is cooped up in a hot railway carriage with several lively children and their inept aunt on an hour's journey.[56] One immediately sympathizes with the bachelor. This basic situation frames the storytellers' stories. At the end,

---

[55] Saki is the pseudonym of Hector Monro, a Scottish writer and journalist. Munro decided on the pen name Saki early in his writing career. Saki was a character in The Rubáiyát, an eleventh-century volume of Persian poetry by Omar Khayyám that Monro admired.

[56] Scholars claim that the aunt in this story is based on two aunts who raised Munro from early childhood and were excessively strict and insensitive.

Saki returns us to the basic situation as the bachelor alights from the train mentally shuddering at the aunt's incompetence.

I ask students to state the implication in this passage: "Both the aunt and the children were conversational in a limited, persistent way, reminding one of the attentions of a housefly that refused to be discouraged…. The bachelor said nothing out loud." The *inference* is clear: The bachelor finds the foolish chatter of the carriage's other occupants extremely annoying. In all literature classes, I often ask students to make inferences about the text. I tell them that, to read intelligently, one must read between the lines. The meaning of literature often resides, as it were, in the white space. I ask the class what one may infer about the *setting* of a railway carriage. Some students realize that the enclosed space and stifling atmosphere increase the bachelor's annoyance at the aunt's inability to control the children. He cannot escape from them, as implied by the reference to the compartment's communication cord.[57]

The two storytellers
The tale includes two storytellers. The unimaginative, narrow-minded aunt tells a predictably moralistic story about a good little girl who is saved from being gored by a bull because everyone admires her goodness. The children find it boring. One child inevitably questions whether the girl would have been saved if she hadn't been good, a question that has immediately occurred to the bachelor. Then there's the absurdity of the aunt's response: Because she was a good child, her rescuers ran faster than they would have done if she'd been bad!

To preserve his sanity, the bachelor takes over the story telling. The creative, unconventional second storyteller tells a story about a little girl whom he ironically describes as "horribly good" who is gored to death by a wolf. It captivates the children. The bachelor has an indispensable quality for a storyteller: a vivid imagination. He promptly responds to each child's questions with amazing creativity. The children are impressed when he fills his imaginary park with creatures such as pigs and fish and parrots "who said clever things at a moment's notice." And, of course, they love the graphic description of the wolf's devouring good little Bertha. The consensus: They've never heard a more beautiful story!

Theme
We talk about the story's *theme*. What makes it unconventional? Students point out that Bertha's goodness is the cause of her horrible death, so the bachelor's story reverses the

---

[57] A communication cord on British trains runs along the length of a train and can be pulled in an emergency in order to stop the train.

common belief that goodness is rewarded. Saki implies a strong opinion about stories the young will and will not sit still for: They like imaginative, unpredictable stories that do not tack on a moral. They don't like dull stories about good children being rewarded for their goodness. It is, of course, essential that students recognize the theme of a literary piece; whether or not they agree with it is another matter altogether. In this case, they may object, quite rightly, that it's important to tell young children stories with important lessons embedded in them that mold their characters. Within the context of "The Story-Teller," that fundamental truth is not Saki's concern.

Ironic ending

Students should recognize the *irony* of the superior story's outcome. Goodness is not rewarded. On the contrary. The tinkling of Bertha's medals for goodness causes her death. And since the park is some distance from the town, there is no one around to rescue her. The class should not miss the further irony of this story being told by a bachelor: His single state does not preclude his knowledge about children's taste in stories.

<h1 align="center">"Young Ladies Don't Slay Dragons"</h1>
by
<h1 align="center">Joyce Hovelsrud[58]</h1>

This amusing story shares some similarities with "The Story-Teller." Like Saki's story, it conveys a central idea, it deals with children's stories—in this case, fairy stories, and its *theme* is satiric. It's also fun to read.

Students have already read the story before we discuss it, but in this case I assign parts and different students read the dialogue spoken by the cast of characters. Then we discuss traditional fairy stories about beautiful princesses. There's always an ogre, a witch or some sort of evil creature who captures the princess, and a brave prince who rescues her, proposes marriage, and carries her off on his white horse to live happily ever afterwards. Everyone agrees. Yes, that's a typical story line for fairy tales. Like "The Story-Teller," "Young Ladies Don't Slay Dragons" is *satire*. Similar to Saki's story that derides the sort of story adults like to read to small children, Hovelsrud's story satirizes traditional fairy stories; in other words, it makes fun of them by reversing conventional characters and situations.

Reversals

When students are told that Hovelsrud's story is also based on *reversals*, they realize that the author is reversing typical aspects of fairy tales. In other words, she satirizes them. The class shares ideas about the satire and makes these points:

- The king is inept and unable to control his kingdom.
- The princess is not helpless but enterprising and boyish.
- The dragon is not the ferocious beast of fairy tale. He talks in clichés and chats with the princess.
- The princess, not a prince, kills the dragon.
- She kills the dragon with a lead pipe not the traditional sword.
- Instead of slaying the dragon, the prince appears out of the ashes of the dead beast.
- The prince does not give long speeches declaring his love. He is entirely passive. He merely proposes and rides away with the princess.

So how do these reversals contribute to the satire? They make fun of traditional fairy stories with an amusing situation, dialogue, and characters. We also laugh at allusions to nursery

---

[58] I have been unable to obtain dates or any other information about this author.

rhyme: The queen is eating bread and honey, and king is counting out his money. Finally, there is no suspense. It's all very down-to-earth. Hearing about the menacing dragon, the princess makes her plans and efficiently deposes of him.

Theme

When I ask for suggestions about the story's *theme*, the class agrees that the tale illustrates the imaginary, unrealistic nature of fairy tale. Students enjoy their involvement in this amusing story.

"The Bridge"
by
Nicolai Chukovski[59]
1904–1965

"The Bridge" is another very different tale that illustrates the importance of *theme* or the author's main idea. It is set in modern Russia. Like Doris Lessing's story "The Tunnel," it is a rite of passage theme to which teenagers can relate because they are growing into adulthood and making discoveries about themselves.

Rite of passage

I remind students about universal *rites of passage* such as graduation, first job, and marriage. People experience other individual or particular rites of passage. The story's *title* overtly refers to the bridge from which the girl falls, but symbolically it refers to the bridge from Kostya's childish fears to his maturing self as he overcomes his fears about adult life. Kostya bridges or crosses the gap between childhood and young adulthood. At the beginning of the story, Kostya's immaturity is established. I ask the class for details that substantiate this point.

Characterization

We review methods an author uses to convey character. Students find examples of *direct* and *indirect characterization* including Kostya's thoughts, appearance, and actions as well as others' reactions to him.

Suspense

The writer builds *suspense* as Kostya bicycles after the girl. Young people understand the challenge. Kostya must catch up with her. We follow the two of them with mounting horror as the girl bicycles across a half-constructed bridge with a river swirling below. The climactic moment is emphasized by its placement in a single paragraph. At this point, we exchange ideas. What would you do to save someone from drowning? One student suggests knocking the person unconscious. Most students think it's pointless to rescue the bikes. Of course, Kostya does so to increase the girl's admiration. He succeeds. Her respect represents a dramatic contrast to his grandmother's opinion of him. Students recognize his growing self-confidence and the girl's adoration.

---

[59] Chukovski was a Russian writer of historical fiction and short stories.

Explicit theme

Young people often confuse a story's *theme* with its *plot*. I remind them of the difference:

- The plot refers to the sequence of events.
- The theme is the central insight about life or human nature that the plot reveals.

Students should understand that a theme can be *explicit*, as it is in this story, but is usually *implicit*. The author of this story explicitly states the theme: Kostya has discovered something new about himself—he has acquired a new-found confidence and is able to control his future. He makes a second discovery: He feels a dawning sense of affection for a girl. These new emotions mark Kostya's rite of passage to maturity. I tell the class that one way to identify a story's theme is to decide how the protagonist changes or what he or she learns as a result of the events described. Then I ask students to write out a thematic statement.[60] Before they do so, I tell them that a theme never includes specific details drawn from a literary piece. A theme states the main idea that the piece with all its details conveys. One could state the theme of this story in different ways:

1. In the face of danger or challenge of some sort, even the most fearful person can acquire self-confidence.
2. Only via a challenging experience can one achieve self-confidence.

The class is certain of one point: The change in this Russian boy will be permanent.

---

[60] Students should be instructed to write out the theme of a literary work in one sentence.

Irony
"The Ransom of Red Chief"
by
O. Henry (William Sydney Porter)
1862–1910

At this point, we turn to discussion of an *ironic tone* in a literary piece. O. Henry, a pseudonym for William Sydney Porter, was a prolific writer of humorous, clever short stories often characterized by surprise endings. "The Ransom of Red Chief" is one of his best-known stories. It describes a kidnapping scheme gone awry. Young people like it because it's amusing, and the protagonist is a mischievous ten-year-old. Two bad guys need money for a fraudulent scheme and decide to kidnap the only child of Mr. Dorset, a well-to-do gentleman whom they're certain "would melt down for a ransom of two thousand dollars."

The most difficult aspect of literature for students of all ages to recognize is the writer's *tone*. It's easy to distinguish verbal tone. I demonstrate a verbal tone by repeating a sentence several times to the class using different tones of voice. It's much harder to recognize tone in a piece of writing. There are as many different tones as there are human emotions, but an *ironic tone* is the default literary tone. I remind the class about the ironic outcome of Saki's story: The death of good little Bertha results from the clinking of her medals for goodness.

Irony

We discuss *verbal, situational,* and *dramatic irony;* I define and compose examples of each type and write them on the board:

> **verbal irony**: a discrepancy between what someone says and what he means e.g.: Mother to son after he spills red soda over her white linen table cloth moments before guests arrive for dinner: "You're a big help."

> **dramatic irony**: a discrepancy between what a character says and what the reader knows to be true e.g.: The reader knows the wife's husband is listening outside the door when her would-be lover tells her, "Your husband is a fool. He has no idea how to make you happy."

> **situational irony**: a discrepancy between the reader's expectations about events and what actually happens e.g.: During a kidnapping story, we expect the victim to be terrified and the ending to be tragic; instead the victim thoroughly enjoys himself and torments his abductors.

O. Henry's description of kidnappers at the mercy of their victim is a classic example of *situational irony*.

When Bill and Sam stake out their victim, he's entertaining himself by throwing rocks at a cat:

> "Hey, little boy!" says Bill. "Would you like to have bag of candy and a nice ride?"
> The boy catches Bill neatly in the eye with a piece of brick.

That response should have warned the bumbling kidnappers they've chosen the wrong victim. Of course, one could talk about stereotypes or conflict or foreshadowing, but I'd rather retain students' interest by enjoying the story's irony. I ask the class to supply other examples of irony. They break into small groups, look through the story, and write down instances such as the following:

- Far from being terrified, the boy takes advantage of his situation and has fun impersonating a savage Indian chief who immediately subdues his kidnappers, one of whom he intends to scalp.
- The kidnappers are terrorized by their victim.
- The boy resists the idea of returning home. In fact, he makes his kidnappers promise they won't take him back to his dad.
- The victim is not missed by anyone in his hometown.
- The kidnappers' demands for a ransom become increasingly smaller as they grow increasingly desperate.
- Bill attempts unsuccessfully to send the boy home.
- The kidnappers fail to obtain ransom money for the boy.
- Mr. Dorset is not inclined to expedite his son's return and demands $250 to be persuaded to take the boy back!

Allusion
We pause to discuss the ironic *allusion* to Herod. What's the point? Well, it's obviously amusing *hyperbole*, but Bill ironically implies that he admires Herod for killing all the young Jewish boys and wishes he could pronounce the same fate for his young victim.

Ending
The finale is hilarious. We are given a vivid picture of the kidnappers imploring the father to hold onto his son long enough for them to escape from a terrifying child who takes his kidnappers captive and names himself Red Chief.

"The Necklace"

by

Guy de Maupassant[61]

1850–1893

"The Necklace" is a highly anthologized story. Its setting is Paris in the 1880s. Its meaning is mainly conveyed via *irony*.

Madame Loisel

Before dealing with the ironic content, we talk about the characters of the two protagonists. From the opening paragraph, the writer shows us the emptiness of materialistic values via the personality of Madame Loisel. It is important, however, that students understand that the culture of nineteenth-century France differed radically from that of contemporary America. Women, for example, did not work; given her middle-class status, Madame Loisel had no other option than to marry a man with a nondescript job, that of a government bureaucrat, and to live a fairly drab life. Of course, she should have cheerfully made the best of her circumstances. She should have been content.

In the first few paragraphs, de Maupassant uses *direct characterization* to introduce us to Madame Loisel. The piling up of negatives and the details listed alert us to her discontent. I ask students to think about someone they know or have read about who is poor but contented with his or her lot. I suggest that they compare that person to this woman. I also tell the class to pay close attention to these first paragraphs: "She grieved incessantly over the shabbiness of her apartment, the dinginess of the walls, the worn-out appearance of the chairs, the ugliness of the draperies. All these things…gnawed at her." We realize that this unhappy woman is casting her eyes over her home noticing only its defects. Instead of being happy with her circumstances, she dreams of the luxury and admiration that she so conspicuously lacks. Monsieur Loisel's personality contrasts strikingly with hers. While her husband appreciates the stew they eat for dinner, discontent gnaws at her soul. I want to shake her and tell her not to distress her husband with her unhappiness. I want to tell her to love him and cook him another savory stew! The class agrees that many people are like this woman—self-pitying, unhappy with their circumstances, craving the admiration of others. Madam Loisel's dissatisfaction is further conveyed via negative *hyperbole*: "She had no evening clothes, no jewels, nothing." At

---

[61] Scholars consider Guy de Maupassant to be the father of the modern short story and the finest French writer of the short story genre. He wrote some three hundred stories depicting aspects of nineteenth-century French life.

the evening party, the self-absorbed woman enjoys brief moments of glory: "She danced madly, wildly, drunk with pleasure, giving no thought to anything in the triumph of her beauty, the pride of her success."

Monsieur Loisel

In fact, this woman is greatly blessed. Monsieur Loisel is a devoted husband. He is so self-sacrificing and generous that he gives his wife money he'd been saving for a rifle so that she can buy an evening dress for a grand reception. And when his wife remains discontented, the husband suggests she borrow some jewelry from her friend. Throughout the paragraphs that describe the party and Madame Loisel's success, the class should notice the lack of reference to Monsieur Loisel until we are told that while his wife dances the night away, he has been dozing in a chair. We note that it is he who has brought wraps to shield her from the cold after they leave the party. It is he who wants to call a cab, and when they discover the loss of the diamond necklace, it is he who searches the streets of Paris for the rest of the night while she slumps vacantly in a chair at home. It is he who reports the loss to the police, to the newspapers, to the cab companies. And it is he who dictates to her the fabricated excuse she will tell her friend. When the couple purchases another diamond necklace to replace the one she has lost, Monsieur Loisel uses his father's inheritance to cover half the cost and borrows the rest. Certainly, this man is unselfish and caring, but I ask the class about his attitude to his wife. Invariably, students fault him for his excessive indulgence.

Symbolism

The necklace is not simply an item in the story. It takes on a deeper meaning than a mere piece of jewelry. From the title onwards, it *symbolizes* materialistic desires. Its being of little value suggests the worthlessness of materialistic aspirations. If Madame Loisel had accepted her lot in life in instead of pining for luxury, she would not have sunk into poverty and premature old age.

Irony

Like the story of Red Chief, this is a story with various *ironies*. It's ironic that Madame Loisel's dissatisfaction with her lack of luxury ultimately leads to a wretched lifestyle and, more importantly, to the deterioration of her circumstances and her husband's character. Because the Loisels lie to the friend about the loss of the necklace, Madame Loisel turns to menial labor in the face of abject poverty. The husband sacrifices his integrity and his reputation: "He signed notes, made ruinous deals, did business with loan sharks, ran the whole gamut of moneylenders. He compromised the rest of his life, risked his signature without knowing if he'd be able to honor it." The couple is reduced to a life of squalor. A subtler irony involves the change in the wife's character. Before the loss, she is vain, lazy, and dissatisfied with every aspect of her life. After she loses the necklace, she gradually becomes humble and industrious. Nevertheless, the loss of a supposedly expensive piece of jewelry reduces her to poverty and hardship.

The ultimate irony is eventually revealed: Their misery is needless because the jewelry they lost is a fake diamond necklace of little value. The irony becomes more poignant when we reflect that the loss is the direct result of Madame Loisel's habitual discontent with her middle-class status and her longing for wealth and prestige.

Ending
The clever ending takes us by surprise. It's powerful, but students sometimes wonder why we are not told of Madame Loisel's reaction to the revelation that the necklace is worthless. That detail would have defeated the purpose. Instead, the author allows us to imagine the woman's shock and mortification. Students sometimes ask why the Loisels don't tell Madame Forestier about the loss. They apparently assume the necklace is valuable; it doesn't occur to them that their wealthy friend would own costume jewelry. We are certain of one fact: They lack the strength of character to tell their friend the truth.

Title
When I ask students to comment on the title, they realize that the necklace, which has little value, symbolizes the vain pursuit of material possessions.

Theme
The story's *theme* is universal: Longing for wealth and discontent with one's circumstances will inevitably lead to misery.

Essay

I ask students to write an essay on this topic: Discuss this story's ironies in terms of Madame Loisel's character.

To help students write a well-organized essay, I again ask them for ideas as I write their suggestions on the board. Here are some sample notes:

- Madame Loisel's embarrassment and humiliation at owning no jewelry for the reception ultimately results in wretchedness.
- She doesn't want to call a cab on a cold night because she is embarrassed about her shabby wraps.
- She is more concerned about returning a supposedly valuable necklace to her friend than being truthful about its loss.
- Because she is untruthful to her friend when she cannot return the necklace, she risks losing Madame Forestier's friendship.
- Instead of becoming the cultured, refined woman she dreams about, she becomes coarse and harsh.
- Culminating irony: she learns that the supposedly valuable necklace she and her husband have worked so hard to replace is worthless.

I remind students about well-developed essays. (See notes on the "To Build a Fire" essay.) The class breaks into groups to exchange ideas, and everyone writes notes on the topic. Students complete their notes and write an outline for homework that could center on these points:

- Mme. Loisel's discontent
- the disintegration of her character
- the final revelation

They write the essay in class the following day.

"The Sniper"
by
Liam O'Flaherty[62]
1897–1984

Historical background

This story is universally popular. It's fast-paced, straightforward, and has an unexpected ending. Unlike "The Necklace," we deal with this tale rapidly. Students should grasp its historical background. It is set on a rooftop in Dublin, Ireland, in the 1920s during a civil war between Irish republicans who wanted Ireland to be free of British rule and become a republic and Irish nationalists who wanted only limited independence.[63]

The sniper

I ask students how the author engages our sympathy for the republican sniper. They are quick to note several instances. We admire the sniper's subterfuge with the cap trick. He is also bitterly remorseful after he has killed his enemy. At that point, the sniper hates the thought of war and death and killing another man.

The ironic ending

Then there's the ending. It's effective because we're totally unprepared for it. We are jolted by the tragic outcome. Like the end of O. Henry's kidnapping tale, this ending is an example of *situational irony*. Students often question why it's situational irony. Well, the reader expects a less tragic outcome.

"The Man He Killed"

After discussing "The Sniper," I distribute copies of a poem by Thomas Hardy (1840–1928), "The Man He Killed." Students silently read the poem then write a paragraph that explains the connection between story and poem. Here are the first two stanzas of Hardy's poem:

> Had he and I but met
> By some old ancient inn,
> We should have sat us down to wet
> Right many a nipperkin![64]

---

[62] O'Flaherty was an Irish novelist and short story writer who became involved in Ireland's civil war.

[63] The nationalists eventually won the war. The conflict resulted in a massive loss of life and an embittered country.

[64] a glass of ale

But ranged as infantry,
And staring face to face,
I shot at him as he at me,
And killed him in his place....

In their paragraphs, students should point out how both pieces ironically illustrate the pointlessness of war and the horror of young men killing one another. The sniper in O'Flaherty's story is undoubtedly overcome with remorse and revolted by Ireland's civil war. Hardy's poem causes us to realize a similar irony: In peacetime, the two young soldiers could have been good friends; in war, they must kill or be killed. Both O'Flaherty and Hardy imply that war requires men to become calloused to the horror of taking another man's life.

Point of View
"The Open Window"
by
Saki (H. H. Monro)

An essential decision a fiction writer must make concerns a story's *point of view* or the perspective from which a writer chooses to tell the story. Who is going to relate the events? Students should appreciate that the narrator of a story is not synonymous with the author.

We review the basic literary perspectives:

1st **person**: The story is told in the first person from one character's perspective. This choice of narrator always raises the issue of reliability: Is the narrator telling the whole truth about events?

3rd **person limited**: The story is told in the third person, but the perspective is limited to the thoughts and feelings of one character.

3rd **person omniscient**: The story is told in the third person by an omniscient author who allows the reader to know the thoughts and feelings of several characters.

In order to review the three main perspectives, I compose and distribute the following paragraphs in order to differentiate among the three of them:

3rd **person omniscient**:

Angie and Frankie were in love, but Frankie could never pluck up enough courage to tell Angie of his devotion. He was too timid and shy. He kept imagining how awful he'd feel after declaring his love for her and having her scream with laughter only to reject him—and then, at school the next day, make fun of him in front of all the other guys. No, Frankie decided, even Angie wasn't worth that kind of harassment. So, he adored her from afar. As a matter of fact, Angie adored him, absolutely idolized the boy in spite of his double chin and bifocals and long hair. She thought, although her friends could never figure out why, that Frankie was really sweet. She wished he'd ask her out. . ..

3rd **person limited**:

Frankie was really in love with Angie, but he could never pluck up enough courage to tell her of his devotion. He always felt too timid and shy. He kept imagining how awful he'd feel after declaring his love for her and then having her scream with laughter and reject him—and then, at school next day make fun of him in front of all the other guys. No, he decided, even gorgeous Angie wasn't worth that kind of harassment. He decided he'd just have to adore her from afar. He simply couldn't imagine asking her out. . ..

1ˢᵗ person:[65]

One day after school, I decided that Frankie is actually in love with me and not with that snobby Janie Perkins. Of course, I reminded myself, Frankie isn't good looking with his thick glasses and long hair, not to mention that double chin. In fact, he's downright homely when you stop to think about it. But the point is—yes, the point is—he's totally crazy about me, and well, that's rather nice. Besides, none of the other 9ᵗʰ grade girls have a boyfriend. I just wish he'd get around to asking me out. Trouble is, he's such a wimp; he'll never get around to it. I'll just have to drop a few hints—to get the relationship going. . ..

I point out differences among the three points of view. Students should understand that a *third-person omniscient* perspective is all-knowing. That is, the author, using the third person, knows what each character is thinking and allows the reader to know the thoughts and feelings or all or several of them. In the first example, we know how Frankie and Angie think and feel and, very briefly, Angie's friends.

A *third-person limited* perspective means that the author, using the third person, focuses exclusively on the thoughts and feelings of one character. Events are limited to one person's perceptions. In the second example, we only understand how Frankie thinks and feels.

In the third example, events are told from a *first-person* perspective. We only know about Angie's thoughts and feelings as she relates them in the first person. I remind the class about the issue of reliability. In the example above, Angie's reliability is questionable because she is self-centered, thus probably incapable of analyzing things objectively.

"The Open Window," another widely anthologized story by Saki, is mainly told from the *third person limited point of view.* We learn about events almost exclusively via the perspective of Framton Nuttel. How do we know that? I ask students to read passages that reveal Mr. Nuttel's thoughts. We are, as it were, inside his head as we learn the following information:

- Mr. Nuttel lacks confidence in his sister's cure for his nerves.
- He regrets having no acquaintance with the people in the neighborhood.
- He wonders whether Mrs. Sappleton is married or widowed.
- He's relieved when Mrs. Sappleton comes into the room and interrupts Vera's account of the alleged tragedy.
- He attempts to talk about less gruesome subjects than the alleged deaths of Mrs. Sappleton's husband and brothers.

---

[65] Students should remember that a first-person narrator always raises the question of reliability: To what extent is the narrator telling the truth about facts he relates? Is he entirely honest or objective about those facts? To what extent, if any, is the author withholding information about the facts we are told?

- He realizes that Mrs. Sappleton is paying him very little attention.
- He becomes fearful when the niece gazes out of the window in apparent horror.

It's helpful to ask students to write down phrases that relate to Mr. Nuttel's thoughts and feelings so that they can more easily grasp the perspective, phrases like these: "Privately he doubted…. Framton wondered whether…. It was a relief to Framton…."

We are not told about the thoughts and feelings of the niece, the aunt, or Mr. Nuttel's sister. We *infer* that both the niece and Mrs. Sappleton find their visitor insufferably dull. We also infer a great deal about Vera's personality. She is self-possessed, clever, with a vivid imagination. She immediately sizes up the visitor, realizes he is gullible, and decides to have some fun at his expense. Students should understand the importance of Saki's last sentence: The niece is particularly adept at spinning fantastic stories on the spur of the moment.

I point out the brief switch in perspective. After Mr. Nuttel frantically escapes, Saki switches to an *omniscient point of view* as he describes the cyclist who almost collides with Nuttel and relates the brief conversation between the Sappletons and Vera. Why is the switch effective? It allows us to grasp the aunt's reaction to their visitor and to further appreciate Vera's vivid imagination.

We talk about the effectiveness of Saki's perspective. The class should realize that the point of the entire story would be diminished if it were told by the niece or her aunt. Because we are inside the mind of Mr. Nuttel, we are made keenly aware of his nervous personality. He is the ideal target of Vera's outrageous lie.

Characterization

In addition to point of view, we briefly discuss *characterization*. We know very little about the aunt. The author implies that she is a confident and accomplished hostess. How do we know that? She converses easily with her guest although he's a complete stranger. She is insensitive. Why? She is indifferent to the man's nervous condition, real or imagined. We pay more attention to Vera. She's an unusual teenager. For one thing, she exudes self-confidence. She's also unkind. How can we deduce this? She takes advantage of a dull-witted guest. First, she ascertains his lack of knowledge concerning her aunt and their neighbors then she immediately invents a tale about her aunt's husband and brothers who were supposedly lost in a hunting accident. Vera tells Mr. Nuttel that her aunt never believed that they died but is convinced they will return through the open window in the front room. Why does Vera tell such an extravagant lie? She is bored by the visitor and entertains herself by telling a preposterous story about her supposedly mad aunt while she watches Mr. Nuttel's predictable reaction.

We are made even more aware of Vera's resourcefulness when she lies extravagantly about the visitor's fear of dogs. Saki's ending cements in our minds Vera's ingenuity. Students interject that they believed Vera's story about the tragedy. Yes, we all do when we first read it. That's the point. Vera dupes Mr. Nuttel and the reader into believing her fiction. She makes the visitor think her aunt is mad then she takes advantage of his nervous state and causes him to believe he's seeing ghosts when the aunt's husband and brothers return from their hunt. It's a clever story.

"The Cask of Amontillado"
by
Edgar Allan Poe
1809–1849

This well-known story by the master of horror fiction provides another impressive example of the function of *point of view*. Edgar Allan Poe was a brilliant Romantic writer whose life was marked by tragedy.[66] I don't share young people's love for Poe's tales of horror, but many students like this story and choose to read a collection of Poe's tales for the next book report. The language is esoteric, so obscure words should be defined during discussion. It has a grisly *setting*—the crypt or underground cemetery of an Italian city some centuries ago during carnival time. People often stored wine such as amontillado in the cool environment of the catacombs.

Point of view

From the first few sentences, we realize the point of view is *first person* and the narrator is speaking to another person. This perspective always raises the question of reliability: Is the narrator's account of events dependable? It's a given that everyone has some sort of bias and that no one will record a series of events exactly as they occurred. Someone else will record them differently. When reading about events from a first-person perspective, we can usually determine that the person is not, on the whole, being entirely accurate. Poe's opening paragraph suggests that this narrator is vindictive and deceptive and that he is giving an unreliable account of the alleged wrongs his friend has inflicted on him. We strongly suspect that Fortunato's insults are trivial if not purely imaginary.

The first paragraph reveals certain important facts. The class should understand that the speaker, Montresor, is an Italian nobleman and that he is consumed with desire to avenge insults leveled at him by an ironically named friend, Fortunato. We also learn that Montresor is determined that he will punish his victim with impunity and that his victim will grasp that Montresor is having his revenge upon him. In the third paragraph, we are told about Fortunato's fatal flaw—his pride at being a connoisseur of fine wine.

---

[66] Poe's father deserted his mother when Poe was a baby; one year later, his mother died. He was cared for but never adopted by the Allan family. Poe had to leave the University of Virginia because of gambling debts and was later dismissed from West Point. His wife died after a long illness. All his life, he batted poverty, poor health, alcoholism, and emotional instability. Poe's stories and poetry reflect his tragic life. They are overwhelmingly gloomy and pessimistic. His worldview is distorted and biblically unsound.

We gradually realize that Montresor's gruesome revenge proves him to be insane as he recounts the grisly murder. Why is the first-person perspective effective? For one thing, it allows us to follow the macabre events from the viewpoint of the murderer himself. We realize that the protagonist is brutally cunning and proud of the way he dispenses with his enemy— walling him up alive in a catacomb. Because this is a first-person narrative told by the murderer, we recognize his vile cunning, his thirst for revenge, and his lack of mercy more effectively than we would if the story were told by an omniscient narrator.

Irony

Apart from the perspective, the story abounds in *irony*. I ask two boys to reread some of the dialogue. Then the class breaks into groups, and each student writes down instances of verbal and dramatic irony. Here are some examples:

verbal:

- Fortunato: "I drink...to the buried that repose around us."
- Montresor: "And I [drink] to your long life."
- Fortunato: "I shall not die of a cough."
- Montresor (after Fortunato is shackled to the walls of the recess): "Once more let me *implore* you to return."

dramatic:

- Fortunato's name is ironic.
- Fortunato is wearing a colorful jester's costume as he stumbles to his grave.
- The setting of the murder is carnival time.[67]
- Fortunato's pride in his knowledge of wine results in his death. He walks to his death because he is anxious to give his expert opinion of a bottle of amontillado.
- Montresor's insignia and motto are ironic.[68]
- Fortunato's lack of understanding versus our knowledge of his doom provides an extended example of dramatic irony.
- Fortunato is incapacitated and unaware of Montresor's intentions because of his love of wine.

---

[67] The setting reminds one of Mardi Gras in New Orleans.

[68] A family's insignia is its coat of arms. Here's the irony: The victim asks about Montresor's insignia and motto unaware that they foreshadow his impending death. The insignia depicts a huge foot (Montresor) crushing a serpent (Fortunato) that bites the heel of the foot. The serpent has bitten or offended the foot, but the foot will kill the serpent. Translated fairly loosely, the Latin motto means "No one injures me and gets away with it," but after Montresor commits the grisly murder, he ironically suffers horrendous guilt for the rest of his life.

- Montresor feigns concern for Fortunato's health.
- Both men are masons, members of a secret society whose principles include brotherhood and charity.
- The trowel that Montresor shows his victim, supposedly a sign of the Freemasons, is the tool used to enclose Fortunato in his tomb.

Several other questions should be addressed. Students invariably ask why Montresor shows his victim the trowel he will use to wall up Fortunato in the crypt. We must assume the madman is overly confident about the risks he takes. Young people also question why Montresor is able to kill Fortunato so easily. They should realize that Fortunato's smug knowledge of wine lures him to his death and that Montresor ensures that the other man drinks a great deal of wine as they move through the catacombs to Fortunato's hideous interment. A further *irony* is involved here: Montresor is determined to punish Fortunato for numerous unnamed injuries by committing the perfect revenge. He elaborates on this point: He must punish his victim with impunity, and his victim must perceive that Montresor is accomplishing his revenge. In these two objectives he surely fails. He becomes burdened through the years with guilt that weighs more and more heavily on his conscience until at last he must confess his crime, and Fortunato has no idea that Montresor is exacting revenge on his victim. We discuss the irony of Montresor's revenge in some detail.

Audience

The class exchanges ideas about the person to whom Montresor is speaking—a friend perhaps but more likely a priest to whom he is confessing his crime. We know that guilt torments him to some degree as he commits the gruesome murder: "My heart grew sick." One hopes that guilt has plagued him so acutely for the last fifty years that now, perhaps moments before death, he feels he must unburden himself and repent of his egregious crime.

A church crypt,
Italy

"The Hat"

by

Jessamyn West[69]

1902–1984

This is another tale that is useful for teaching the importance of *point of view*. Boys aren't enthusiastic about the story, so we don't spend a great deal of time on it. "The Hat" is told from an *omniscient viewpoint*. We understand the thoughts of several people—both of Cress's parents and Cress herself. I break the class into groups to locate and write down examples of this point.

We look for examples of humor in the story. There are plenty. It's amusing to read about Mr. Delahanty's perplexity over his daughter's choice of hat and his incomprehension when Cress requests that he give the hat his stamp of approval. And why on earth would his daughter want to wear a hat to the beach in the first place! Cress is like so many thirteen-year-old girls we've all known—dramatic and romantic and absorbed in her undying love for Edwin. However, the most amusing moment involves Cress's acute embarrassment when she undoubtedly wants, in her mother's words, "to stick her head in that bucket of fish and end everything." However, Sir Lancelot comes to her rescue with his valiant assurances. Someone asks what is so gallant about Edwin's behavior. He saves the day for Cress. He's a shy person, always a victim, but he stands before a large crowd and identifies with Cress's humiliation; he manages to deflect her embarrassment by suggesting that the color dyes in the offending hat are not harmful to the fish. Ecstatic, Cress knows she'll keep the hat for the rest of her life. "Why?" (From a boy.) A girl looks at the offender witheringly. "The Hat" turns out to be a fun read.

Test
Because the short story unit test is the first literature test for high school students, I hand out a list of short story topics to help 9th grade students prepare for the unit test. A list of topics and a test on the short story unit are included in the handouts.

Review questions
On the following page is a set of review questions for the short story unit. After I distribute the questions, students break into small groups to discuss the answers to each question before

---

[69] Jessamyn West was a Quaker who wrote many short stories and novels including *Friendly Persuasion*, which was made into a popular movie. "The Hat" is an excerpt from her novel for girls entitled *Cress Delahanty*. The episode is autobiographical. West is recounting a similar incident in her own childhood.

recording responses in their notebooks. I tell them they can write notes or full sentences as they respond to each question. They use their literature books and their notes as they work on the questions for approximately twenty minutes during several class periods. They complete the questions as a homework assignment and submit them the next day for grading.

****

During the Short Story Unit, students choose and begin to read a novel for the first book report of the school year. They have approximately six weeks to complete their books and write essays on them during class. Throughout the year, students read and write about books chosen from the 9th grade reading list. (See reading list in the handouts.)

Review questions on the short story unit[70]

"Through the Tunnel"

1. Briefly describe the two settings in "Through the Tunnel." In your response, refer to the colors that describe both settings. What do the colors describing the settings suggest?

   [The bay looks dangerous, and the sea looks menacing. The colors describing the bay and the description of the French boys suggest danger. The beach seems safe because it's crowded with people, and the colors that describe the mother as she sunbathes seem warm and comforting.]

2. How do the two settings suggest Jerry's conflict?

   [The contrast between the bay and the beach suggests Jerry's internal conflict. His mother remains on the crowded beach, but Jerry wants to swim in the dangerous looking bay. The contrast in settings suggests that Jerry wants to acquire some independence from his mother and to prove himself by facing something dangerous and overcoming the danger; at the same time, he wants to reassure his mother by remaining with her and preventing her from becoming anxious about him.]

3. Briefly describe the relationship between Jerry and his mother. Does it change by the end of the story?

   [Jerry's widowed mother is overly protective of Jerry, an only child. She realizes she tends to shield him too much. Jerry is aware of his mother's anxiety about him, but he wants to assert his independence from her. By the end of the story, he has proved to himself that he can accomplish something dangerous, so he no longer feels the need to affirm his independence and is happy to comply with his mother's wishes.]

"To Build a Fire"

4. As precisely as possible, state the setting of "To Build a Fire."

   [The setting is a deserted trial in the Yukon, northwestern Canada, where the temperature drops to seventy-five degrees below zero, during the nineteenth century when gold was discovered there.]

---

[70] Because of the number of stories discussed in the short story unit, I provide more questions than a teacher will want to include in one set of review questions.

To answer these and subsequent review questions, students work in small groups. They use their notes and literature books as they work on the questions for about twenty minutes during several class periods.

Suggested responses are provided in brackets for this set and subsequent sets of review questions.

A student booklet that accompanies this teaching guide contains all 9th grade review questions and tests with answers omitted.

Any of these questions could be used for a graded discussion of the short story unit.

5. Who or what is the antagonist in this story?

   [the bitter cold]

6. List aspects of the man's personality that contribute to his death.

   [The man is unimaginative, unwise, lacks caution, is cold-hearted towards his dog.]

7. What precautions should the man have taken to ensure that he was successful in building a fire?

   [He should have built a fire out in the open not under a snow-laden tree. He should have made sure his hands were not frozen before he attempted to build a fire so that he could light matches and build up his fire to avoid its going out.]

8. What else should the man have done to increase his chance of survival?

   [He should not have traveled alone. Before setting out, he should have determined the extreme to which the temperature would drop. He should have taken the main trail. He should have dressed in warmer clothes.]

9. How do we know that the dog has a better instinct for survival than the man?

   [The dog's instincts constantly alert it to the danger of walking in such a frigid temperature. It bites out the ice forming between its toes. It wants to stay near the first fire the man succeeds in building. It senses danger when the man attempts to kill it and backs away. At the end of the story, it runs off to camp for food and warmth.]

10. In your opinion, what is this story's climax?

    [Most students decide that the climax occurs when falling snow extinguishes the man's fire.]

"Top Man"

11. What is the setting of "Top Man"?

    [The story is set on a fictional mountain in the Himalayas in South Asia known as K3.]

12. Explain how the setting provides the story's conflict.

    [The men are pitted against the mountain in a valiant attempt to ascend to the summit.]

13. Apart from their nationalities, list several differences between the two protagonists.

[Nace is an experienced mountaineer; Osborn is comparatively inexperienced. Nace is prudent; Osborn is reckless. Nace is self-sacrificing; Osborn is selfish.]

14. In your opinion, who is "top man"? Explain your choice.

[Opinions vary. Students who cite Nace as "top man" refer to his wisdom, skill, and self-sacrifice. Students who cite Osborn refer to his generous tribute to Nace.]

"Antaeus"

15. Explain the allusion in the title of Borden Deal's story. How does the allusion apply to T.J.?

[The mythical Antaeus was a giant whose strength came from the earth. When Hercules lifted him off the ground, Antaeus lost his strength, and Hercules killed the giant. T.J. resembles Antaeus in that he gains his emotional strength in a rural setting or, in other words, when he is in contact with the earth.]

16. What is the essential difference between T.J. and the city boys?

[T.J. has lived in a rural area all his life and feels out of place in an urban environment. The other boys have grown up in a city and cannot relate to a country boy's inability to adapt to city life.]

17. Explain why T.J. is a good leader.

[T.J. gives the other boys a reasonable goal; he motivates the city boys to achieve something difficult. He provides a good example by working harder than them. He encourages them to imagine their goal. His enthusiasm motivates them to continue the hard work.]

"A Christmas Memory"

18. List methods of indirect characterization the author uses to convey the old woman's personality.

[To convey the woman's personality, the author uses physical description, speech, actions, other people's reactions, lists of things the woman has and has not done.]

19. What main aspects of the woman's personality are conveyed via lists?

[The lists reveal her unworldliness and her quaintness.]

20. What do the kites in the final paragraph symbolize?

[The kites represent the close friendship between the boy and the old woman.]

"Thank you, M'am"

21. What is your opinion of Mrs. Jones in "Thank you, M'am"?

[Students consistently admire this woman. She is straightforward, generous, and doesn't hand Roger over to the police. She wants to teach Roger a lesson in moral behavior that he will never forget.]

22. Why does Mrs. Jones tell Roger that she has done things she's ashamed of?

[She wants the boy to know that people can change and improve their characters.]

23. What main method of indirect characterization does Langston Hughes use to convey Mrs. Jones's personality?

[speech]

"The Storm"

24. Characterization is not a key element in this story; however, we learn something about the husband and the wife's personalities. List one or two traits that define each of them.

[In addition to being miserly, Ben tends to be morose and short-tempered. Janet is indecisive and naïve.]

25. How does Janet's attitude to the storm change?

[While she alone in the house, the storm terrifies her. When she realizes her husband is a murderer, she rushes out into the dubious safety it provides.]

"The Story-Teller"

26. Identify this story's setting. Why is this particular setting indispensable to the meaning?

[The story is set in an oppressive railway carriage on a hot day. The setting conveys the bachelor's annoyance at his companions in the carriage—specifically, the children's endless questions and the aunt's inability to control them.]

27. Why is the bachelor a better storyteller than the aunt?

[The bachelor's story is fascinating and holds the children's interest. The aunt's dull and predictable story bores them.]

28. Why is the theme of the bachelor's story unconventional?

[His theme is unconventional because he describes the death of a good child who is devoured by a ferocious wolf.]

29. What is ironic about Bertha's death?

[Bertha hides in a bush and would probably have escaped, but the wolf hears her medals for goodness clanking against one another. He immediately finds her and devours her.]

"The Bridge"

30. In terms of Kostya's personality, explain why "The Bridge" is a rite of passage story.

[Kostya is an excessively shy, withdrawn, insecure boy who hides from other people. He dreads leaving his grandmother to go to technical school. After the experience of rescuing the girl, he acquires a new-found self-confidence.]

31. You may remember that we recognize a story's theme by observing what the protagonist learns throughout the events described. Write out a one-sentence theme for this story.

[Only experience can result in a person's acquiring self-confidence.]

"The Ransom of Red Chief"

32. What type of irony is involved in the story entitled "The Ransom of Red Chief"?

[situational irony]

33. Explain the story's central irony.

[The would-be kidnappers must pay the father of their victim in order to persuade him to take his son back.]

34. List other ironies in this tale.

[Red Chief has fun being kidnapped and doesn't want to go home.
He torments his captors rather than the other way around.
The kidnappers, particularly Bill, are victimized by their victim.]

"The Necklace"

35. Drawing from details in the story, explain your opinion of Madame Loisel.

   [Students habitually decide that Mme. Loisel is self-pitying and needlessly discontented. Instead of grieving about her shabby apartment and dreaming of luxury, she should have been happy with her circumstances. She dreams of wealth and prestige and wants others to admire her. She is selfish; for instance, she accepts the money her husband had saved for a rifle to buy herself a new dress, and she allows her husband to search for the lost necklace while she remains at home.]

36. What is your opinion of Monsieur Loisel?

   [Students appreciate the husband's self-sacrificing personality and his enduring love for his wife; however, they comment that he should not have indulged her so much and he should not have been willing to engage in nefarious business transactions in order to repay a debt.]

37. What lesson does this story teach?

   [Desire for wealth and dissatisfaction with one's circumstances will lead to unhappiness and often ruin.]

"The Sniper"

38. Summarize what you know about the historical background of "The Sniper."

   [The story is set in Dublin, Ireland, in the 1920s during the civil war between Irish republicans who wanted Ireland to free itself from British rule and Irish nationalists who wanted limited independence from Britain.]

39. What type of irony is involved in this story? Explain.

   [situational irony; we do not expect such a tragic outcome.]

"The Open Window"

40. From what point of view is this story mainly told? Explain how we recognize the point of view.

   [The story is told from a third person limited point of view. Almost all events are told from Mr. Nuttel's perspective.]

41. What point of view does the author adopt in the last few paragraphs? Why is the switch effective?

[At the end, Saki switches to an omniscient point of view. This switch allows the reader to learn the aunt's reaction to the visitor and to further appreciate Vera's vivid imagination.]

42. What does Mr. Nuttel assume when the three hunters walk through the open window?

[He assumes that the hunters are ghosts.]

"The Cask of Amontillado"

43. List several examples of dramatic irony in Poe's horror story "The Cask of Amontillado."

[Fortunato's name is ironic.
Fortunato is wearing a colorful jester's costume as he stumbles to his grave.
The setting of the murder is carnival time.
Fortunato's pride in his knowledge of wine results in his death. He walks to his death because he is anxious to give his expert opinion of a bottle of amontillado.
Montresor's insignia and motto are ironic.
Fortunato's lack of understanding versus our knowledge of his doom provides an extended example of dramatic irony.
Because of his love of wine, Fortunato is incapacitated and unaware of Montresor's intentions.
Montresor feigns concern for Fortunato's health.
Both men are masons, members of a secret society whose principles include brotherhood and charity.
Montresor's trowel, which is supposedly a sign of the Freemasons, is the tool used to enclose Fortunato in his tomb.]

44. List several examples of verbal irony.

[Fortunato: "I drink…to the buried that repose around us."
Montresor: "And I to your long life."
Fortunato: "I shall not die of a cough."
Montresor: "Once more let me *implore* you to return."]

45. Is Poe's narrator reliable or not? Explain.

[As the story progresses and Fortunato is interred in his grave, we realize that Montresor is insane and has probably imagined or exaggerated the injuries Fortunato has inflicted upon him; therefore, he is a thoroughly unreliable narrator. He is a madman consumed with desire for revenge.]

"The Hat"

46. What is the point of view adopted in "The Hat"?

[omniscient]

47. How can you identify this point of view?

[The reader is allowed to know the thoughts of several people such as Cress and both her parents.]

48. State one or two of Cress's main personality traits.

[She is lively, romantic, and imaginative.]

Unit II
The Novel

After the Short Story Unit, I introduce freshman students to the novel. The word means "new" since the novel is a relatively new genre that essentially emerged as recently as the eighteenth century as opposed to poetry, an ancient literary genre that predates Homer. The novel is obviously longer than the short story and involves more people and events. The first novels that were written several centuries ago catered to the desire of the rising middle class to read something that suited their taste, something less sophisticated than the poetry and essays that had been written up to that period in history, something that was a nice, long story about people living out their daily lives. Broadly speaking, a novel is a fictional representation of a specific group of human beings who interact with one another and who live in a specific locale.

The novelist uses the basic elements of the short story—*plot, setting, characterization*—but these elements are usually more extended in scope. Whereas a short story usually includes one setting, one major conflict, one set of characters, and one theme, a novel often includes several of each element. Like the short story writer, the novelist has something important to say and conveys his or her insights about life, human nature, or human experience via story telling. A good novel, or for that matter a good short story, often deals with the motives, actions, and experiences of people to whom we can relate, although this is obviously not the case with both novels I read with the 9th grade class. The resulting narrative is significant, it instructs us or it moves us, and it has stood the test of time. Scholars consider Daniel Defoe's *Robinson Crusoe* to be the first novel. Students should also know about the *novella*[71] as a genre, which is too long to be considered a short story and too short to be considered a novel. Famous novellas include Dickens's *Christmas Carol,* Herman Melville's *Billy Budd,* and Hemingway's *Old Man and the Sea.*

I usually discuss two novels with a freshmen class, Ray Bradbury's *Fahrenheit 451* and George Orwell's *Animal Farm.* Both books are dystopian fiction, and both convey a significant cultural theme from which young people can benefit. Students usually read a novel before class discussion begins. I assign each novel and give them several weeks to complete it.

---

[71] little novel

Fahrenheit 451

by

Ray Bradbury[72]

1920–2012

Many novels are suitable for 9th grade students, but I've always thought that Bradbury's *Fahrenheit 451* is an important book to explore with students entering high school for this major reason: It alerts the reader to a significant cultural development, *the declining impact of the written word*. That development should worry young people growing up in today's world, a world in which timeless books are increasingly becoming a rarity.[73] Bradbury's book awakens freshman students to the reality that precious books of the ages are steadily vanishing. High school students need to be aware of this deeply troubling reality. However, I should insert a significant caveat about the book: It contains profanity and coarse language, a distressing circumstance that will deter some teachers and parents from including the book in a freshman curriculum. I wish there were an edition with the offensive language omitted.[74] Despite this considerable disadvantage, I consider the novel to be a valid choice for the reason

[72] Ray Bradbury was a prolific American novelist who wrote fantasies, mysteries, horror, and science fiction.

[73] Bradbury's theme, the decline of the written word, is introduced via the title that refers to the temperature at which paper burns.

[74] Ballantine Books published an edition of the novel in 1967 with all coarse language removed. When Bradbury heard about it, he was outraged, and the objectionable language was included in the next edition.

I have mentioned in addition to its being beautifully written as well as its wisdom. There is much wisdom in this short novel about family and books and intellectual life, issues that are important to discuss with freshmen students. In terms of methodology, I introduce the book to the class and ignore the inappropriate language during class discussion. I read a few paragraphs to get students interested and ask them to read on through the book during the next two weeks.[75] After that, discussion begins. I buy classroom sets of any novel we study and loan students a copy to ensure we're all on the same page when we read or refer to a passage.

Decline of books

I talk with the class about the growing disinterest in the written word, a situation which has steadily intensified since the advent of electronic media. Libraries today need additional funding and are not usually frequented by young people in search of books to read for pleasure. Apart from Amazon Books, Barnes and Noble, and Books-A-Million, many other bookstores struggle to remain in business. Borders, B. Dalton, Walden Books, Oxford Bookstore, and others are defunct. Think about the reading public. With the exception of academics and students under pressure from teachers, many people tend to buy beach reads. The consensus seems to be that folks are too busy to sit down and read a classic book. Everyone has twenty-four hours a day to fulfill responsibilities and enjoy leisure hours. Everyone makes different choices. Reading for pleasure seems to have been crowded out.

When I visit a bookstore, I look for the classics and find a few of them on an obscure shelf vastly outnumbered by volumes of lurid Young Adult (YA) fiction. Some school systems teach via computers or other mobile devices in addition to books. Librarians and bookstore employees routinely inform me that young people favor romance or fantasy, particularly books that are dark and full of angst. Many teens favor graphic novels and books that have been made into movies. I am assured that most teens are no longer interested in the classics. Before we talk about Bradbury's prophetic book, 9th graders should be aware that the classics are no longer in favor. I want to teach them to feel very, very concerned when they realize that classic literature is becoming an endangered species.[76] As Bradbury comments in his Coda to *Fahrenheit 451*, "There is more than one way to burn a book."[77]

---

[75] Throughout my years of teaching, I have found that high school students enjoy being read to.

[76] When I use the term classic literature, I am referring to books that by common consent have stood the test of time and are most excellent. Authors such as Austen, Hawthorne, Emerson, Thoreau, Hardy, and Dickens come to mind.

[77] Ray Bradbury, *Fahrenheit 451* (New York: Ballantine, 1991), 176.

Dystopian fiction

I tell the class that Bradbury wrote his book during the Cold War era and that it was first published in 1953. *Fahrenheit 451* is a *dystopian* novel, which means that instead of describing an ideal or utopian world like Sir Thomas More's *Utopia*,[78] it depicts a world that is the stuff of nightmares. It describes a futuristic totalitarian state set in an unnamed American city in which televisions in every home instruct the citizens of the state in all they are allowed to know. The novel is about censorship. Book ownership is forbidden. It presupposes an American fire department that reverses its role: Houses have been fireproofed, so instead of protecting people and their homes, firemen are responsible for burning books. The firemen are the state's censors. Students should grasp the significance of the *title*, the temperature at which paper burns.

We review the focus of the three parts into which the book is divided. Part 1 centers on Montag as book burner; Part 2 describes Montag's grief at the destruction of knowledge; Part 3 centers on his joining a community of scholars who preserve books.

Characters

We talk about the main characters. At the start of the novel, Guy Montag enjoys destroying mankind's history. I want the class to feel outraged. He mindlessly burns the literature of the ages. However, his satisfaction with his work is a façade he's adopted all his life. He meets a seventeen-year-old who makes him realize that he is, in fact, deeply unhappy. Clarisse McClellan represents what teachers dream about—a student who has something that can rarely be taught— intellectual curiosity. Bradbury implicitly contrasts the beautiful simplicity of Clarisse's life with the ugliness of Montag's world. In sharp contrast, Mildred, like others in Bradbury's world, is alienated from all that is good and meaningful. She can only fill her life with distractions that prevent her from facing the sterility of her existence. The fire chief, Captain Beatty, is the novel's educated but satanic *antagonist*. The class should understand that Beatty's comments about books and happiness are full of distortions and falsehoods. The Mechanical Hound is like a "hit man."[79] Its job is to pursue and kill its prey—nonconformists who resist the state. It's the tool of a totalitarian government that wields complete control over citizens of the state.

Education in Bradbury's world

We discuss the pseudo-education that prevails in Bradbury's fictional world. The fruit of this non-education—a mere regurgitation of facts—is predictable. Teenagers don't talk about

---

[78] *Utopia*, the title coined by More (1477–1535) for his satiric novel, is based on a Greek word that means "nowhere." More was the first person to describe a "utopia" or an ideal world.

[79] In his Afterword, Bradbury tell us that the hound is modeled on Sir Arthur Conan Doyle's Baskerville hound.

important issues and routinely commit violent acts. These young people haven't been taught to adopt moral behavior or to enjoy what is true and meaningful. During an interview included in the fiftieth anniversary edition of the novel, Bradbury talks about his own education in the 1920s. All students were proficient readers and writers by the end of first grade. One is reminded of America's founding fathers who were proficient in reading, writing, and arithmetic before they started school. Bradbury's book reverses this model. From childhood, the young people of *Fahrenheit 451* are manipulated by the state via an impoverished education system.

Conformity

At this point, I refer the class to the *epigraph* by Juan Ramón Jiménez[80] that exhorts the reader to resist conformity. We examine the reason why books in this society are destroyed. Beatty assures Montag that books promote conflict and unhappiness. Therefore, ridding the world of books ensures conformity and happiness; people become equal to everyone else. They are not of course. Some people have more wealth, more intelligence, more attractiveness than others. But because everyone in Bradbury's world must be reduced to the lowest common denominator, people are taught not to think but to accept the status quo. In order to train people to become robots, books must be eradicated. History is rewritten to enforce compliance. It is, of course, essential that young people recognize these false precepts and that they understand the inestimable value of books. Books contain ideas that cause us all to reflect and to grow intellectually. Non-readers, on the other hand, can more easily be brainwashed into believing anything they are told; if such brainwashing occurs, these people remain robots who mindlessly obey the laws of the state.[81]

This explanation of Bradbury's world is crucial for students to grasp—or begin to grasp. The focus of much education today is to teach conformity not academics, and revisionist historians are everywhere. I tell the young people I teach that conformity is the mindset of contemporary America; differences among people—intelligence, financial circumstances, sexual orientation—are becoming blurred. We are told we should share the wealth, take from the rich and give to the poor, give everyone the same chance. Politicians talk of income equality as a goal for American society. People are created equal in the eyes of God, but all people are not equal in terms of ability, advantages, heritage, and so on. The concept of wealth sharing is a socialist principle that has been endorsed and adopted by many of today's politicians in order to maintain their prestige and to secure votes.

---

[80] Jiménez was a Spanish poet and Nobel Prize recipient.

[81] C. S. Lewis brilliantly distinguishes between readers and non-readers in his essay "The Few and the Many," *An Experiment in Criticism* (New York: Cambridge University Press, 1961), 1–4. I place on the classroom wall a list of the contrasts Lewis makes between readers and non-readers for students to stare at all year.

I am reminded of Alan Bloom's opening thoughts in his classic analysis of contemporary culture that was published some thirty years ago.[82] Bloom argues that the crisis of the twentieth century in America is an intellectual crisis. Students, says Bloom, are being taught to fear intolerance and to espouse the virtue of openness. Bloom points out that they cannot defend this mindset because they have been trained to simply adopt it.[83] He goes on to say that rather than being trained in rigorous academics, students are indoctrinated with the social propaganda of toleration. They are ignorant about the past. They cannot engage in rational debate but merely cite their opinions as proof of any argument.[84] How much more relevant is Bloom's warning today. Like Bradbury's characters, we live in an age devoted to instant gratification and tolerance for all lifestyles, all worldviews. Remove books from a society, take away people's ability to think, suppress their nurturing instincts and all that makes life meaningful, and people will be reduced to mindless robots. Bradbury's totalitarian state keeps people content by urging them to buy four walls of mindless television and discouraging conversation. That's why houses in Bradbury's world have no porches or rocking chairs.

Questions students raise

Students have questions about the fate of the woman who loves her leather-bound books. Like the sixteenth-century martyrs to whom Beatty refers, the woman probably hopes that her rejection of the government's oppressive system, which includes book burning, will change her world.[85] I read this section to the class so that young people grasp the horror of it all. Bradbury's words should make them want to go home and *read*. Young people don't always understand the reason for Beatty's fate. Bradbury appears to suggest that the fire chief has become sickened by his job and wants to end it all. The class also questions why Bradbury inserts the incident about Montag's brush with death. It conveys an attitude that results from the state's indoctrination of its citizens—an utter lack of respect for human life. Students tend to question why an innocent victim is killed. The police must save face by televising the rebel's alleged death, or they'll have mass rebellion on their hands.

---

[82] Alan Bloom, *The Closing of the American Mind* (New York: Simon and Schuster, 1987).

[83] Ibid., Introduction 25–26.

[84] Ibid., 27–28.

[85] Beatty quotes the words that Hugh Latimer spoke to Nicholas Ridley as both men were burned at the stake for heresy in 1555. These men wanted to spread the Protestant religion throughout England during the reign of Queen Mary who unsuccessfully attempted to eradicate Protestantism in England. Bishops Latimer and Ridley were martyred for their beliefs.

Community of scholars

The class should appreciate the implicit *contrast* between a world devoid of books and the tiny community of scholars who treasure books. The mythical phoenix to which Granger alludes *symbolizes* the scholars' work. As the phoenix bird dies and rises from its ashes to live again, so man always rises from the ashes to redefine his culture. Young people should take note that the book Montag steals is the Bible that he starts to memorize, and the novel ends with his memorizing verses from Ecclesiastes and Revelation.[86]

Significance of *Fahrenheit 451*

Most freshman students are affected by this novel. It teaches them to value good literature and a good education. The elderly English professor Faber talks to Montag (often via ear radios) about mankind's need of books that have value, in other words, books that reveal truths about life. I take the opportunity to impress teenagers with the importance of reading good literature rather than much YA fiction currently available.

I share with the class Bradbury's implication in his coda about a cultural atrocity, abridged books. The day about which Bradbury so eloquently prophesied is upon us. Public libraries, school libraries, and bookstores display many rewritten or abridged books on their shelves. Some young people begin to get the point, but what can they do about it? Plenty. Keep on reading. "I don't like reading." Read until you do like it. Read until you can't survive without books. Talk to your friends and parents about books. "I can't find books I like." Parents and librarians will help you. You can refer to a reading guide that will help you pick books that suit your interests.[87] Some students understand. A few of them will ponder Bradbury's terrifying implications.

Freshman students may not scratch the surface of the novel's meaning, but some of them will begin to appreciate Bradbury's prophetic message and transfer to upper high school classes with a clearer sense of books' importance to their well-being. Most of all, I want them to understand how *Fahrenheit 451* relates to today's world and how it indicates disturbing trends in contemporary culture. Armed with this knowledge, some of them may eventually attempt to thwart the anti-intellectualism of our culture. I also tell the class that Ray Bradbury was a prolific writer. He wrote many novels and dozens of short story collections. In one of these collections, he explored the central idea that he disturbingly dramatized in *Fahrenheit*

---

[86] The final section of the book includes quotations from Eccles. 3:1,3, and 7 and Rev. 22:2.

[87] I have already mentioned *The Book Tree: A Christian Reference for Children's Literature*, a guide for young people that helps them select books they enjoy.

451—the appalling reality of censorship and ignorance. Some young people decide to read these macabre tales. They are titled *A Pleasure to Burn*.[88]

As we finish discussing the novel, I give students some fascinating information Bradbury shares with his readers. He wrote *Fahrenheit 451* in a typing room in the basement of the library at the University of California at Los Angeles (UCLA). He shoved dimes into one of the typewriters as he feverishly typed and completed his book in nine days.[89]

Essays

1. Discuss parallels between *Fahrenheit 451* and our contemporary world.
2. With reference to certain sections of the novel, discuss the reasons for Mildred's mindless existence.
3. Guy Montag is a dynamic character. Discuss how he feels about his job at the beginning of the novel, what causes him to change his attitude, and what he does as a result of that new outlook.
4. With reference to the novel, discuss how Bradbury targets censorship of the written word.

The class divides into small groups to exchange ideas and take notes on one of the topics. As a homework assignment, they refine their notes and make an outline. During class the next day, I review each student's ideas. The following day, they write their essays during class.

Test

A test on the novel and a student's essay on topic #1 listed above are included in the handouts.

---

[88] *A Pleasure to Burn* was first published by HarperCollins in 2010. One hundred of Bradbury's short stories have been collected into another volume, *The Stories of Ray Bradbury* (New York: Alfred A. Knopf, 1980.)
[89] Ray Bradbury, Afterword, *Fahrenheit 451*, 168.

Review questions on *Fahrenheit 451*[90]

1. Why is the title of this book appropriate?

    [The title refers to the temperature at which paper burns; thus, it is thoroughly appropriate for a novel about eradicating books.]

2. How and why are the people in the world of this book controlled?

    [A totalitarian government controls the masses via television, a pseudo-education system, and censorship. Because books cause people to think, to understand their past, and to oppose the state, book ownership is forbidden.]

3. Provide some adjectives that describe Clarisse McClellan's family.

    [Clarisse's family members are perceptive and happy.]

4. Why is Clarisse important to Guy Montag's change of character?

    [Clarisse causes Montag to understand the importance of books and the horror of a totalitarian state in which people are controlled, their lives censored. Clarisse is also concerned about the violence perpetrated by her generation. After Montag meets Clarisse, he realizes that the work he does as a fireman is horrific and that he and Mildred are deeply unhappy.]

5. Briefly describe the Mechanical Hound. What is its function?

    [The Mechanical Hound is an electronic device controlled by a central command. Its function is to hunt down and kill enemies of the state.]

6. In what way is the woman who owns leather-bound books like the sixteenth-century martyrs, Bishops Latimer and Ridley?

    [The woman is like these sixteenth-century martyrs because she probably hopes that her rejection of the system will decrease the abolition of learning in her world.]

---

[90] To answer these and subsequent review questions, students work in small groups. They use their notes and literature books as they work on the questions for about twenty minutes during several class periods.
Suggested responses are provided in brackets for this set and subsequent sets of review questions.
A student booklet that accompanies this teaching guide contains all 9th grade review questions and tests with answers omitted.
Any of these questions could be used for a graded discussion of the novel.

7. What is the function of the fire chief, Captain Beatty, in this novel? What is Beatty's opinion of Montag?

   [Captain Beatty is the story's ruthless antagonist. He suspects that Montag is becoming disillusioned by his fireman's job; Beatty is determined to expose the rebellious fireman.]

8. Why is Montag's alleged death televised?

   [Via television screens in every home, the government broadcasts the death of a man, supposedly Montag, as a warning to everyone that rebels against the state will be eliminated.]

9. What is Granger's function?

   [Granger is a scholar who leads a group of fellow scholars bent on memorizing books in order to ensure their survival in a world that destroys books.]

10. What does the novel imply about education?

    [A totalitarian government superintends education in Bradbury's world in order to maintain control of the populace. The result is non-education.]

11. What does Bradbury's book have to say about history?

    [The book conveys the crucial importance of preserving history, which in Bradbury's nightmare world has been rewritten.]

12. What does the book imply about parenting in the world Bradbury describes?

    [In Bradbury's world, parents no longer nurture their children; on the contrary, they regard children as an inconvenience.]

13. What important insight or insights have you gained from reading *Fahrenheit 451*?

    [Students usually comment that Bradbury taught them the value of books, a good education, and an inquiring mind. They also realize that the novel emphasizes the importance of preserving the history of one's culture. Some of them comment that the book warned them against the danger of watching mindless television programs.]

****

Graded discussion

During the unit on this novel, I schedule at least one graded discussion in order to vary teaching procedures and to ensure class comprehension of important issues the book raises. As mentioned in the introduction, I use the graded discussion technique in the 9th and 10th grade classrooms. It's another way to ensure that homework is completed and to elicit student responses. Here's the procedure: The night before class, I write down a list of students' names and a long list of thought-provoking questions about the material. In class the next day, students respond to each question by raising their hands, and if a response is reasonable, I place a check mark by the name. I try to ensure that all students get many opportunities to respond. They can enlarge on a previous response or ask a related question. They may not repeat material covered in a previous answer. That night, I assign grades based on the number of each student's responses. Freshman students like the activity. It tends to become lively, and it ensures that everyone adds to the discussion. As already noted, review questions on the novel could be used for this activity.

Animal Farm

by

George Orwell (Eric Blair)

1903–1950

Orwell's best-known novel, *1984*, is inappropriate reading for 9th grade students, but *Animal Farm* is a good read for a freshman class since it raises questions that are similar to those raised in *1984* but without the nightmare vision and sordid content of the other book. Like *Fahrenheit 451*, both *1984* and *Animal Farm* are *dystopian* novels. They depict a decidedly negative, often horrific picture of the world.[91] But perhaps the best reason for including *Animal Farm* in a 9th grader curriculum is this: It's fun to read. One of the main reasons for reading good literature is that it's enjoyable.

Facts about the author

Students should know that the author's name was Eric Blair and that he used the pseudonym George Orwell for his writing. After serving in the Imperial Police in Burma, Orwell returned to England, repudiated the upper-class system, and became an avid socialist; however, he

---

[91] Orwell wrote *Animal Farm* in 1945. He published *1984* in 1948, several decades before the year contained in the title. Both *Animal Farm* and *1984* are prophetic; both novels warn the reader about the horrors that face a populace enslaved by a totalitarian government.

never embraced communism or any other form of totalitarianism.[92] He was a champion of the working class and hated its exploitation by Britain's upper class. Orwell was aware that revolutionary causes can evolve into a type of totalitarianism, which, as he realized, presents a formidable threat to freedom. He watched Stalin oppress the Russians just as severely as they had been oppressed under the czars. Orwell wrote *Animal Farm* specifically to warn his countrymen that England too could become enslaved by a totalitarian government, although his overall purpose was to alert people everywhere to the dangers of dictatorship.

The novel's genres

To some degree, students should be familiar with three literary genres into which *Animal Farm* falls: It is a fable, a satire, and an allegory.[93] We apply the three genres to the novel:

- It is a *fable* with animals that represent Russian leaders and peasants. Its moral is a warning against totalitarianism. The use of this genre allows Orwell to tell his story from the farm animals' perspective thus gaining the reader's sympathy for them and the Russian peasants they represent.

- It is a *satire* of Soviet communism. It humorously satirizes totalitarian governments that persecute and enslave people in order to warn England and other nations to guard against oppressive leaders.

- It *allegorizes* the Russian Revolution of 1917. Orwell's allegory points out that one oppressive tyrant will be replaced by another—as happened in Russia when Stalin replaced Lenin—if the populace is not well-educated and informed.

Students should realize that Orwell is not merely condemning Soviet communism; he condemns totalitarian government in any country. And he is pointing out that people need to be well-educated if they are to keep potentially aggressive rulers in check. The animals of *Animal Farm* are so ignorant that the literate pigs take advantage of the other animals' naiveté in order to overturn the goals of the animals' rebellion. That is Orwell's prophetic warning to his reader.

---

[92] Totalitarianism is the total control of people by their government.

[93] A *fable* is a brief story involving animals with a moral. The most famous fables are those of Aesop, purportedly a Greek slave living around 600 BC, and the fables of the seventeenth-century French writer, Jean de La Montaigne. *Satire* is a genre that uses humor to expose some weakness or vice in human institutions or mankind in order to generate reform.

An *allegory* is a story with characters, setting, and events that represent someone or something else.

Orwell's animals

I pass around a sheet that lists the characters and whom they represent; for example, Old Major represents Vladimir Lenin and Napoleon is Joseph Stalin.[94] We refer to a complete list in order to appreciate the allegory.[95] Orwell connects the pigs to historical figures in order to warn mankind of the dangers inherent in all totalitarian governments. Orwell's animals also represent a *microcosm* or miniature version of humanity, stereotypes of mankind. Boxer is the obtuse, exploited worker who labors for the good of society; Mollie is the vain, foolish female. As for the pigs, Napoleon is the tyrannical leader, Snowball is the popular idea man, and Squealer is the manipulative talker. Students question the purpose of these stereotypes. (If they don't, I ask them for an explanation.) Orwell humanizes ordinary farm animals to strengthen his implication that people anywhere can be subjected to tyranny.

Propaganda

Propaganda is a key issue to discuss with a freshman class. Students usually understand that propaganda refers to ideas that are spread deliberately, often deceitfully, in order to influence people's thoughts and emotions. I ask the class for examples of commercial propaganda. An attractive young woman stands near a late model sports car, for instance; a handsome sports celebrity is pictured wearing a particular brand of running shoes. In fact, most commercial products are designed to appeal to our self-serving desire to be permanently young, athletic, and beautiful. The pigs use propaganda—popular slogans, loaded words, appeals to fear—to keep the ideals of the rebellion ever present in the animals' minds.

Revisionist history

Students should notice Snowball's courage during the Battle of the Cowshed, which Napoleon later denies.[96] This is a blatant example of *revisionist history*.[97] They should understand Squealer's revisionism regarding plans for the windmill. The uneducated farm animals don't realize Napoleon will become another tyrant just like Mr. Jones. His dogs enforce his despotic rule, and his propaganda agent Squealer slyly alleviates the animals' fears. As the animals' history is rewritten, Snowball becomes Napoleon's scapegoat.[98] The most blatant piece of

---

[94] Napoleon's name suggests that Orwell also modeled Napoleon on the despotic French military leader Napoleon Bonaparte (1769–1821) in addition to despots in general.

[95] Detailed lists that compare the animals to people in Russian history are available at several websites.

[96] See ch. 5.

[97] Revisionist history is history that is rewritten.

[98] Students should know that a scapegoat is someone we blame if something goes wrong.

revisionist history involves the most industrious member of the animal community.[99] Orwell inserts these events to imply the danger of rewriting history.

Sugarcandy Mountain

Most students question the presence of Moses who talks constantly about Sugarcandy Mountain. The raven's task is to provide hope of a better life for the animals in the hereafter, thus discouraging rebellion. Orwell's bird blatantly contrasts with the godly law-giver of the Old Testament; his references to a pseudo-religious Sugarcandy Mountain present a flippant contrast to the Promised Land, the land God promised to Abraham and his descendants.[100]

One tyrant replaces the other

Ultimately, the rebellion is forgotten. One tyrant has replaced the former tyrant. The commandments are subsumed into one, Orwell's ultimate irony![101] The twentieth-century philosopher George Santayana has famously remarked that "Those who cannot remember the past are condemned to repeat it." After we have discussed the novel, I ask students to write a short paragraph applying this insight to the novel. Here is one student's response:

> These words directly relate to *Animal Farm*. After Napoleon has been reigning for many years, the animals cannot remember what life was like when Mr. Jones was their master. The gullible farm animals have been so brainwashed that they are willing to believe whatever they are told; they forget their past—Old Major's teachings, the original wording of the commandments of animalism, the Battle of the Cowshed, for instance—and are thus unaware that their current leaders are as tyrannical as the farmer who has been replaced. The pigs achieve this takeover via Squealer's sly propaganda and cunning manipulation of language. Orwell's satire brilliantly demonstrates the truth of Santayana's words.

Manipulation of language

Orwell's attack on the manipulation of language is another important issue.[102] Orwell suggests that tyrants use euphemistic language to promote their agenda. In other words, they soften the language they use with the workers in a community in order to mask the reality that powerful

---

[99] See ch. 9.

[100] Gen. 17:8.

[101] In an essay on George Orwell by the incomparable C. S. Lewis, Lewis comments, "The great sentence 'All animals are equal but some are more equal than others' bites deeper than the whole of *1984*. Thus the shorter book does all that the longer does. But it also does more." In that essay, Lewis strongly asserts his preference for *Animal Farm* over *1984*. "George Orwell," *C. S. Lewis on Stories and Other Essays on Literature*. Ed. Walter Hooper (New York: Harcourt Brace Jovanovich, 1982), 103.

[102] The misuse of language is a complex topic and one that some teachers may prefer to omit from discussion of the novel during a 9th grade course.

men control those workers' lives, and they manipulate the masses into thinking all is well. I ask students for examples of *euphemisms* commonly used today.[103] I also share with them a partial list of euphemisms that one bright class composed:

> *car accident*: inadvertent vehicular contact
>
> *a disobedient child*: a youthful person with a strong personality
>
> *failure*: success at going the wrong way
>
> *theft*: a form of borrowing
>
> *jail break*: a prisoner succumbing to his desire to leave a captive establishment earlier than originally planned by others
>
> *starvation*: getting rid of excess weight in excess
>
> *expulsion*: the mutual decision of two parties that it is in the best interests of one of the parties not to return

These euphemistic definitions may be amusing; they are also wordy, indirect, and inoffensive. By definition, "euphemism" means the substitution of an expression that is considered offensive for one that is acceptable. Politicians and ordinary citizens use euphemisms, sometimes quite harmlessly; as a technique for tyrants, however, euphemisms become dangerous. And that is Orwell's point. When young people write essays, they should be trained to adopt direct, vigorous prose and to avoid beating about the bush with euphemisms or any other form of circumlocution.

Freshmen students won't appreciate Orwell's essay "Politics and the English Language," but I discuss this well-known piece with 12th grade students in connection with *1984*. You may want to share with 9th grade students Orwell's list of rules for good writing included in that essay.[104] Young people should understand the vital importance of their education, without which they too could become, as it were, like Boxer—unable to realize he is being manipulated by animals much cleverer than he. They should understand the key ideas that permeate Orwell's book. For example, we must be trained to think lucidly in order to express ourselves forcefully and to recognize the manipulation of truth in all its ugly forms. Furthermore, if citizens of any

---

[103] For example, instead of mentioning that someone has died, we say "he has passed on"; a lie is referred to as "a manipulation of the truth"; poor people are "economically disadvantaged"; a slum is "substandard housing"; a garbage man is "a sanitation engineer." During war, civilians killed or wounded are referred to as "collateral damage," and prisoners are "detainees."

[104] I reproduce the six rules and display them on the classroom walls. They convey invaluable advice for the writer.

country are uneducated and unable to reflect wisely on current events, that country's rulers could subjugate the people and subject them to tyranny.

Essays

1. Explain Squealer's function in *Animal Farm*. Refer to incidents in the novel throughout your response.
2. Explain how the pigs are traitors to the animals' original ideals.
3. Napoleon is obviously the novel's antagonist. Explain whether or not the novel has a hero.

Test

A test on the novel is included in the handouts.

Review questions on *Animal Farm*[105]

1. Mention some facts you have learned about the author of this novel. Include the reason why he wrote *Animal Farm*.

   [The author's real name was Eric Blair. He used George Orwell as a pseudonym for his novels. He attended Eton, a prestigious English school, and served in the Imperial Police in Burma. On his return to England, he became a socialist, but he strongly disliked communism and totalitarianism, both of which he realized are threats to freedom. He hated the exploitation of working-class people by England's upper class. He watched a powerful leader, Stalin, rise to power and oppress the Russian people as badly as they had been oppressed by the czars. To demonstrate how people in England or in any other country can be oppressed by a totalitarian government, Orwell wrote *Animal Farm*.]

2. Why does Old Major call man the enemy of all animals?

   [According to the old boar, man abuses animals by starving and overworking them, eventually killing them.]

3. Define these terms and apply them to the novel: fable, satire, allegory.

   [**A fable** is a short story about animals that contains a moral. The animals in Orwell's novel represent Russian leaders and peasants. Its moral consists of a warning against a totalitarian form of government like that of Russia.

   Satire is writing that uses humor in order to expose weakness or vice in human institutions or mankind in order to effect reform. Orwell uses humor to satirize totalitarian governments like that under Soviet communism, which persecuted and enslaved people. Orwell intends to warn nations to guard against oppressive leaders.

   An allegory is a story in which characters, setting, and events represent someone or something else. Orwell's book is an allegory of the 1917 Russian Revolution. It points out that an oppressive tyrant will be replaced by another tyrant. This happened in Russian when Stalin replaced Lenin.]

4. Define the main character traits of these animals: Mollie, Boxer, Clover, Benjamin.

   [Mollie is vain; Boxer is dull-witted and hard-working; Clover is motherly; Benjamin is cynical.]

---

[105] A student booklet that accompanies this teaching guide contains all 9th grade review questions and tests with answers omitted.

Any of these questions could be used for a graded discussion of the novel.

5. What point is Orwell making by giving some animals specific character traits?

[The animals represent a cross-section of human nature; thus, they convey Orwell's concern that people in any community world-wide can be oppressed by a tyrannical government.]

6. In *Animal Farm*, Orwell makes the same point about education as Bradbury does in *Fahrenheit 451*. Explain.

[Both Orwell and Bradbury are implying that people in any country must be well-educated in order to think for themselves, evaluate events correctly, and combat tyranny.]

7. Define this term: propaganda.

[Propaganda is the use of ideas that are circulated in order to influence people's actions and emotions.]

8. Name some examples of propaganda used in this novel.

[Old Major's opening speech depicts the animals as downtrodden victims of their enemy, man. The animals' history is rewritten; the Seven Commandments are changed; false confessions are extorted from so-called traitors. Other propaganda techniques include appeals to the animals' fears, the use of slogans, and loaded diction.]

9. What is Squealer's function?

[Squealer is Napoleon's propaganda agent who uses propaganda in order to suppress insurrection.]

10. Name the people in Russian history that these animals represent: Old Major, Mr. Jones, Napoleon, Napoleon's puppies.

[Lenin, Czar Nicholas II, Stalin, Stalin's secret police]

11. What do the Seven Commandments represent?

[the Communist Manifesto]

12. Define this term: revisionist history.

[Revisionist history defines history that is rewritten or falsely recorded.]

13. Referring to Snowball, give some examples of the way the animals' history is revised.

[Snowball is accused of acting as Jones's secret agent during the Battle of the Cowshed; it is maintained that he displays cowardice during that battle, that he is not decorated afterwards, and that he is responsible for destroying the windmill. All these assertions are false.]

14. Why do the pigs allow Moses to remain at the farm?

[The raven's talk of Sugarcandy Mountain gives the other farm animals hope of happiness after death thus preventing their rebelling against the pigs.]

15. What does the windmill symbolize?

[The windmill symbolizes tyrants' exploitation of the working class. Despots invent an activity to keep workers employed so that those subordinates become too tired to question their tyrannical masters' schemes.]

16. Is there a clear protagonist and antagonist in *Animal Farm*?

[Most students decide that the novel does not include one character who is the protagonist; instead, the farm animals collectively are the novel's protagonist; they always cite Napoleon as the antagonist.]

17. What is Orwell's main concern in this novel?

[Orwell is concerned about the rise of totalitarian governments and writes this novel in order to demonstrate the importance of freedom and personal dignity.]

Unit III

Drama

William Shakespeare
1564–1616

Shakespeare's birthplace,
Stratford-upon-Avon,
Warwickshire

Facts about Shakespeare

Having studied the short story and the novel, we turn to drama, which is usually the most well-liked unit in a 9th grade course. A popular play to study among freshman students is undoubtedly *Romeo and Juliet*.[106] We read all plays together during class.

I review with the class the known facts about the Bard of Avon. These few facts are based on public records. William Shakespeare was born in Stratford-on-Avon, a market town on the River Avon, in 1564, possibly on April 23. He was baptized on April 26, 1564 and died on April 23, 1616 at fifty-two years old.[107] He probably attended the local grammar school. In 1582, he married Anne Hathaway, eight years older than Shakespeare, by whom he had a daughter, Susanna, and two twins, Hamnet and Judith. After the births of Shakespeare's children, we know nothing about him until the year 1592 when he was living in London and had become a successful playwright, actor, and poet. When Shakespeare left Stratford to travel to London, his wife and children remained in Stratford and lived there all their lives.

---

[106] Other good choices include *A Midsummer Night's Dream, As You Like It*, and *The Merchant of Venice*.

[107] In the sixteenth-century, infants were baptized three days after their birth, so Shakespeare's birth date is assumed to have been April 23, 1564, which is a nice coincidence because he died on the same date in April fifty-two years later. Also, April 23 is St. George's Day, St. George being the patron saint of England.

By 1594, Shakespeare was a leading member of an acting company, The Lord Chamberlain's Men, and became prosperous as a prominent playwright and actor. In 1596, his son died. In 1597, Shakespeare purchased New Place, the second largest house in Stratford. He became a shareholder in the Globe Theater built in 1599 on the south side of the Thames River. In 1603, James I became king of England, and Shakespeare's acting company changed its name to The King's Men. In 1607, his daughter Susanna married a Dr. John Hall and gave birth to Shakespeare's only granddaughter a year later. In 1616, his daughter Judith married Thomas Quiney, a wine merchant. Subsequently, Shakespeare's line died out leaving no direct descendants. At some point early in the seventeenth century, Shakespeare retired from London to live in the house he had bought in Stratford. As noted, he died on April 23, 1616. In 1623, seven years after his death, two friends collected his 37 plays, 154 sonnets, and 2 narrative poems and published the first collection of his works, the First Folio.

That is all we know definitively about the greatest writer who has ever lived.

I do not expect students to memorize these facts. I expect them to be familiar with Shakespeare's birth and death dates and to realize how few facts are known about his life because most records no longer exist. "He was a monument without a tomb," said his friend Ben Jonson. Students should be familiar with another of Jonson's tributes: "He was not of an age but for all time." I ask students to memorize these lines and tell me what they mean.[108]

We watch a fifty-minute video, *William Shakespeare: A Life of Drama*, produced by A & E. Students take notes, and after the video, they talk about aspects of Shakespeare's life that most interest them.

---

[108] Jonson was asserting that Shakespeare does not need a memorial because he will be forever remembered by his works and that Shakespeare's works are relevant to and enjoyed by not just his contemporaries but every age to come.

**Globe Theater
on the south bank of the River Thames,
London**

A theater in Shakespeare's day was very different from today's modern theater with its stage raised above the seated audience and curtain that separates actors from audience. The Globe and other London theaters were much more accessible with one stage projecting into the audience that stood on all three sides of the platform.[109] The theaters in Shakespearean England also had a curtained inner stage and an upper balcony. A trap door in the floor of the main stage allowed for the entrance of ghosts from hell. Plays were performed in the afternoon, and a flag indicated a performance. There were few sets or props and certain no technology for lighting, microphones, or other enhancements such as modern theatrical productions employ. The scene was almost entirely suggested by the dialogue. Groundlings stood "cheek by jowl" in front of the main stage, and wealthier patrons sat in seats around it. If one were a prominent nobleman, one could sit on the stage itself. All parts were performed by boys, since plays were considered to be a low type of entertainment unsuitable for women to participate in.

Shakespeare's play about young love is the most famous love story ever written.

---

[109] Elizabethan theater goers were not as polite as today's audiences. They were often rowdy and boorish. Members of the audience sometimes threw rotten vegetables at the actors if they disliked the play!

Shakespeare's poetic techniques

Freshmen students should know that Shakespeare wrote his plays predominantly in a meter called *iambic pentameter*. A line of poetry is composed of feet or units of rhythm in verse. An *iambic* foot is composed of one unstressed syllable followed by one stressed syllable. *Pentameter* is a poetic line made up of five feet. I write examples of iambic pentameter on the board. The capitalized words are emphasized, and the slash indicates the end of each foot:

> My GRAVE / is LIKE / to BE / my WED/ ding DAY
> Is THERE /no PI / ty SIT / ting IN / the CLOUDS

Students write out other lines and scan them in order to acquire a solid grasp of iambic pentameter rhythm. It is this meter that gives Shakespeare's poetry its stately cadence.

In order to further appreciate Shakespeare's poetry, young people should be familiar with *end-stopped* and *run-on lines*. An end-stopped line is punctuated at the end of the line; a run-on line is not. Here's an example of both:

> **end-stopped lines**: Rebellious subjects, enemies to peace,
> Will they not hear? What, ho! You men, you beasts,
> hear the sentence of your movèd prince.

> **run-on lines**: On pain of torture, from those bloody hands
> Throw your mistempered[110] weapons to the ground
> And hear...

Memorization

I tell students they will memorize one soliloquy of approximately twenty-five lines that they write out in class and submit for a grade. (Twenty-five lines? *All* of them?) A list of soliloquies to memorize is included at the end of the unit on the play. I give this assignment for all Shakespearean drama and distribute suggestions about memorization:

- Look through the speech to be sure you know what it means. It's difficult to memorize what you don't understand.
- Memorize the first two lines, thoroughly.
- Move on through the speech a few lines at a time always memorizing from the beginning.

---

[110] bad-tempered

- Repeat the whole speech aloud to someone who will correct you. Twice.
- Now you're ready to write it down.

Students have two weeks to memorize their speeches. As they come to class, they hand in a copy of the speech they have memorized, write out the speech, and submit it for grading. This procedure obviates my having to thumb through the play to find the passages they have memorized.

Romeo and Juliet

It certainly does not detract from Shakespeare's genius to point out that his plays are usually based on other literature. He found material for his plays in the work of other writers. *Romeo and Juliet*, for example, is based on a sixteenth-century narrative poem by Arthur Brooke entitled *The Tragical History of Romeus and Juliet* first published in 1562. The class reads the play while listening to Caedmon unabridged audio cassettes starring Claire Bloom and Albert Finney. This procedure brings the play to life far more readily than having students (or myself) stumble through the poetry. I stop the tape whenever questions arise; otherwise, I play it for a couple of pages as we follow along in the book. Apart from one short section at the end of Act IV, we read the entire play. The time span is five days, and the setting is the cities of Verona and Mantua, Italy, during the fourteenth century.

Act I

Prologue

Scholars cannot explain why Shakespeare decided to include a prologue before the first two Acts that recapitulates the plot.[111] The prologue, which is a sonnet and precedes Act I, does indeed summarize the main events of the play. Of particular significance is Shakespeare's reference to the feud that causes the lovers' deaths. In his prologue, Shakespeare emphasizes not the tragedy of young love but the fatal grudge operating in the hearts of two families. The two young people are "star-crossed" or fated to die because of this hateful animosity. It would seem that the interminable hatred of vindictive adults appears to be Shakespeare's concern and the focus of his play. One needs to stress for 9th grade students that *Romeo and Juliet* is not a mere love story gone tragically wrong but an exploration of the long-term effects of hatred.

Scene 1

The class should note that Act I contains the play's *exposition* and that the *setting* is fourteenth-century Verona. A dramatist has only *dialogue* to convey information; the opening interchanges between the Capulets and Montagues serve to alert us to the two families' longstanding quarrel, the cause of which has been long forgotten. Even the servants of the warring families are involved; the Capulets' servants Sampson and Gregory deliberately provoke an argument with the Montagues' servants Abram and Balthasar that leads to fighting. After the fathers of both families are sternly reprimanded by the ruler of Verona and threatened with death should such a riot reoccur, we learn from Benvolio and Lord Montague that Romeo has recently become listless and depressed.

---

[111] It has been frequently observed that Shakespeare's prologues share the same function as an ancient Greek chorus by commenting on the action for the audience. However, the omission of a prologue at the beginning of the last three Acts appears to be inexplicable.

This sorrowful description foreshadows Romeo's appearance. Romeo is suffering from unrequited love for a young woman who does not appear in the play. Romeo is a typical Petrarchan lover, which means he adopts a melodramatic, idealistic attitude to love.[112] Why does Shakespeare include in his play a lady we never meet? He does so in order to depict Romeo's transient love for Rosaline that contrasts with his genuine love for Juliet; Shakespeare also includes Rosaline in order to demonstrate Romeo's impulsive personality. One could point out the *oxymorons* that emphasize his conflicting emotions, but the term needs defining. An oxymoron is a figure of speech that contains two seemingly contradictory terms in order to create emphasis.[113] We talk about the personality of Romeo's friend. Benvolio lives up to his name, which means "goodwill," and is the sort of friend we all want, sympathetic and sensible. He gives love-sick Romeo wise advice about his friend's unrequited love for Rosaline: "Examine other beauties."[114]

Scene 2

A situation occurs that will become one of many stumbling blocks for the lovers: Count Paris asks Juliet's father for permission to marry his daughter. Capulet somewhat reluctantly agrees. He invites Paris to a ball that he will hold that night. Every freshman class raises two complaints that involve Juliet: She is thirteen thus far too young to marry, and no girl in her right mind would allow her parents to choose her husband. That's when I repeat Samuel Taylor Coleridge's advice: *When you read literature, you must willingly suspend your disbelief.* In other words, today's reader cannot apply a contemporary attitude to a literary work but must bear in mind the customs of the period during which the work was written.[115] In sixteenth-century Europe, girls often married at Juliet's age, and arranged marriages were common.

It is also important to note that Juliet's parents are realistically depicted human beings. In the talk about marriage, Lord Capulet is concerned about Juliet's youthfulness and wants his daughter's happiness. He has lost all his other children:

> Earth hath swallowed all my hopes but she....[116]

---

[112] A Petrarchan lover is steeped in melancholy and obsessed with love for an unattainable lady.

[113] Commonplace oxymorons include an open secret, an everyday miracle, and a cheerful pessimist. Examples of oxymorons in this scene include the following: "loving hate...heavy lightness...cold fire, sick health." *Romeo and Juliet*, I.i.175, 77, 79. Line numbers will vary based on the edition one uses.

[114] *Romeo and Juliet*, I.i.227.

[115] Coleridge was thinking specifically of a work of fantasy, but his dictum can and should be applied to all genres of literature.

[116] *Romeo and Juliet*, I.ii.14.

And he is concerned that Juliet should approve of the marriage:

> My will to her consent is but a part.
> And she agreed, within her scope of choice[117]
> Lies my consent….[118]

The class should also note a significant coincidence: Romeo happens to hear that Rosaline will attend the Capulets' banquet and decides to appear in spite of his being a hated Montague. His sensible friend Benvolio unsuccessfully attempts to convince him that he will meet other girls at the party who are more beautiful than Rosaline:

> I will make thee think thy swan a crow.[119]

Scene 3

Observing Juliet and her mother interact in this scene, students realize that their relationship is formal and somewhat distant. The Nurse reacts in a more caring way than Lady Capulet to the proposal that Juliet should marry the Count. The Nurse lost her own daughter Susan and has cared for Juliet and been her companion from Juliet's babyhood. Juliet appears to be closer to the Nurse than her mother. Most readers dislike the Nurse. She is garrulous, coarse, and annoying—both to the reader and to Lady Capulet. Juliet is a submissive daughter, but one wonders why Shakespeare made her so insipid.

Scene 4

This scene dramatizes a universal situation: Boisterous young men are on their way to a party. The lighted torches add to the festive mood. They are all wearing masks, as was the custom, a circumstance that hides Romeo's identity from the Capulets. Shakespeare's audience loved *puns*;[120] Romeo's speeches are full of them. To Mercutio's assertion that he should dance at the party, Romeo responds,

> You have dancing shoes
> With nimble *soles*; I have a *soul* of lead
> So stakes me to the ground I cannot move.

And when his light-hearted friend insists, he cries,

---

[117] among the other men she could choose to marry

[118] I.ii.16–18.

[119] Ibid., 89.

[120] A pun is a play on words based on the sound of the words.

I am too *sore* enpiercèd with his[121] shaft

To *soar* with his light feathers; and so *bound*[122]

I cannot *bound*[123] a pitch above dull woe.[124] [Italics added.]

We talk about *foil characters*. Both Benvolio and Mercutio are foils for Romeo since they both in different ways contrast with Romeo thus helping us to better understand his personality. Romeo is impractical unlike level-headed Benvolio; he is also overly emotional, a passionately romantic introvert, unlike Mercutio who is an extrovert and realistic about affairs of the heart:

If love be rough with you, be rough with love.[125]

Both young men help us to better understand Romeo's Petrarchan attitude to love. Mercutio loves to joke around, sometimes absurdly, often to excess. Although Mercutio is doing his best to cheer up his love-sick friend, the others get tired of his non-stop babbling about Queen Mab:[126]

Peace, peace, Mercutio, peace![127]

One could also argue that Juliet's suitor, the calm and rational Count Paris, is another foil for Romeo.

Shakespeare makes good use of *foreshadowing*. We are constantly aware of the lovers' ultimate doom. On the way to the Capulets' party, Romeo is full of misgivings about his future:

…my mind misgives

Some consequence yet hanging in the stars

Shall bitterly begin his fearful date

With this night's revels, and expire the term

Of a despisèd life, closed in my breast,

By some vile forfeit of untimely death.[128]

---

[121] Cupid's

[122] tied up

[123] rise

[124] I.iv.14-16, 19-21.

[125] Ibid., 27.

[126] Due to its length, I usually avoid reading much of Mercutio's Queen Mab speech. Students find it a little monotonous.

[127] I.iv.95.

[128] Ibid., 106-11.

The language suggests that Romeo is fatalist about future events. He explicitly refers to his "despisèd life" and "untimely death." In the next scene, Juliet cries,

> My grave is like to be my wedding bed.[129]

Scene 5

There isn't much *comic relief* in this tragedy, but the servants' frenetic preparations for the Capulets' party provide a little. The dancing begins as our anticipation rises. At that point, Romeo sees Juliet:

> I ne'er saw true beauty till this night.[130]

From this moment, Romeo forgets Rosaline and falls passionately in love with Juliet. The initial romantic mood, however, is dashed as fiery Tybalt realizes that a hated Montague, "that villain Romeo," has crashed the party. Like any other host, Lord Capulet is annoyed by Tybalt's noisy ranting and concerned that it will upset his guests; in any case, as far as Capulet is concerned, Romeo apparently intends no harm, so it's easier for the old man to allow him to remain than force him to go. Tybalt is so infuriated that he leaves in a fury.

When the two young people begin to talk, Juliet doesn't realize Romeo is a Montague since he's wearing a mask. She is immediately attracted to his witty flirtation. Freshmen students always object to the suddenness of the couple's falling in love and to Romeo's switching his affections so rapidly. They should realize that Romeo is young and passionate and, as already mentioned, that Shakespeare probably includes Rosaline in the play to emphasize Romeo's inability to handle his emotions with any maturity. If Benvolio had fallen in love with Juliet, the play would doubtless have been short and ended happily. As the party ends, the lovers are stunned that the object of their love is a hated enemy of their respective families. I ask the class why Shakespeare makes the party so brief. Students should understand that the consummate dramatist allows nothing to diminish the tragedy that unfolds. All events focus on the tragic story of the "star-crossed lovers."[131] However, students should realize that human error, particularly the parents' interminable enmity, plays a significant part in the tragedy that unfolds. Although the lovers are doomed to die, their own actions and those of others play a significant role in causing their tragic deaths.

---

[129] I.v.136.

[130] Ibid., 54.

[131] To call the lovers "star-crossed" for an Elizabethan audience was to indicate that their lives were predestined by Fate to end tragically. Most of Shakespeare's contemporaries believed that the star under which they were born largely determined their fate; in other words, the day, month, and year of their birth determined their fate according to a malign star.

The major issues in Act I are these:

- exposition in the opening scene
- Tybalt's character
- Benvolio and Mercutio as foils for Romeo
- complications for the lovers presented by Prince Escalus, Count Paris, and Tybalt
- foreshadowing

Act II

The Prologue summarizes events in Act I.

Scene 1

The next two Acts comprise *complications* for the lovers and the play's *turning point*. When starting to read this scene, the class should note that love-stricken Romeo hides in the orchard outside Juliet's house. Assuming Romeo still dotes on Rosaline, the irrepressible Mercutio mocks his friend's passionate attitude to love. Giving up all hope of finding Romeo, Mercutio and Benvolio leave the Capulets' grounds.

Scene 2

This is the celebrated balcony scene. Shakespeare gives Romeo a lengthy speech full of conventional metaphors that profess his love for Juliet. When Juliet realizes Romeo is in the orchard below her, she is immediately concerned for his safety since he is a hated Montague. Students should notice the two lovers' different personalities: Juliet is sensible and practical. She is also modest and embarrassed that Romeo has overheard her frank words of love for him:

> Thou knowest the mask of night is on my face;
> Else would a maiden blush bepaint my cheek
> For that which thou hast heard me speak tonight....[132]

It's a lovely speech. As mentioned earlier, one assignment I give students when studying Shakespearean drama is to memorize a passage of about twenty-five lines. Juliet's speech would be an excellent choice for girls.

The young people have fallen deeply in love. Disinclined to tell their feuding parents of their love, they make plans to be married by Romeo's confidant and adviser, the Friar, although

---

[132] II.ii.85–87.

Juliet is afraid that Romeo's protestations of love are insincere and is more cautious than he, urging him to wait:

> I have no joy of this contract tonight.
> It is too rash, too unadvised, too sudden;
> too like the lightning...."[133]

Again, we realize that Juliet is more sensible than Romeo. The Nurse's constant interruptions emphasize the danger of discovery that the lovers face, and more ominous *foreshadowing* ends the scene as Juliet declares,

> Yet I should kill thee with much cherishing.[134]

Juliet is evidently suggesting that her love will cause Romeo's death.

Scene 3
Shakespeare gives Friar Laurence a long speech, excessively long perhaps, to indicate the priest's knowledge of herbs.[135] Understandably shocked that Romeo has switched his affections from Rosaline to another girl whom he wants to marry, the Friar chides Romeo's inconstancy. However, he agrees to Romeo's request because he assures himself that marriage to Juliet may end the longstanding feud between the two families.[136]

At this point, I introduce an important topic: The lovers' deaths are caused for two reasons—*coincidence* and *human error*. Scholars fault Shakespeare for emphasizing the element of coincidence or fate in this tragedy; certainly, one cannot speculate about the playwright's reliance on mere chance that plays a fairly significant part in the tragedy.[137] I ask the class to start listing examples of both issues in their notebooks. The Friar's willingness to marry the lovers is an outstanding example of human error. It's a tragic mistake. The possible termination of the parents' antagonism is hardly sufficient reason to withhold from them knowledge of their children's imminent marriage. Students are unanimous in the opinion that Friar Laurence should have tried to dissuade the lovers from such a hasty marriage, and he should certainly have told the parents about their children's love for each other and their wedding plans. Lord

---

[133] Ibid., 117–18.

[134] Ibid., 184.

[135] In Act IV, the Friar makes a potion presumably with herbs that puts Juliet into a coma.

[136] See II.iii.90–92.

[137] One must bear in mind that the play is one of Shakespeare's early tragedies and that he has not yet matured into the author of towering tragedies such as *Macbeth, Hamlet, Othello,* and *King Lear.*

Capulet seems to be a reasonable man: He refrains from insisting that Romeo leave his party, and he tells Count Paris that Juliet's consent to their union is important to him.[138] In any case, the Friar's acquiescing in the marriage is unwise and immoral. Students begin to compose lists with the headings "coincidence" and "human error"; throughout our study of the play, they continue to record the many instances of both factors that contribute to the lovers' deaths.

Scene 4

Tybalt, an accomplished swordsman, has challenged Romeo to a duel, a development that will end in tragedy. In the meanwhile, Mercutio keeps up his usual light-hearted banter, bandying names of famous lovers[139] and continuing his light-hearted attempt to brighten Romeo's mood. Having forgotten his unrequited love for Rosaline and engrossed in his new love, Romeo exchanges jests and puns with Mercutio. The garrulous Nurse continues to be annoying although, as Shakespeare doubtless intended, she adds *comic relief*. She agrees to give Romeo's message to Juliet and to see that Juliet joins Romeo at Friar Laurence's cell to be married.[140] Romeo tells the Nurse that his servant will bring her a rope ladder by which Romeo can gain access to Juliet's room after the marriage. Like the Friar, the Nurse is dreadfully wrong to collude with the lovers over their marriage. She knows Juliet's parents wish their daughter to marry Count Paris; in any case, she should certainly have made them aware of Juliet's intended marriage to Romeo, son of the Capulets' hated enemy. The Friar and the Nurse, the young couple's close friends and confidants, act with appalling lack of wisdom or morality.

Scene 5

Having waited three hours for the Nurse to return, Juliet now impatiently endures the Nurse's protracted recital of Romeo's plans. At this point, everything seems to bode well for the lovers.

Scene 6

Friar Laurence feels uneasy about the marriage he is to perform, as indeed he should. About to be married, the lovers are happy. References to death, however, continue to *foreshadow* their tragic fate as we note in the words first of Romeo then the Friar:

---

[138] See I.ii.17–19.

[139] The lovers to whom Mercutio alludes are these: the Italian poet Petrarch and Laura, the lady to whom he wrote poetry; Dido, Queen of Carthage, who fell in love with Aeneas, hero of Virgil's *Aeneid*; Cleopatra, Queen of Egypt, who loved Antony; Helen of Troy whom Prince Paris abducted, an event that caused the Trojan War; Hero who loved Leander and whose tragic story was made famous by Ovid and Christopher Marlowe; Thisbe whose love for Pyramus is recorded in one of Ovid's *Metamorphoses* and whom Shakespeare made famous in *A Midsummer Night's Dream*.

[140] A friar's cell would be a room assigned to him in a hermitage or monastery.

Then love-devouring death do what he dare…

These silent delights have violent ends
And in their triumph die….[141]

The major issues in Act II are these:

- the lovers' differing personalities
- the Nurse and the Friar's involvement in the lovers' decision to marry
- foreshadowing

Act III
Scene 1

Students should understand the events that lead to Mercutio's death. Always sensible, Benvolio attempts to persuade Mercutio to leave the neighborhood since the weather is hot,[142] and the Capulets are close by, circumstances that will provoke another fight. When Mercutio, true to form, mocks his wise friend, and Tybalt arrives looking for Romeo, Benvolio again attempts to convince Mercutio to leave. Romeo arrives and is reluctant to accept Tybalt's challenge; the last thing the new bridegroom wants is to get involved in a duel, even when Tybalt gives him a pretext by insulting him— "thou art a villain."[143] Mercutio is annoyed that Romeo ignores Tybalt's insults— "O calm, dishonorable, vile submission!"[144]—and gets angry enough to draw his sword challenging the obnoxious Tybalt to a duel. At this point, I stop the tape and ask three boys to stand in front of the class with books in hand and act the parts of the three young men. (On a previous day, I ask them to bring in plastic swords.) This strategy allows the class, especially kinesthetic and visual learners, to better appreciate the sequence of events. Mercutio and Tybalt fight, Romeo comes between them to stop the fight, and, seizing his chance, Tybalt mortally wounds Mercutio then runs off. In his dying moments, Mercutio repeatedly curses the Capulets and Montagues— "A plague a' both your houses!"—and dies off stage moments after uttering a pun: "Ask for me tomorrow, and you shall find me a *grave* man."[145] [Italics added.]

Mercutio's death is the direct result of his own impetuous behavior and Tybalt's rage. Mercutio should have listened to Benvolio. But the situation exacerbates. Romeo is horrified at the turn

---

[141] II.vi.7, 9–10.

[142] Hot weather tends to make people irritable.

[143] III.i.60.

[144] Ibid., 72.

[145] Ibid., 96–97.

of events. In an instant, he realizes several facts, all of them contributing to the tragedy that has just occurred: Romeo caused Mercutio's death by intervening in the sword fight, Mercutio dies because Romeo refuses to accept Tybalt's challenge, and Mercutio is killed by Juliet's cousin. The enormity of all this enrages Romeo to such a pitch that when Tybalt returns (Oh, why did he have to return?), he furiously kills Tybalt.

We discuss the *decorum principle*. I tell the class that this is a dramatic principle determined by the ancient Greek philosopher Aristotle who decreed that all violence in drama should occur off stage. Shakespeare has Mercutio die off stage and Tybalt on stage perhaps because Mercutio is a frivolous but likeable young man, and Tybalt is unattractive. In other words, an audience would find it less bearable to witness Mercutio's death than Tybalt's. A more important reason, though, is that Tybalt's death is the play's *turning point*; thus, Shakespeare gives it prominence by having it occur on stage. I make sure the class realizes that a play's turning point occurs when the protagonist can no longer avoid his doom. Up to this point, Romeo could have left Verona and eventually arranged for Juliet to join him; however, now he's a murderer and worse still an exile, as Benvolio instantly makes clear to him.[146] When Benvolio explains the tragedy to Prince Escalus, he attempts to mitigate Romeo's involvement and place the culpability squarely on Tybalt's shoulders.

Romeo's permanent exile is an appalling complication for the lovers. Why is he exiled from Verona? Well, he's killed the nephew of Lady Capulet, a member of a prestigious family. We wonder when the lovers will see each other again. Another point to discuss is Romeo's *tragic flaw*. Freshmen students need to appreciate Aristotle's decree that great tragedy is caused by a particular weakness in the protagonist's character. I attempt to guide the class towards a decision that Romeo's flaw is his rashness. He is rash to marry Juliet in such haste; he is rash to intervene in a dangerous sword fight; and, of course, he is rash to kill Tybalt.

Scene 2
The first twenty-five lines of Juliet's speech that open this scene is another option for the girls' memorization project. Shakespeare uses the Nurse's obtuseness to create *dramatic irony* as Juliet struggles to deal with the meaning of her ambiguous wailing. Juliet's brief happiness is shattered; her *oxymoronic speech* conveys her anguish and despair:

> Beautiful tyrant! Fiend angelical!
> Dove-feathered raven! Wolfish-ravening lamb![147]

---

[146] See III.i.133–34.

[147] III.ii.75–76.

When Juliet desperately decides to hang herself, the Nurse assures Juliet that she will tell Romeo to join his bride that night. A point to emphasize with students is this: The fact that Romeo has killed a member of Juliet's family makes it even more difficult for the lovers to tell their parents about their marriage.

Scene 3

Both the Friar and the Nurse have nothing but bad news for Romeo—exile and Juliet's sorrow. Although Romeo is naturally grief-stricken, students fault him for his rashness and loss of control that convey his immaturity. He succumbs to self-pity, he grovels on the ground, and when he hears that Juliet is distraught, he attempts to commit suicide.[148] Many young people are unimpressed by Romeo. The class should carefully follow the Friar's plan: Romeo will briefly comfort Juliet then leave for Mantua. The Friar will reconcile the two families, tell them of the marriage, and ask the Prince to pardon Romeo so that he can return to Verona, and the lovers will live happily ever afterwards. But this is not a fairy tale, and that's obviously not what happens.

Scene 4

The Capulets and Paris continue to be unaware of Juliet's marriage to Romeo and naturally assume she is grieving over Tybalt's death—a further instance of *dramatic irony*. Another complication arises when Lord Capulet decides his daughter will marry Paris in three days' time, on Thursday. In the circumstances, this appears to be a reasonable decision. We know Lord Capulet approves of the Count as a son-in-law, and apparently Paris genuinely loves Juliet. Also, Juliet has given no indication that she is unhappy about marrying the Count.

Scene 5

This is a powerful and emotionally challenging scene. The brief conversation between the lovers again emphasizes Romeo's tragic flaw—his rashness as well as Juliet's practical realism. Again, Shakespeare *foreshadows* the tragic ending when Juliet refers to death:

> Methinks I see thee, now thou art so low,
> As one dead in the bottom of a tomb.[149]

Dramatic irony continues with Lady Capulet's assumptions that her daughter is distraught over Tybalt's death and that the news of marriage to Paris will cheer Juliet. Also ironic is Lady Capulet's repeated belittlement of Romeo. When Juliet refuses to marry the Count, her parents' reactions are horrifying. Her father heaps abuse on her and disowns her:

---

[148] The class should note the stage direction: "He offers to stab himself…"
[149] III.v.55–56.

Graze where you will, you shall not house with me....
And you be mine, I'll give you to my friend;[150]
And you be not, hang, beg, starve, die in the streets
For, by my soul, I'll ne'er acknowledge thee.[151]

At these appalling words, Juliet's grief is heartbreaking. A few lines later, her mother too abandons her daughter:

Talk not to me, for I'll not speak a word.
Do as thou wilt, for I have done with thee.

One should realize, however, that Lord Capulet is not usually abusive; when he heaps abuses on Juliet, his wife cries,

Fie, fie! What, are you mad?[152]

In other words, Lord Capulet's reaction is uncharacteristic. Also, he is deeply saddened by Tybalt's death and frustrated by his daughter's apparent willfulness. Juliet's parents are unwise, but they are not mere stage villains.

Equally horrifying is the Nurse's insensitive comparison of Romeo to Paris and her brazen suggestion that Juliet commit bigamy by marrying Paris. The Nurse has always been Juliet's friend, but from this point on, she loses Juliet's respect. Juliet is deserted by everyone she has depended on. As far as she is concerned, her situation is hopeless. If the Friar can offer no suggestions, she will commit suicide. I ask the class about the Capulets' parenting skills. The invariable consensus is that Juliet's parents are insensitive and overbearing and that they don't stop to discover what their daughter really feels. If they had been more compassionate and loving, they would surely have found out about her marriage to Romeo. This scene provides an opportunity to talk with teenagers about the alleged generation gap and the need to maintain a close relationship with one's parents.

The major issues in Act III are these:

- the turning point
- the Nurse and the Friar's responses to Juliet and Romeo respectively
- the Capulets' treatment of their daughter

---

[150] Count Paris
[151] III.v.189, 192–4.
[152] Ibid., 157.

- the developing characters of both lovers
- Romeo's tragic flaw

Act IV
Scene 1

I ask students why Shakespeare made Act IV exclusively Juliet's Act. Perhaps he centers on Juliet not Romeo at this point in the play because he wishes to develop her character as the play's protagonist. Certainly, Juliet faces her ordeal alone. Turning to Friar Laurence, it is *ironic* that both Juliet and Count Paris seek him out for opposing reasons—Paris to request that the Friar officiate at his marriage to Juliet and Juliet to seek the Friar's help in preventing her marriage to the Count. After a brief conversation with Juliet, Count Paris leaves. It is the last time he will see Juliet alive.

Juliet shows admirable restraint and maturity as she faces one grim situation after another. In the previous Act, she deals valiantly with her parents' insistence that she marry Paris. While she talks with the Count, she displays admirable composure, but when he leaves, she gives vent to her despair and is close to committing suicide. However, she agrees to the Friar's plan. Two scenes later, she courageously faces the unknown by drinking the Friar's potion. There is much to admire in Juliet.

I make sure that the class appreciates the Friar's ingenious plan that will prevent Juliet's marriage to the Count. He will give Juliet a drug to induce in her a deathlike coma for forty-two hours. Her parents will discover her apparently dead, and she will be buried the family vault. A messenger will travel to Mantua to instruct Romeo to rescue Juliet from the Capulets' vault and take her back to live with him in Mantua. Teachers should be prepared for teenagers' objection that this plan is needlessly complicated. The Friar should simply have told the parents about their children's marriage.

Scene 2

The class must grasp a further complication when Lord Capulet advances the wedding by one day. His wife is dismayed since her mind runs on practical matters such as adequate time for wedding preparations. I always smile at her husband's magnanimous remark— "I'll play the housewife for this once."[153] This hasty alteration in the wedding date is an example of coincidence, one that will prove to be fatal for the lovers. Juliet will still be in a coma when Romeo arrives at her grave, and, because he does not receive the Friar's message, Romeo will assume she is dead.

---

[153] IV.ii.43.

Scene 3

After Juliet persuades her mother to leave her alone so that she can swallow the potion, Shakespeare makes Juliet's torment very real. During her long soliloquy, her mind darts from one horrifying possibility to another. We look over the speech again and note the dreadful scenarios she imagines: Perhaps the liquid won't work, maybe it's a poison that will extricate the Friar from any involvement in the marriage, perhaps she'll regain consciousness before Romeo arrives and suffocate in the vault, or perhaps she'll go insane with horror at being entombed with other dead Capulets. It is also important to note that curtains hide Juliet as she falls on her bed unconscious, a detail that delays the discovery of her apparent death and builds suspense.

Scene 4

This scene is a superb example of *dramatic irony*: The Capulets joyfully prepare for their daughter's marriage to the Count while the bride lies on her bed apparently dead. The scene creates sustained suspense.

Scene 5

The Nurse's sorrow is noisy and repetitive, but it is heart-breaking to witness the parents' grief when we recall that the last time they were with Juliet, they abused and disowned her. The Friar can only rebuke the parents with glib assurances that their daughter is in a better place. I usually disregard the musicians' lines that end the scene, although the interlude does provide some relief from the tragic events. I tell the class that the irritating Nurse has spoken her last lines in the play.

We evaluate Juliet's parents. They certainly love their only child. Lord Capulet has already mentioned that their other children have died, and they want their only remaining child to marry well; however, they are unreasonable when Juliet doesn't agree to marry the man they have chosen for her, and they fail to communicate adequately with her.

The major issues in Act IV are these:

- examples of dramatic irony
- trials Juliet must face
- the Friar's plan

Act V

Scene 1

Act V includes the play's *climax* and *dénouement*. Students should note that the *setting* is now Mantua and that Romeo does not realize Juliet is in a coma rather than dead as his servant reports. The Friar's plan has failed. Romeo has not received his message for reasons that Shakespeare will soon reveal. When Balthasar tells Romeo that Juliet is dead, the rash husband immediately decides to commit suicide. Knowing about an apothecary nearby whose poverty will probably compel him to sell poison, Romeo finds the man's shop is closed. By a strange coincidence, however, the man himself happens to walk by at that precise moment. Shakespeare stretches our credulity here. In any case, as Romeo suspected, the impoverished chemist breaks the law and sells the poison. Romeo rushes off to kill himself at Juliet's tomb, another example of his rash behavior. Students occasionally find it disturbing that both Romeo and Juliet resort to the use of drugs. However, Romeo takes a drug on his own initiative while Juliet is persuaded to do so; also, Romeo resorts to a drug as a means of suicide, while Shakespeare would have us believe that Juliet does so to achieve reunion with her husband. One could argue that these contrasts support the implication that Juliet is more mature than Romeo.

Scene 2

The scene switches back to Verona where we now learn that another friar who was supposed to deliver Friar Laurence's message to Romeo has been quarantined at a house in which everyone is stricken with the plague. Students should know that the "infectious pestilence" to which Shakespeare refers is the Black Death that killed millions of people throughout Europe in the fourteenth century, the time period during which the play takes place. Another coincidence involves Friar John. Of all the houses in Mantua where he could have stayed, he lodges at one so plague-ridden that neither people nor letters could leave the residence. Thus, Friar John could not deliver the letter to Romeo that explained Juliet's coma. Friar Laurence immediately foresees a fatal outcome, and he too hurries to Juliet's vault to rescue her and hide her at his cell until Romeo is contacted.

Scene 3

A few days beforehand, I assign parts and select students to act the final tragic scene as they read their lines. The tape is switched off, and the front of the classroom is cleared of desks. I ask the actors to wear costumes—cloaks, plastic swords, a long brown tunic for the Friar. A *complication* opens the scene: Count Paris arrives to place flowers on Juliet's grave, which is usually placed center stage with Tybalt's corpse nearby.[154] When Romeo arrives, the grieving husband must have a reason to be alone, so he tells his servant he wishes to remove a ring from Juliet's finger as a memento. Horrified at Romeo's sacrilegious attempt to open Juliet's tomb, the Count recognizes Romeo as Tybalt's murderer and attempts to arrest him.

Students sometimes wonder why Shakespeare has Romeo kill again. Romeo's words convey his longing to be alone with Juliet, and the other man's unwelcome presence incites him to commit another desperate act. After stabbing him, Romeo realizes it is Paris he has killed and is confused at the Count's talk of Juliet, although he vaguely remembers Balthasar talking of a marriage between Juliet and Paris. He places the corpse in Juliet's tomb. Then he sees Juliet lying there still so beautiful:

> Shall I believe
> That unsubstantial Death is amorous…[155]

Romeo is distraught with grief, but we wish he had realized that Juliet looks so lovely because she is still living. It is a poignant speech, a good choice for boys to memorize.

Two more coincidences occur: Friar Laurence arrives seconds after Romeo's death, too late to tell Romeo that Juliet is not dead, and the Count's servant arrives immediately after Juliet stabs herself. Both lovers' deaths occur moments after someone appears and could possibly have prevented their suicides. I ask students their opinions about the Friar's haste to get away, with or without Juliet. They realize he panics and wants to avoid being implicated in the lovers' deaths and find his action contemptible. It is obviously cowardly to leave Juliet to her certain fate.

Shakespeare now brings on stage all the main characters except Romeo's mother who has died of grief at her son's exile and the Nurse whose annoying presence would detract from the tragedy. Students wonder why Shakespeare includes the Friar's long, unnecessary explanation that begins, "I will be brief"! The audience has followed the antecedent events, but perhaps Shakespeare wants us to witness the parents' reactions to their children's tragic deaths.[156] The Prince magnanimously admits he shares culpability and should have ended the two families' hostility earlier:

---

[154] The class should note that most of the main characters in the drama converge at the Capulets' vault in addition to the supposedly dead Juliet—Count Paris, Romeo, Friar Laurence, Prince Escalus, the Capulets, and Lord Montague.

[155] V.iii.102–3.

[156] Some producers of the play cut the Friar's speech.

And I, for winking at your discords, too
Have lost a brace of kinsmen [Mercutio and Paris].[157]

Inevitably, we think of the irresponsible Friar and Nurse and the Capulets' cruel abandonment of their daughter. How tragic it is that Romeo and Juliet are "sacrifices of [their parents'] enmity." The fathers' promises of permanent memorials are magnanimous, and we are thankful the long feud is over, but at what a cost. In this final scene and indeed throughout the play, Shakespeare's focus is the tragic result of long-standing hatred. The Montagues and Capulets have lost their most precious possessions, their children. Romeo and Juliet had to keep their love and subsequent marriage secret because of their parents' hatred for one another. This need for secrecy led to their deaths. As the highest-ranking character, the Prince delivers the closing lines:

For never was a story of more woe
Than this of Juliet and her Romeo.

The major issues in Act V are these:

- examples of dramatic irony
- coincidences
- the play's climax
- the tragic resolution

---

[157] V.iii.294–95.

Plot diagram

I distribute a plot diagram that students complete by adding events that comprise the *exposition, complications, turning point, falling action, climax*, and *dénouement*.[158] (See template of a plot diagram in the handouts.) I give them several days to complete these charts before handing them in for grading. Here are some sample notes:

- **exposition:**   we are made aware of the feud between the Montagues and Capulets

- **rising action / complications:**

  a quarrel breaks out between the servants of both families
  Paris becomes a suitor for Juliet
  Romeo attends the Capulets' ball
  Romeo and Juliet fall in love
  Friar Laurence agrees to marry the lovers
  Tybalt challenges Romeo to a duel
  the lovers are married
  Tybalt mortally wounds Mercutio

- **turning point:**   Romeo kills Tybalt

- **falling action:**

  Prince Escalus banishes Romeo from Verona
  Romeo leaves for Mantua
  Lord Capulet arranges Juliet's marriage to Paris
  Friar Laurence gives Juliet a drug simulating death
  Lord Capulet advances the wedding day
  Juliet takes the Friar's drug
  the Capulets bury their supposedly dead daughter
  Friar John cannot give Romeo the message about Juliet's coma
  Romeo thinks Juliet has died
  Romeo kills Paris

- **climax:**

  Romeo drinks poison
       OR
  Juliet awakes to find Romeo dead and stabs herself

- **dénouement:**

  Friar Laurence explains the circumstances of the lovers' deaths
  the fathers are reconciled

---

[158] You may wish to refer to more detailed instructions about a plot diagram that are included during discussion of Doris Lessing's short story "Through the Tunnel."

We complete the play with further discussion of several issues.

1. **The climax**: Which of the lovers' deaths is the more climactic or are both deaths equally climactic? Or does the climax occur earlier in the play? Students' opinions vary on the most climactic moment—Romeo's or Juliet's death. Some argue that Romeo's death that follows his long speech is the play's climax and that Juliet's death is by comparison anti-climactic. Others argue, with great plausibility, that the climactic moment is also the play's turning point, Romeo's killing Tybalt. From then on, the tragic outcome is inevitable.

2. **The lovers' personalities**: I ask the class whom of the two lovers they most closely relate to. This is not an open and shut case with the boys choosing Romeo and the girls Juliet. Boys and girls alike often decide that Juliet is more interesting because she is more realistic and has more problems to confront.

3. **Human error and coincidence**: The issue I emphasize is the extent to which both human error and coincidence contribute to the lovers' deaths. Most students decide that the lovers' deaths are caused by other people's errors, chiefly the feuding parents. Two young people die because of long-standing, bitter enmity between their families.

Essay

Students write notes on the third point and use them to plan an essay on this issue. Here are some sample notes on the issue of human error:[159]

Human error:
- Lord Capulet and Lord Montague do nothing to end the long-standing feud.
- Prince Escalus fails to effectively end the feud.
- Tybalt does not control his anger and kills Mercutio.
- The Capulets lack sensitivity regarding Juliet's refusal to marry Paris and act heartlessly and irrationally.
- The Friar fails to give Romeo wise counsel.
- The Friar marries the lovers.
- The Nurse colludes in details that concern Juliet's hasty marriage.
- The Nurse suggests that Juliet marry Paris and commit bigamy.
- The lovers fail to consult their respective parents about their marriage.

An outline could focus on these points: the feuding families, Tybalt's anger, the Friar and the Nurse's compliance in the marriage, the lovers' secrecy.

---

[159] See student essay in the handouts.

Occasionally, students explore the issue of coincidence:

Coincidence:
- Romeo hears that Rosaline is a guest at the Capulets' party, information that motivates him to attend.
- The Capulets advance the day of Juliet's wedding to Count Paris.
- The apothecary's shop is closed, but the man appears at his shop the moment Romeo arrives to purchase poison.
- Friar John is detained and prevented from giving Romeo the message about Juliet's being in a coma.
- Friar Laurence and the watchman arrive seconds after Romeo and Juliet respectively kill themselves.

An outline could include the following points: the Capulets' ball, Juliet's wedding date, the Friar's message, the lovers' deaths.

Memorization

I assign speeches for memorization:

Girls:
"Thou knowest the mask of night is on my face" (II.ii.85–106).
OR
"Gallop apace, you fiery-footed steeds" (III.ii.1–25).

Boys:
"But soft! What light through yonder window breaks?" (II.ii.2–25)
Romeo has other long speeches; boys could memorize part of his final speech at Juliet's grave.[160]

Test

A short test on poetry devices, a test on the entire play, and a student's essay on the play are included in the handouts. Review questions on *Romeo and Juliet* are listed on the following pages. After the drama unit, we tackle another challenging genre, epic poetry.

---

[160] Students may be interested to know that Shakespeare's *Romeo and Juliet* is the basis of a modern musical, *West Side Story,* set on the West Side of New York City. Like the play, the musical tells the tragic story of two "star-crossed" lovers.

Review questions on *Romeo and Juliet*[161]

1. Why do you think Shakespeare includes Rosaline in this play?
    [Rosaline is included in the play in order to convey Romeo's immaturity. Romeo immediately switches his affections from Rosaline to Juliet the moment he meets Juliet.]

2. List the main character traits of these young men: Benvolio, Mercutio, Tybalt.
    [Benvolio: rational, practical, and wise
    Mercutio: impetuous and frivolous
    Tybalt: fiery and vengeful]

3. In what ways is Benvolio a good friend to Romeo?
    [Benvolio is a loyal friend to Romeo throughout the events of the play. Since Rosaline is apparently indifferent to Romeo's love, Benvolio attempts to persuade Romeo to switch his affection to another girl. After Romeo kills Tybalt, Benvolio urges his friend to escape from Verona to avoid death. When Benvolio explains to Prince Escalus how Tybalt died, he attempts to mitigate Romeo's involvement and suggests that Tybalt was to blame for the tragedy.]

4. How do Mercutio and Romeo differ in their attitudes to love?
    [Mercutio adopts a frivolous attitude to love that contrasts with Romeo's highly romantic approach.]

5. Both the Nurse and the Friar could have averted the young lovers' deaths. Explain how they should have acted differently.
    [Both Nurse and Friar should have informed the lovers' respective parents of their children's marriage plans. Instead, they both colluded with the lovers in those plans, and the Friar marries them without their parents' knowledge.]

6. Apart from Mercutio, name another character who is Romeo's foil, and explain why he is a foil character.
    [Benvolio's prudence and practicality contrast with Romeo's rash, impractical approach to life that extends to his love for Juliet.]

7. Reread the following passage and state its purpose:

    > . . . my mind misgives
    > Some consequence yet hanging in the stars
    > Shall bitterly begin his fearful date
    > With this night's revels and expire the term

---

[161] A student booklet that accompanies this teaching guide contains all 9th grade review questions and tests with answers omitted.

Any of these questions could be used for a graded discussion of the play.

Of a despisèd life, closed in my breast,

By some vile forfeit of untimely death.

[On his way to the Capulets' banquet, Romeo is overwhelmed by misgivings about his future. The passage is an example of foreshadowing. In these lines and throughout the play, Shakespeare foreshadows the lovers' deaths.]

8. Reread Romeo's lines spoken to the Friar and state the device Shakespeare uses here:

> Do thou but close our hands with holy words,
>
> Then love-devouring death do what he dare—
>
> It is enough I may but call her mine.

[The passage is another instance of foreshadowing.]

9. What is ironic about the Friar's reason for marrying the lovers?

[The Friar agrees to marry the young couple in order to end the feud between their respective families, but only the deaths of the respective parents' children will end the conflict. The end of the bitter feud comes at far too great a cost.]

10. What is Romeo's punishment for killing Tybalt?

[Romeo is exiled from Verona.]

11. Mention some ways in which the lovers' personalities are different.

[Romeo is impractical, impulsive, and passionate; Juliet is practical, thoughtful, and has a more stable personality.]

12. When Juliet discovers Romeo's punishment, she weeps. Her mother responds: "Evermore weeping for your cousin's death?" Lady Capulet's comment is an example of _____ (complete the sentence).

[dramatic irony]

13. What is this play's turning point? Explain why this event is indeed the turning point.

[Romeo's killing Tybalt is the play's turning point. From that moment, Romeo's fate is doomed. He can do nothing to extricate himself from exile and the tragic events that follow.]

14. Give a valid reason for Shakespeare's making Act IV exclusively Juliet's Act.

[Act IV dramatizes the challenges that Juliet must endure and overcome. She has been compelled to marry Romeo secretly because of her parents' hostility to his family. She must now deal with her parents' desire that she marry Count Paris when she is already married to Romeo. She must also endure her new husband's banishment from Verona. She must drink the Friar's potion with no knowledge of its effect on her. We respect her courage as she deals with these trials alone more than we would if Romeo were with her.]

15. Lord Capulet moves the date of Juliet's marriage to Count Paris closer by one day. Why is this decision fatal to the lovers?

    [When Juliet's wedding to the Count is advanced by one day, there will be insufficient time for Juliet to take the Friar's drug and awake from it, and for Romeo to arrive at the Capulets' vault in order to take Juliet to live with him in Mantua.]

16. Name several reasons why Juliet is reluctant to drink the drug the Friar has given her.

    [She imagines that the drug will not work or that it is poisonous and will kill her; she may regain consciousness before Romeo rescues her and will suffocate in the vault; she will wake up, and surrounded as she will be by dead Capulets, she will go mad.]

17. Are the Capulets villains or are they bad parents? Explain your opinion.

    [Students usually make these points:

    Lord and Lady Capulet are not simply stage villains. They love their daughter, but they are not particularly good parents because they do not take time to consider their daughter's wishes in their choice of a husband for her, and they verbally abuse her when she refuses to marry the Count. They fail to communicate well with their daughter.]

18. List several of the play's coincidences.

    [Romeo hears that Rosaline is a guest at the Capulets' party, information that motivates him to attend.

    The Capulets advance the day of Juliet's wedding to Count Paris.

    The apothecary's shop is closed, but the man appears at his shop the moment Romeo arrives to purchase poison.

    Friar John is detained and prevented from giving Romeo the message about Juliet's being in a temporary coma.

    Friar Laurence and the watchman arrive seconds after Romeo and Juliet respectively commit suicide.]

19. Why is it generally more satisfying to read or watch a play in which human error plays a larger role than coincidence as events unfold?

    [Students generally decide that tragedy in people's lives is far more likely to be caused because of mistakes people make rather than coincidental occurrences. Therefore, tragedy caused by human error is more believable and more satisfying.]

20. What is the cause of Lady Montague's death?

    [She is heartbroken at Romeo's exile.]

21. At the end of the play, how are Lord Capulet and Lord Montague reconciled?

    [The fathers agree to have monuments built that will honor their children.]

22. In your opinion, which moment is the play's climax?

[Students often state that Romeo's killing Tybalt is both the play's turning point and the climax. They sometimes decide that Romeo's death is the play's climax or that both lovers' deaths are equally climactic.]

23. Do you think Romeo or Juliet is the more convincing character? Explain.

[Most students think that Juliet's characterization is more convincing. They state that Romeo seems too extravagantly romantic and is too determined to marry a girl he has only just met. Although Juliet accepts his marriage proposal, she is more moderate and reasonable, therefore more convincing as a person than Romeo.]

24. What action should the lovers should have taken that would probably have averted their tragic deaths?

[Students unvaryingly make this point:

Both young people should have informed their respective parents of their desire to marry instead of marrying secretly without their parents' permission.]

25. Briefly state why you think future 9ᵗʰ grade students should study this play.

[Most students realize that this tragedy is relevant to any culture in any time period because people throughout the world suffer the pangs of forbidden love and parental abuse. Also, the play depicts the nature of young love, which is often rash and short-lived. Above all, the tragedy of *Romeo and Juliet* powerfully reveals the fatal results of long-standing hatred.]

Unit IV

Epic Poetry

the *Odyssey*

by
Homer[162]
ca. 800–700 BC

Homer

The Odyssey is one of the finest adventure stories ever written. In Leland Ryken's words, it "is one of the foundational stories of Western literature—a veritable model of storytelling technique."[163] However, I do not read the entire epic with freshman students. During class, we read and discuss incidents for which the *Odyssey* is most famous, and I summarize other sections for the class.[164] It is essential to show students a map of Odysseus's journey home from

---

[162] No one knows whether Homer was, in fact, the author of the two epics attributed to him. Scholars believe Homer lived during the eighth or ninth century BC and that he came from Ionia in the Mediterranean. He was supposedly a blind poet. He inherited the stories recounted in the two epics that were recited orally by professional bards. The stories were eventually written down to become the most important literary works of the ancient world.

[163] Leland Ryken, *Realms of Gold: The Classics in Christian Perspective* (Wheaton, IL: Harold Shaw, 1991), 24.

[164] See line numbers listed for the sections in each Book that I read with the class.

Troy to Ithaca. One can find an excellent map and time line of Odysseus's journey at several websites.[165] When students notice the close proximity of Ithaca to Troy, they question why the journey took ten years to complete. They should understand that Odysseus was blown off course many times by the sea god, Poseidon, for reasons that will become apparent. They should also realize that we know almost nothing about Homer. Perhaps he never existed, but tradition has it that he was a blind Greek minstrel who authored the *Iliad* and the *Odyssey* around 750 BC. The epics were not written down; minstrels or bards traveled to local communities and recited them, a custom that is referred to as the oral tradition of poetry. Centuries later, the epics were recorded.

Chronologically, the *Iliad* precedes the *Odyssey*, but I cover the *Odyssey* in the introductory course and the *Iliad* during the world literature course because the *Odyssey* is more accessible for younger students. The earlier epic describes the Trojan War fought in approximately 1200 BC over Helen, wife of the Greek King Menelaus. When the Trojan Prince Paris abducted Helen, Menelaus and his brother Agamemnon sailed for Troy and engaged in a ten-year war to restore Helen to her husband. The second epic describes Odysseus's return journey home to Greece after defeating the Trojans.[166]

Several books have proved invaluable to my reading Homer with high school students. I highly recommend *Heroes of the City of Man: A Christian Guide to Select Ancient Literature* by Peter J. Leithart. This is an invaluable resource for the study of ancient literature. Leithart devotes a chapter each to the *Iliad,* the *Odyssey,* the *Aeneid,* and *Oedipus Tyrannus* or *Oedipus Rex* (*Oedipus the King*), as well as several other Greek dramas. Two other fine resources are written by Leland Ryken. One book included in the *Christian Guides to the Classics* series is titled *Homer's The Odyssey*; the other is titled *Realms of Gold: The Classics in Christian Perspective.*

We talk first about the epic as a genre. Students memorize the definition of an epic: An epic is a long narrative poem about the exploits of an epic hero who embodies or represents the values of his culture. The class should also know that epic heroes were superhuman and could therefore accomplish extraordinary feats, which in classic epics was a battle.

Young people should become familiar with the following details that are antecedent to the *Odyssey*:

---

[165] The map at www.tripline.net includes explanations for each step of the hero's odyssey and a detailed time line of Odysseus's journeying.

[166] The word *odyssey* is used today to indicate a long journey that often involves a quest or mission.

- It was Odysseus's idea to build the massive Trojan horse that hid half the Greek army.
- Odysseus was one of the Greeks who hid in the body of the wooden horse.
- The wily Greeks persuaded the Trojans to bring the horse into the city so that they could climb out of the horse once they were in the city and conquer Troy. This incident is mentioned only briefly in the *Odyssey* because this epic centers on Odysseus's journey home.
- The rest of the army pretended to sail away but returned at night to join the other soldiers and enter the city of Troy.
- The Greeks conquered Troy, and those that survived the war returned home.

Students do not read epic poetry on their own. During class, we read long sections of Robert Fitzgerald's translation of the *Odyssey*, which many scholars claim is the finest available.[167] This translation is reproduced in various literary anthologies. Ryken points outs that titles for the books of the epic are added by translators or editors;[168] for instance, some editors of the Fitzgerald translation title Book 1 "A Son Seeks a Father." I distribute a list of people and gods mentioned in the epic to which we refer as we encounter them.[169] (See handouts for a list of characters in the *Odyssey*.) I tell students not to be overwhelmed by the many names but to become familiar with the principal characters. I mention that epics traditionally include twenty-four books and that we will be reading exciting excerpts for which the *Odyssey* is most famous.

Book 1: lines 1–18; 142–68; 299–344[170]
Invocation

As Ryken points out, the *Odyssey* falls into three sections. Books 1 to 4, referred to as *The Telemachia*, deal with Telemachus's travels to locate his father;[171] Books 5 to 12 describe Odysseus's journeying; Books 13 to 24 cover Odysseus's return home to restore order in Ithaca.[172] Epic poetry traditionally begins with an *invocation*, which is a supplication or prayer.

---

[167] Fitzgerald's translation is copyrighted, so I limit quotations to a few brief phrases.

[168] Leland Ryken, *Homer's The Odyssey* (Wheaton, IL: Crossway, 2013), 17.

[169] The ancient Greeks were polytheists; that is, they believed in many gods. Their gods were supposedly omnipotent and immortal, but they behaved much like some human beings and were corrupt. Nevertheless, ancient Greeks prayed to and sacrificed to the gods in order to gain their favor.

[170] I cite the lines in each Book of the *Odyssey* that I read with a 9th grade class. The lines are based on the Fitzgerald translation.

[171] At one level, the episodes involving Telemachus can be read as a rite of passage or a coming of age story. Like Jerry in "Through the Tunnel" or Kostya in "The Bridge," Telemachus matures significantly.

[172] Ryken, *Realms of Gold* (Wheaton, IL: Harold Shaw), 28.

The first eighteen lines of the *Odyssey* comprise an invocation to Calliope, the Muse of epic poetry. I show the class an illustration of the nine Muses. A beautiful painting of the Muses in Apollo's temple by Richard Samuel hangs in London's National Portrait Gallery.[173] One can find other paintings as well as artefacts depicting the Muses at many websites.

Homer begins by asking his Muse to inspire him to recount the adventures of "that man skilled in all ways of contending." This expression is an *epithet* or a colorful phrase that students should memorize since Odysseus's main characteristic is his resourcefulness. Epithets were mnemonics or prompts for the bard as he recited the poetry. Students find many examples of epithets to note down as we read the epic.[174] Historical examples include Alfred the Great, Richard the Lionheart (King Richard I), Honest Abe, and Stonewall Jackson. One should note that, in Homer's summary of Odysseus's adventures in these first eighteen lines, he exonerates the hero from causing the deaths of his sailors. The men died because they rashly ate the sacred cattle of the sun god, Helios.

As already noted, the first four books deal not with the hero but with his son Telemachus.[175] At this point, twenty years have elapsed since Odysseus left Troy for home, and the goddess-nymph Calypso has imprisoned him for seven years on her island of Ogygia. We look at the map of Odysseus's journeying and notice that much of his voyaging is over, so one wrongly assumes he will arrive fairly soon in Ithaca. A copy of the map, much enlarged, goes on the classroom wall in order that the class can follow the hero's sea voyage throughout our reading of the epic.

Chaos in Ithaca

On Olympus, the gods have been debating the hero's fate.[176] When Athena[177] persuades her father Zeus to free Odysseus from his captivity, Zeus sends the messenger god Hermes to Ogygia to free Calypso's prisoner. Athena then disguises herself as Mentor, an old family friend, and arrives in Ithaca, where chaos reigns. During her husband's twenty-year absence,

---

[173] One can view Samuel's painting at www.npg.org.uk or www.greekmyths-greekmythology.com.

[174] Some examples include the following: Homer refers to the sea as "the wine-dark sea" and to dawn that is constantly "spreading out her finger tips of rose"; Telemachus is referred to as "clear-headed Telemachus," Penelope as "faithful Penelope," Hermes as "the Wayfinder," and Persephone as "the iron queen."

[175] I am using modern spellings for names rather than adhering to Fitzgerald's authentic Greek spelling.

[176] The class should know that ancient Greeks believed in a so-called Fate that allegedly determined man's destiny. The gods had limited power in that they could thwart Fate for a while but could not entirely change a man's destiny. Odysseus was fated to return to Ithaca, so he did not drown with the rest of his men and was eventually reunited with Penelope in spite of Poseidon's interference.

[177] Athena or Pallas Athena was the Greek goddess of wisdom, crafts, and warfare.

Penelope has been pestered by suitors demanding her hand in marriage while they devour Odysseus's food and wine. Leithart comments, "By devouring Odysseus's substance, they are eroding the basis of his power," which, Leithart asserts, is their plan. By slaughtering the king's cattle, eating his food, and slurping his wine, the suitors are virtually ensuring that Odysseus will lack the resources to maintain power and pass that power on to his son.[178] The epic thus starts *in medias res,* in the middle of things or at a crucial moment, as all good stories should.

Ancient Greek mores: hospitality

Young Greek boys learned about their culture by studying epics with a long oral tradition such as Homer's *Odyssey.* The class writes notes on ancient Greek cultural mores. One of these is the emphasis on *hospitality,* which Leithart maintains is a major topic throughout the epic.[179] Telemachus immediately invites Athena, the disguised goddess, to join the feast and to state her business later. When the young man laments the dilemma he faces with the rowdy suitors, Athena counsels him to discover whether his father is still alive by talking to two men—Nestor, King of Pylos and Menelaus, King of Sparta, Helen's husband. If Odysseus is dead, Telemachus should give his father a suitable funeral and kill the suitors. Quite an assignment for an inexperienced young man. As Leithart asserts, these riotous men are violating the hospitality extended to them by Penelope and Telemachus and wantonly consuming Odysseus's wealth and Telemachus's inheritance.[180] Zeus will eventually ensure that they are punished by death. As Leland Ryken points out, Homer's main *theme* is justice.[181]

Book 2: lines 1–14; 96–123; 271–300

Telemachus confronts the troublesome situation at the palace. However, he is a naïve teenager and lacks the ability to rid the palace of these mature men who harass his mother and restore order to his father's kingdom. Leithart comments that order in Ithaca will only be restored by "the wiles and cunning of an Odysseus."[182] Telemachus does not have his father's strength or resourcefulness. He lacks the confidence to deal with an intolerable situation. As already indicated (see footnote 171), the story of Telemachus is a rite of passage or a coming of age story that describes the boy's maturing.

---

[178] Leithart, *Heroes of the City of Man: A Christian Guide to Select Ancient Literature* (Moscow, ID: Canon Press, 1999), 163.

[179] Leithart, *Heroes of the City of Man,* 154.

[180] Ibid.

[181] Leland Ryken, *Homer's The Odyssey,* 68.

[182] Leithart, *Heroes of the City of Man,* 151.

Penelope's subterfuge

Now we come to Penelope's ruse. Penelope appears to be as wily as her clever husband. The most arrogant of the suitors, Antinous, complains to Telemachus about the clever trick. Penelope has promised to marry one of the suitors when she finishes weaving a funeral shroud for her father-in-law, Laertes; however, for the last three years, she has unraveled her day's weaving each night. Leithart makes some fascinating comments about Penelope's weaving:

> This trick is significant on several levels. The loom is typically a woman's instrument; men employ swords and spears, while women work on the loom. Penelope's trick is a typically feminine deception, using the one weapon she has in her armory. Weaving, moreover, is often an image of fate and destiny… in pagan literature the fates "weave" the mantle of the world.…Penelope is quite literally "weaving" the fate of the suitors, for by delaying her decision, she is leaving time for Odysseus to "weave" a web to entrap the suitors. Appropriately, she is working on a funeral shroud, rather than the wedding veil that the suitors hope for. Ironically, the suitors have forced her to finish the web, sealing their own fate.[183]

The chief suitor Antinous demands that Penelope choose one of them and end the conflict among them. I show the class a stunning painting by a sixteenth-century Italian painter, Bernadino Pintoricchio, that depicts Penelope at her loom.[184]

Telemachus prepares to find his father

Realizing that Mentor is Athena in disguise, Telemachus turns to the goddess for help in dealing with his dilemma. Athena encourages the boy and foretells the suitors' fates. Obeying Athena's instructions, Telemachus decides to set sail for Pylos then Sparta for news of his father while Athena finds a ship and crew for him. We refer to the map to check the locations of Pylos and Sparta in southern Greece. Telemachus and Athena prepare for the journey.

Book 3: lines 7–40; 71 –77; 132–39; 233–49
King Nestor of Pylos

Telemachus and Athena find King Nestor's men making a sacrifice to Poseidon. This activity is an example of another ancient Greek custom, *piety*. Students should know that Poseidon is furious with Odysseus because the hero had earlier blinded the sea god's son, the one-eyed giant Polyphemus. As a result of Poseidon's anger, Odysseus is constantly blown off course and will take ten years to journey back to Ithaca. Nestor, famous for his wisdom, is a typical old warrior reminiscing about past glory. At this point, students exchange comments about aging grandfathers at the Thanksgiving dinner table who recount lengthy stories about their glory days. Much like other elderly gentlemen, Nestor rambles on about the past. He does not,

---

[183] Ibid., 166-67.

[184] The painting can be viewed at www.nationalgallery.co.uk.

however, have any knowledge of Odysseus's whereabouts having last seen him in Troy. Again, the emphasis on *piety* and *hospitality* is evident: We hear about the best meat served to the gods, and Nestor defers his questions until his guests have eaten dinner.

Delayed entrance of the hero

Another device of epic poetry is the *delayed entrance of the hero*. Homer does not introduce us to Odysseus until Book 5 but whets our curiosity about the hero as Nestor praises him. With all the talk of Odysseus throughout the first four books, Homer increases our curiosity about the legendary hero.

Book 4: lines 116–57

King Menelaus of Sparta and Helen

Telemachus next visits King Menelaus now reunited with Helen whom students remember was the cause of the Trojan War. Students should note the description of the famous beauty as she comes from "her scented chamber." Homer compares her to Artemis.[185] Homer's Helen is languid and seductive. The description of her also implies that she is indolent as well as self-deprecating—a few lines later, she calls herself a "wanton." The multi-faceted beauty is a seductress, as are Circe and Calypso, but Homer's Helen is not typical of all his women, a point that introduces yet another aspect of ancient Greek society, the *role of women*. Women in general were passive creatures, subject to the will of their husband. They stayed at home. They were clever like Penelope, but they did not participate in affairs of state. They tended to their children, managed their households, and acted as a gracious hostess for their guests. It is also interesting to note that several women in this epic are associated with weaving. We have noted Leithart's comment about Penelope's weaving, which is a trap that will seal the fate of the men who harass her. Penelope weaves cloth as do Calypso and Circe in Books 5 and 10 respectively.

As Menelaus talks about Odysseus's adventures, the young man misses his father and weeps. Telemachus now learns that his father is living with the nymph Calypso but longs to return home. Homer tells us that Penelope's suitors plan to kill Telemachus on his return to Ithaca.

Book 5: lines 48–89; 155–71; 203–29; 513–19

Odysseus and Calypso

At this point in the story, Homer introduces his hero. Athena has again persuaded Zeus; this time she has convinced her father to send the messenger god Hermes to Ogygia to release Odysseus from Calypso's spell. Students frequently ask how Calypso can keep Odysseus

---

[185] Artemis, Apollo's sister, is Greek goddess of the hunt.

captive. Since Calypso is a goddess, she has divine power. An *epic* or *Homeric simile*, a well-known convention of epic poetry, compares Hermes to a cormorant or seagull.[186] Students should know that an epic simile extends throughout several lines of poetry. In the following lines, sensory imagery describes Calypso's lair. The air is scented with a cedar wood fire and pungent trees. Even the messenger god is fascinated by the beautiful enchantress as she sits in her cave singing and weaving. As already noted, Calypso is a seductress, as opposed to Penelope who embodies the ever-faithful wife. A double standard existed in ancient Greece: Odysseus has two lovers, Calypso and Circe, whereas Penelope is expected to exemplify the faithful wife. However, Homer gives Odysseus no alternative; resistance to these goddesses would result in terrible punishment, and he would never return to his kingdom.

When we first meet the exiled hero, he is grieving over his long absence from home. Hearing Hermes's instruction from Zeus, Calypso is enraged but has no other choice than to release the king of Ithaca. Since Calypso cannot disobey Zeus's command to give up Odysseus, she provides the king with refreshments and a raft and bids him farewell; but she warns him that if he could foresee the problems that await him on his voyage, he would not wish to leave her. Calypso then makes a remark that is characteristically feminine. Comparing herself to Penelope, she asks Odysseus whether she is less desirable than his wife. Girls relate to this. And most boys understand Odysseus's dilemma. How can a man respond to such a question? But, as Ryken observes, Odysseus always rises above his circumstances via "his wit and intelligence."[187] Always resourceful, the hero quickly assures the nymph that Penelope's beauty is far inferior to Calypso's because the goddess is immortal whereas Penelope is a mere mortal. Odysseus is the consummate diplomat.

A well-known romantic water color of the parting of man and goddess, *Farewell to Calypso* by the nineteenth-century artist Samuel Palmer, depicts Odysseus sailing away, while on the shore Calypso waves goodbye, her arms outstretched towards him.[188] Poseidon sends a storm that destroys Odysseus's raft; the hero drifts on a stormy ocean for several days, but with Athena's ever-present help, the hero arrives exhausted on the shore of Scheria, home of the Phaeacians.

Book 6
Odysseus at Phaeacia[189]
We do not read Book 6. I summarize for the class the domestic scene involving Princess Nausicaa. This is the last of Odysseus's adventures but the second one we read about. Odysseus

---

[186] Book 5, 56–59.

[187] Ryken, *Realms of Gold,* 24.

[188] The best site to view this painting is www.whitworth.manchester.ac.uk.

[189] pronounced "fee-A-sha"

has landed on the island of Phaeacia. He asks a young woman, who happens to be the king's daughter Nausicaa, for directions, and the hero arrives at the palace of King Alcinous, where he is hospitably received.[190] It is fortunate that the hero has landed here because the Phaeacians are ship builders and will provide Odysseus with a ship so that he can sail home to Ithaca. I show the class Rubens's painting, *Ulysses and Nausicaa*.[191]

Book 7
Odysseus at Alcinous's court

I also summarize Books 7 and 8 for the class. Book 7 recounts the reception given Odysseus by Nausicaa's father, King Alcinous, at the Phaeacian court, although the king does not know the stranger's identity. Alcinous gives a feast in the hero's honor after which he wants to hear the stranger's story. This is another example of Greek *hospitality* but, more importantly, it provides Homer with a pretext for summarizing the hero's exploits that continued for ten years after Troy's destruction.

Book 8
The minstrel sings about Troy's destruction

After the banquet, Odysseus asks the minstrel Demodocus to sing about the wooden horse. The minstrel sings about Odysseus's brilliant plan involving the Trojan horse and the Greeks' destruction of Troy. As he listens, Odysseus weeps for his companions killed in battle. Demodocus finishes his recital, and King Alcinous demands that the stranger in their midst reveal his identity.

Book 9: lines 20–40; 91–112; 251–585
The Lotus Eaters

We spend some time reading and reviewing Books 9 through 12. The king's request that Odysseus reveal his identity allows Homer to relate the hero's most well-known and most popular adventures that are covered in these Books. As Odysseus identifies himself, he boasts lavishly about his fame. We would find such bragging obnoxious today, but an epic hero was expected to boast about his prowess; the hero's *hubris* or pride is another instance of an ancient Greek custom. Odysseus describes his adventures to the point of his arrival at the land of the Lotus Eaters, an episode on which Tennyson based his famous poem.[192] The Lotus Eaters are creatures who eat the lotus flower, a plant that creates in them permanent feelings of indolence and forgetfulness. The hero must resist the enticement of this plant if he is to reach

---

[190] One must point out the similarity in the names of King Alcinous and Penelope's chief suitor, Antinous.

[191] One can view Rubens's painting at several sites including www.wikiart.org.

[192] Scholars comment that "The Lotos-Eaters" is one of Tennyson's finest early poems.

his homeland. However, Odysseus's legendary curiosity compels him to send a scouting party to find out about the Lotus Eaters; when his mariners eat "this honeyed plant," they lose all desire to leave that land and must be driven back to the ship and tied down.

Polyphemus

Odysseus's next adventure is most popular with a freshman class. The hero encounters a savage brute, a giant sheepherder who sleeps in a cave apart from other men. This is Polyphemus, Poseidon's son. He is one of the Cyclopes, a race of sheepherding giants with one eye in the middle of their foreheads. Throughout his adventures, the hero wants to know about the people he meets; his celebrated curiosity leads him to take his men into the giant's cave and await the monster's arrival. Homer emphasizes Polyphemus's vast size and strength. Young people need reminding that when they read literature, they should visualize the scene. Here Odysseus and his men are holed up in cave with a giant and no means of escape. Having identified for the Cyclops the strangers in his cave, Odysseus reminds Polyphemus of the giant's obligation to guests and asks to be treated courteously or the monster will incur Zeus's anger. Polyphemus reviles the hero and is contemptuous of the gods.

One is inclined to feel a teeny bit sorry for the hero; however, Odysseus is once again resourceful. When Polyphemus asks where the hero left his ship, Odysseus immediately grasps the significance of the question and replies that it has smashed upon the rocks. As dramatically as possible, I read the section that describes the Cyclops eating Odysseus's men.[193] Young people are captivated. Without stopping to think through the situation, they sometimes question why the hero doesn't make short work of the Cyclops. Epic hero though he is, Odysseus can't remove the massive stone slab at the entrance to the cave and escape. Predictably, however, he devises a plan. That night, plying Polyphemus with wine as the giant eats two more men, Odysseus identifies himself as "Nohbdy." Assuring the hero he'll eat him next, the Cyclops staggers backwards in a drunken stupor. At this point, Odysseus and his men thrust a previously prepared hot spike into the Cyclops's one eye. Homer describes the monster's blinding with a graphic epic simile.[194] Students quite enjoy the grisly details. Screaming for help, Polyphemus yells to the neighboring sheepherders that "Nohbdy" had tricked him. Homer had a keen sense of humor.

The hero's plan of escape is masterful. Tying his men to the underbellies of Polyphemus's rams and clinging to the belly of the largest ram himself, he and his men get away from the cave as

---

[193] Book 9, 312–18.
[194] Ibid., 416–23.

"dawn spread out her finger tips of rose." *Dramatic irony* is evident as Polyphemus wonders why his largest ram is last to leave the cave.[195] With more unconscious irony, the Cyclops tells his ram that no one will leave the cave alive and laments that if only the ram could talk, it would tell Polyphemus of his persecutor's whereabouts.

Odysseus's hubris almost gets the better of him. As the hero sails away, he cannot resist taunting the blinded giant. In fact, his bragging enrages Polyphemus to such a point that the Cyclops uproots and hurls a whole hilltop at Odysseus that sends the ship back to shore. Odysseus, all is vanity! Understandably, his mariners are terrified and rebuke him for his foolishness, but the hero ignores them in his "glorying spirit" and can't resist informing Polyphemus that he, Odysseus, blinded him. I show the class a famous oil painting of the episode, *Ulysses Deriding Polyphemus* by J. M. W. Turner.[196]

Interrupting the excitement briefly, I remind the class about *epithets* or descriptive phrases that epic poets use to create variety. Polyphemus refers to Poseidon as "blue girdler of the islands"; both Polyphemus and Odysseus refer to the hero as "raider of cities."[197] One can well imagine the Cyclops's rage. His fate had been foretold long ago, but he expected to be blinded by a giant; instead, his antagonist is Odysseus, a man who is "small, pitiful and twiggy"![198] The Cyclops resorts to prayer, asking his father Poseidon to kill Odysseus's men, to afflict the hero with trials during his voyage, and to give him more problems at home. The Polyphemus episode is universally popular because of its exciting detail and the hero's ingenuity.

Book 10: lines 229–75; 540–53
Aeolus and the Laestrygonians
I summarize for the class events covered at the beginning of this Book before the Circe episode. More trials assail Odysseus. After landing on the island of Aeolus, the wind king captures all the winds in a sack so that Odysseus is not diverted from his course but can sail towards Ithaca; however, his sailors open the sack in order to satisfy their curiosity, and the winds drive them back to Aeolus's island. Several of the crew are eaten by giant cannibals called Laestrygonians.

Circe
Odysseus's next ordeal involves the beautiful witch-goddess Circe who turns men into pigs. The goddess sings beguilingly and weaves beautiful fabric on her loom. Her seductive singing

---

[195] Ibid., 487–88.

[196] The painting can be viewed at www.nationalgallery.org.uk.

[197] Book 9, 551, 576, 578.

[198] Ibid., 562.

lures Odysseus's mariners to her house where she promptly turns them into swine; they are rescued when a wiser sailor, Eurylochus, resists her captivating voice and reports back to Odysseus. Hermes gives the hero a plant that frees the foolish mariners from bondage. However, Odysseus pays a bitter price: Circe beguiles him into remaining with her for a year until Odysseus's men implore the hero to get Circe's help so that they set sail for Ithaca. Circe agrees to help them but warns Odysseus that before returning home he must visit Hades in order to hear Teiresias's prophecy.[199]

Book 11: lines 31– 53; 100–69; 228–55
Odysseus in the Underworld

The class may need to be reminded that Odysseus is still describing his adventures to King Alcinous and the Phaeacians. Students should also know that many mythical figures such as Heracles, Orpheus, and Aeneas descend into the Underworld, which is variously called Erebus, Land of the Dead, or Hades. The ability to make the journey and return to earth alive is a trait of a hero, and the hero's descent into the Underworld is another convention of epic poets. In the opening section of Book 11, Homer implies that the Underworld is located at the ends of the earth far from the land of the living.

Obeying Circe's instructions, Odysseus performs some odd rites in order to bring Teiresias up from the dead. Odysseus makes sacrificial rites to Hades and Persephone, the gods of the Underworld. He digs a pit, pours libations around it, sacrifices animals and lets their blood drip into the pit. At that point, Spirits from the Underworld, young and old, ascend to the pit while Odysseus guards it. The class is confused: Why are the dead drawn to a pit full of animals' blood? I can only comment that ancient Greeks' beliefs about the afterlife were bizarre. We do not read Odysseus's interview with Elpenor[200] but turn to the hero's meeting with Teiresias. Teiresias tells Odysseus that Poseidon will create many difficulties during the journey home to Ithaca in revenge for blinding his son Polyphemus. Teiresias warns Odysseus that he must avoid Helios's sacred cattle, that all Odysseus's mariners will die, that he alone will arrive in Ithaca. It is odd, however, that the prophet fails to warn the hero about the Sirens or Scylla and Charybdis. He does tell Odysseus that he must kill Penelope's suitors, make sacrifices to Poseidon (probably a wise move), and depart on a final voyage to die at sea. After finishing the *Odyssey,* we read Tennyson's poem "Ulysses," which describes the hero's obeying

---

[199] Teiresias, the iconic blind prophet of Thebes, features in other literary works such as Dante's *Inferno* and T. S. Eliot's *Waste Land*, to name two.

[200] Ryken comments that Elpenor died when he fell off Circe's roof, an incident that Homer describes at the end of Book 10. *Homer's The Odyssey*, 41.

these instructions and leaving Ithaca on one more adventure before his death. (See discussion of Tennyson's poem at the end of the unit on the *Odyssey*.)

After Teiresias leaves, Homer includes a tender scene between Odysseus and his mother's ghost. Anticleia died of grief at the lengthy absence of her son. Seeing the spirit of Anticleia, Odysseus attempts to embrace her, but she drifts away from his grasp and bids him leave since she is doomed to remain in Hades. It is important for Christians to note that pagan notions of life after death are desperately sad. What a contrast these notions present when we think about biblical references to heaven, which is a place that Christians longs for.[201] The hero sees many other shades or shadows whom we do not read about including some that students will encounter in other literary texts— Jocasta, Oedipus's mother; Ariadne, daughter of King Minos; and Agamemnon, leader of the Greek army during the Trojan war.

Book 12: lines 46–67; 103–67; 183–219; 246–348
Circle's instructions
After Odysseus returns from Hades to Circe's island, the witch instructs him how to overcome future dangers. She tells the hero how to sail safely past the Sirens, sea nymphs who lure men with their bewitching voices to crash upon their island's rocky shore and drown. He should place wax in his mariners' ears so that they sail on unmindful of the Sirens' singing. He must instruct his men to lash him to the mast so that he can satisfy his curiosity and listen with impunity to the Sirens' seductive singing.[202] Circe next tells the hero how to navigate past two cliffs; on one side lurks Scylla, a female monster with six serpent heads; on the other side is Charybdis, another female monster that creates a huge whirlpool. The map indicates that these creatures are supposedly located in the Strait of Messina between Italy and Sicily. The witch advises Odysseus to have his crew steer the ship away from Charybdis and close to the cliff where Scylla lurks so that he will lose only six men rather than all of his mariners as well as the ship.[203] Finally, Circe warns the hero to steer the ship far away from Helios's cattle. Only then will he return safely to Ithaca.

The Sirens, Scylla, and Charybdis
As Odysseus and his men sail on, the Sirens with their seductive voices fly overhead, but Odysseus is tightly bound to the ship's mast so that he can safely satisfy his curiosity. He orders

---

[201] For instance, the Bible describes heaven as God's "holy habitation," Deut. 26:15 and as "a house not made with hands, eternal in the heavens," 2 Cor. 5:1.

[202] The word "siren" is sometimes used today to refer to a beguilingly beautiful woman.

[203] When one must make a difficult choice between two equally tough alternatives, one is said to be between Scylla and Charybdis.

the sailors to give Charybdis a wide birth but cunningly withholds from them the danger from the six-headed monster, and just as Circe has predicted, Scylla seizes and devours six men. Homer's *epic simile* compares Odysseus's men to writhing fish helplessly hooked with a fisherman's rod.[204] Odysseus is grief-stricken.

Odysseus and the Sirens

Helios's cattle

We do not read the rest of Book 12. I summarize events. Forewarned by Teiresias and Circe, Odysseus forbids his mariners to eat Helios's cattle. Lack of wind dictates that the men remain on the sun god's island a month; when the men have eaten all their food, they ravenously devour the sacred beasts. Zeus sends a thunderbolt that destroys the ship. All drown except Odysseus who drifts north on the open sea—without his men, his ship, and his loot from Troy—until he is thrown ashore on Calypso's island where we first met him. At this point, the hero finishes the story of his adventures that he's been telling the Phaeacians.

---

[204] Book 12, 324–30.

Books 13–15

Odysseus's homecoming[205]

I review for the class the contents of the next three Books. Odysseus sails back to Ithaca in a Phaeacian ship disguised as a beggar and arrives at the cottage of his faithful swineherd, Eumaeus.[206] Odysseus is wise because he is guided by the goddess of wisdom, Athena. It is she who disguises him and instructs him how to proceed in Ithaca. The class should understand that Odysseus uses the surprise element of disguise for two reasons: to determine who among his servants is still loyal to him and to destroy the suitors. The first person the disguised king meets is his swineherd.[207] Meanwhile, Athena tells Telemachus, who remains in Sparta with Menelaus and Helen, to return home, and the king's son heads straight for the swineherd's cottage. The class should appreciate the *dramatic irony* of the hero's return. Some students may question this point. Well, the reader knows, as the characters do not, that the beggar is the long absent king of Ithaca.

Book 16: lines 1–66; 203–61

Reunion with Telemachus

The final Books of the epic focus on Odysseus's reunions on his return home. The first is Odysseus's reunion with his son. We can relate to the father's emotions as his swineherd affectionately embraces Telemachus, overjoyed to welcome the boy home again, while Odysseus stands nearby watching. We wait in suspense for the son to recognize the father he hasn't seen for twenty years. When the omnipresent Athena transforms Odysseus from his beggar's rags to a handsome king, Telemachus, momentarily stunned, embraces "this marvel of a father,"[208] and both men weep over the years they've lost. It's a touching scene.

Book 17: lines 376–422

Reunion with Argos

Homer next describes the reunion of Odysseus and his dog, a faithful hound that immediately recognizes his master. Argos has been ignored during Odysseus's long absence; the dog is old, covered with flies, and lying in a pile of manure. When he hears his beloved master's voice, the neglected dog, unable to wag his tail or move, dies. Homer wrings our heartstrings, but why would he include this incident? A couple of reasons come to mind: It increases the suspense

---

[205] As Ryken points out, Odysseus's homecoming is "one of the most sustained performances of dramatic irony in Western literature." *Homer's The Odyssey*, 47.

[206] Disguise is a common literary motif. One thinks of Shakespeare's *Twelfth Night* and Twain's *Prince and the Pauper*, to name two well-known examples.

[207] A swineherd looked after pigs on a man's estate.

[208] Book 16, 254.

as we anticipate the reunion between husband and wife; more importantly, it indicates the breakdown of order in Ithaca where animals are treated so despicably. For years, Odysseus's kingdom has been ravaged by greedy, indolent men, and when the disguised king returns, he finds Ithaca appallingly neglected.

Book 18

Again, I review the events of this book for the class. After the suitors mock the beggar, Penelope reprimands her son for permitting a stranger to be so shamefully abused. The queen's rebuke is another example of ancient Greeks' commitment to hospitality.

Book 19: 120–93; 240–97; 441–61; 542–52
Penelope and the beggar

Telemachus and Odysseus remove the suitors' weapons from the great hall in order to carry out the hero's cunning plan—one of the many instances of *foreshadowing* throughout the Books describing Odysseus's return. At last, Homer describes the reunion between husband and wife. I assign two students to read Odysseus's and Penelope's lines. Penelope epitomizes hospitality as she talks with the beggar. The *irony* increases as she tells him about the weaving trick and her weariness at dealing with abusive suitors during her husband's long absence. As she listens to the beggar's tales about her husband, she weeps with longing for him while Odysseus has a grand time singing his own praises. The old nurse, Eurycleia, washes the stranger's feet, a custom that implies great honor to guests. When she feels an old scar on the man's leg, she immediately recognizes Odysseus who swears her to secrecy. Why doesn't Penelope notice this incident? Athena has cast a spell on her so that the queen pays no attention to the recognition scene between Odysseus and Eurycleia.

Penelope tests the suitors

Like a fairy-tale princess, Penelope decides to subject the suitors to an impossible test: The man who can bend her husband's great bow and hurl an arrow through the sockets of twelve axe handles will become her husband. For clarification, I sketch on the board a line of axes with sockets in their handles. At this point in the story, students usually ask whether or not Penelope recognizes her husband. After all, she has been told Odysseus is alive and on his way home. Homer does not clarify for the reader exactly when Penelope recognizes her husband. It is reasonable to conclude that by now she recognizes Odysseus, although Homer does not imply this. Why else would she suggest the test of the bow? She surely does not intend to act on her alleged intention to marry one of the suitors; in any case, she knows none of them will be able to string the bow let alone send an arrow through twelve axe handle sockets. It's a moot point. Undoubtedly, faithful Penelope suggests a test that she knows only her beloved husband can win.[209] In any event, she returns to the hall with the axes and Odysseus's great bow with its quiver "spiked with coughing death," as described in a later book.[210]

Book 20

Summarizing Book 20, I tell the class that Odysseus is concerned about the battle with Penelope's suitors, but Athena assures him he will be successful.

Book 21: 41–83; 210–69; 446–99
Contest of the Great Bow

Foreshadowing abounds as the suitors unsuccessfully attempt to win the contest, and the king emerges as the winner. The class should note several details as the epic draws to its climax. Odysseus reveals his identity to two faithful servants—his herdsman and his swineherd—and enlists their aid.[211] He orders them to lock the women in their quarters and bar the outer gate of the castle. As we learn in Book 19, the suitors' weapons have already been removed from the great hall. Like lovers of fairy tale, none of the men succeed; they can't even bend the bow sufficiently to string it. They jeer when the beggar wants to take up the bow, but the gracious queen insists that he be allowed to participate. Now comes the climactic moment as "the man skilled in all ways of contending"[212] enters the contest. Effortlessly, Odysseus sends the arrow through all twelve holes in the axe handles. The victorious king assures his son that he will now "cook their lordships' mutton."[213] (I'd love to know how much liberty Fitzgerald is taking with the Greek here!)

Book 22: lines 1–71; 333–49
Death in the palace

Odysseus takes his revenge on the suitors. He deals first with the chief suitor, Antinous. Just as the man is about to slurp his wine, the king's arrow pierces the man's throat. The stupefied suitor falls dead, blood streaming from his nostrils. (Even the drowsiest student sits up at this point.) The other rioters search in vain for their spears as they yell insults at the beggar. Like all base and cowardly men, the suitors look desperately for a way of escape and blame Antinous for the wretched state of affairs in Ithaca. They attempt to bribe Odysseus with false assurances

---

[209] The impossible feat is another motif common to myth and fairy tale.

[210] Book 21, 63.

[211] The herdsman's name is Philoeteus; as already noted, the swineherd is Eumaeus. I do not require students to remember their names.

[212] Book 21, 460.

[213] Ibid., 492.

of restitution. Odysseus and Telemachus, together with the swineherd and cowherd, make short work of them. We realize that Telemachus has matured into a courageous son worthy of his father. Athena raises her shield with its gorgon's head to strike fear into the despicable suitors.

I summarize the main events that occur during the rest of Book 22. In order to execute justice and restore order to his palace, Odysseus hangs his immoral maid servants who associated with the suitors after the girls have cleaned the great hall. His action conveys the ancient Greeks' conviction that unmarried women should be virtuous. During his return home, in fact throughout the epic, Odysseus manifests his cunning and his sense of justice. I remind the class that Homer's prevailing *theme* is justice.

Book 23: lines 98–133; 173–245; 253–69
Reunion with Penelope

Only in this penultimate book is Penelope told that her husband has returned to the palace and killed the suitors. We've already noted that Homer does not clarify definitively when Penelope realizes that the stranger is her husband; in any case, she decides to subject the beggar to a final test that will determine beyond dispute that he is indeed Odysseus. She instructs the nurse to place their marriage bed outside their bedroom. This command causes Odysseus to lash out at his wife since the bed is immovable, built with the trunk of an olive tree as a bedpost by Odysseus himself, and only he and Penelope know this secret about their bed. Students should understand that the bed *symbolizes* the stability of their marriage. Now Penelope knows that the beggar is indeed her beloved husband. After twenty years, Odysseus is reunited with his faithful and prudent wife. Many readers decide that their reunion is the story's *climax*.[214] It is certainly the most emotional moment in the epic.

Book 24: lines 346–87; 397–411; 592–614
Reunion with Laertes

Homer reserves the last reunion for Laertes in accordance with ancient Greeks' deep respect for fathers. Two boys read the dialogue. Odysseus tells his father he has killed the suitors, and when he shows Laertes the scar on his leg as infallible proof of his identity, his father momentarily faints with joy. Returning to the palace, the two men feast together. In the meanwhile, the suitors' relatives arrive at the palace demanding vengeance for their loved ones' deaths; however, Athena ends the fighting, and peace is restored to Ithaca. Homer's final book is a fitting conclusion to Odysseus's glorious adventures.

---

[214] Other readers find that Odysseus's winning the contest is the most climactic moment in the epic.

After studying the epic, I review with the class the conventions of most epic poetry and ancient Greeks' cultural values:

Epic conventions
- invocation: a supplication or prayer
- epithets: colorful phrases used in place of a name to characterize a person or thing
- *in medias res*: starting in the middle of things or when events have become exciting
- delayed entrance of the hero: readers meets the hero after several events have been described in order to whet our curiosity about him
- epic simile: an extended comparison
- the hero's descent into Hades: the hero makes the obligatory journey into the Underworld

Greek cultural values (Examples of this point are listed under essay #1 below.)
- hospitality
- respect for others
- role of women
- piety
- divine intervention

Students record these items in their notebooks. As mentioned previously, I train students to take copious notes, and, with a freshman class, I routinely walk around the classroom to ensure that they are doing so.

Essays

Here are two essay topics. I assign one of them at the end of the unit:

1. Explain how the epic conveys some of the values of ancient Greek society.

Students break into small groups and discuss several ancient Greek customs writing down examples such as the following:

hospitality:
- Nestor feeds his guests before inquiring about their business.
- Penelope embodies the hospitality she extends to the suitors and the stranger who arrives at her palace.
- King Alcinous gives a feast for Odysseus and provides a ship for his journey back home.

- Penelope's suitors grossly violate this social custom as does Polyphemus when he eats his guests!
- Nausicaa is hospitable to Odysseus: She arranges for refreshments and a bath for him.

respect for others:
- Telemachus regrets keeping Mentor, actually Athena in disguise, waiting.
- Penelope respects the stranger who arrives in Ithaca.
- Odysseus shows great respect for his father by visiting Laertes who lives alone near Ithaca in order to tell him that his son has returned.

role of women:
- Penelope remains quietly at home during her husband's twenty-year absence.
- She is always loyal to Odysseus.
- She embodies the faithful wife who weaves a funeral shroud for her father-in-law in order to avoid marriage to one of her suitors.
- Nausicaa is modest and practical.

piety:
- Telemachus prays to Athena for help with the situation in Ithaca.
- When Telemachus arrives at Pylos, the people are offering sacrifices to Poseidon.
- In Hades, Teiresias instructs Odysseus to make sacrifices to Poseidon after he arrives in Ithaca before departing on a final voyage.

divine intervention:
- Athena transforms Odysseus into a beggar then a royal king.
- Zeus orders Hermes to release Odysseus from Calypso's spell.
- Zeus orders Athena to end the renewed fighting in Ithaca.

An outline should focus on three topics.

2. Referring in detail to several incidents in the epic, explain how Odysseus constantly demonstrates his resourcefulness.

Students break into small groups to exchange ideas and write down examples such as these:

- Odysseus allows Calypso to think that she is more desirable than Penelope.
- He drugs Polyphemus with wine and blinds him.
- He tells the Cyclops his name is "Nohbdy" and his ship has been destroyed.

- He escapes from the giant's cave by tying his men underneath the Cyclops's sheep, and reserving the largest ram for himself, he grips its belly so that the Cyclops doesn't realize he is leaving the cave.
- He orders his men to lash him to the ship's mast and plugs his men's ears with wax so that he can hear the Sirens' singing.
- He devises a brilliant plan to rid Ithaca of Penelope's suitors and restore order to his kingdom.

An outline could include the following topics:

- Odysseus's dealings with goddesses and monsters
- Polyphemus episode
- Odysseus in Ithaca

Test
A test on the epic is included in the handouts.

Review questions on the *Odyssey*:[215]

1. Write out a one-sentence definition of an epic.
   [An epic is a long narrative poem about the exploits of a hero who represents the values of his culture.]

2. In some detail, explain why it is true to say that the *Odyssey* begins *in medias res*.
   [The epic begins in medias res, or in the middle of things, because significant antecedent events have taken place. At the beginning of the epic, Homer tells us that the hero has survived many adventures sailing from Troy to Ithaca and that he is now on the island of Ogygia held captive by the nymph Calypso. We learn about trouble in Ithaca where Penelope is being harassed by suitors.]

3. Like other epic poets, Homer begins his epic with a/ an _____ . Supply one word and define it.
   [invocation; a prayer or supplication to a deity]

4. Does Homer blame Odysseus for the deaths of all his sailors at the hands of the sun god? Why or why not? In your response, name the sun god.
   [Homer does not blame Odysseus for the sailors' deaths. The poet makes it clear that Helios kills them because, in spite of Odysseus's warning, they foolishly eat the sun god's cattle.]

5. We mentioned that Greek boys learned about their culture by studying ancient epics. One convention was the importance of hospitality. List several examples of Homer's emphasis on hospitality in this epic.
   [Nestor of Pylos feeds his guests before inquiring about their business. King Alcinous gives a feast for Odysseus and provides a ship for his journey back home. Nausicaa is hospitable to Odysseus; she arranges for refreshments and a bath for him. Penelope is hospitable to the stranger when he arrives at her palace and insists that he be allowed to participate in the test of the Great Bow.]

6. What information does the *Odyssey* convey about the role of women in ancient Greek society?
   [In ancient Greece, women did not participate in affairs of state but tended to their homes and children. Before marriage, they were expected to be virtuous. After marriage, they were to be faithful wives who supervised their children, managed their households, and acted as gracious hostesses for their guests.]

7. How does Penelope extricate herself from marrying one of the suitors?
   [Penelope plays a clever trick on the suitors. She tells them she will marry one of them when she has finished weaving a death shroud for her father-in-law, Laertes. Every day, she weaves the shroud, but every night she unweaves her work so that she never finishes the shroud.]

---

[215] A student booklet that accompanies this teaching guide contains all 9th grade review questions and tests with answers omitted. Any of these questions could be used for a graded discussion of the epic.

8. Why does Odysseus take ten years to sail the fairly short distance from Troy home to Ithaca?

[Because Odysseus blinded Polyphemus, the sea god's son, Poseidon raises storms so that Odysseus is constantly blown off course and takes ten years to journey back to Ithaca.]

9. Why is it fortunate that Odysseus lands on the shore of Scheria, the land of the Phaeacians?

[Zeus has destroyed Odysseus's ship, but the Phaeacians are ship builders and provide a ship for the hero to sail home to Ithaca.]

10. Odysseus is said to be a "man skilled in all ways of contending." List some examples of the hero's ingenuity.

[Odysseus escapes from Polyphemus's cave by a clever subterfuge. He plies Polyphemus with wine then ties his men under the bellies of the Cyclops's sheep, and clinging to the fleece underneath the largest ram himself, he and all his men escape from the cave. He calls himself "Nohbdy"; when the other Cyclopes hear Polyphemus scream that he has been blinded by "Nohbdy," they assume that no one has hurt him. On another occasion, Calypso compares herself to Penelope and asks Odysseus who is the more beautiful woman. The wily hero assures the nymph that Penelope's beauty will fade because she, unlike the immortal Calypso, is mortal. After his arrival home, Odysseus ensures that the suitors' weapons are removed from the great hall so that he can more easily destroy all Penelope's suitors.]

11. The hero is also boastful. Provide one example of an episode when his hubris is almost fatal.

[After escaping from the Cyclops's cave and starting to sail away, Odysseus cannot resist bragging that it was he, Odysseus, who blinded the giant. This revelation enrages Polyphemus to such a point that the Cyclops hurls a whole hilltop at Odysseus that sends the ship back to shore.]

12. Epic poets often used epithets for variety. Whom or what are the following epithets describing:

"the grey-eyed goddess"

"father of us all" and "the cloud-gatherer"

"the Wayfinder"

"finger tips of rose"

"the iron queen"

[Athena; Zeus; Hermes; dawn; Persephone]

13. Who are the Sirens?

[The Sirens are beautiful nymphs who lure men to their deaths with their irresistible singing.]

14. Mention two people Odysseus meets in Hades.

[the prophet Teiresias; Odysseus's mother Anticleia]

15. Identify these characters: Eurycleia, Argos, Antinous, and Laertes.
    [Eurycleia is Odysseus's old nurse; Argos is Odysseus's dog; Antinous is the chief suitor; Laertes is Odysseus's father.]

16. How is Penelope finally convinced that the stranger who has arrived in Ithaca is indeed her husband?
    [The stranger knows a secret that only she and her husband share. Their marriage bed is immovable because the bedpost is the trunk of an olive tree.]

17. Why is it important that the king returns to Ithaca dressed as a beggar?
    [Athena transforms Odysseus into a beggar's rags on his return to Ithaca so that no one recognizes him and he can use the element of disguise in order to take advantage of the suitors and kill them.]

18. List the men who help Odysseus defeat the angry suitors.
    [Telemachus, the swineherd, and the herdsman]

19. When the relatives of the dead suitors arrive at the palace to avenge their loved ones' deaths, who ends the fighting and how does he or she do so?
    [Directed by Zeus, Athena ends the fighting in Ithaca by admonishing Odysseus that Zeus will become angry if the fighting continues.]

20. Several words from this epic have become part of our everyday vocabulary. Define the following words as they are used today: a muse, nectar, an odyssey, a mentor.
    [A muse is one's inspiration; nectar is a delicious drink; an odyssey is a long, hard journey that often involves a quest of some sort; a mentor is one's close friend and guide.]

Homer's influence

"On First Looking into Chapman's Homer"
by
John Keats
1795–1821

Over the past three thousand years, countless writers have been influenced by the ancient Greek poet. We read poems by John Keats and Alfred, Lord Tennyson that demonstrate Homer's impact. I circulate Keats's poem, "On First Looking into Chapman's Homer." The class should know that it is a sonnet divided into *octave* and *sestet*.[216] The substance of the octave is this: Keats had read widely but had not studied Greek. Although he knew about Homer's epics, he was unable to read them until a friend gave him a translation of the *Iliad* and the *Odyssey* that George Chapman, a sixteenth-century poet, completed in 1616.[217] Here, in part, is the octave:

> Much have I traveled in the realms of gold…[218]
> Oft of one wide expanse had I been told
> That deep-browed Homer ruled as his demesne;[219]
> Yet did I never breathe its pure serene[220]
> Till I heard Chapman speak out loud and bold….

The sestet suggests Keats's exhilaration when he first sits down to read Homer. Having read both epics, Keats compares the intense thrill he felt to an astronomer's discovery of a new planet or an explorer's discovery of the Pacific Ocean. Keats erroneously states that Cortez discovered the Pacific Ocean when, in fact, the Pacific was first discovered by Balboa, but the error does not diminish the impact of this celebrated sonnet.

I read this poem with a freshman class because I want young people to have some appreciation for literature's powerful impact on readers throughout the ages. And I assure them one doesn't have to be a well-known Romantic poet to grasp the wonder and beauty of a literary classic.

---

[216] An octave is eight lines of poetry; a sestet is six lines. Thus, Keats's poem is a Petrarchan sonnet.

[217] The friend was Charles Cowden Clarke, Keats's former teacher.

[218] The phrase "realms of gold" refers to the literature Keats had read. It provided Leland Ryken with the title of his book of literary analysis.

[219] domain or realm

[220] pure air

"Ulysses"[221]

by

Alfred, Lord Tennyson

1809–1892

The other poem we read that conveys Homer's influence on writers through the centuries is Tennyson's "Ulysses." Tennyson picks up, as it were, where Homer leaves off. Homer leaves Odysseus to rule Ithaca. Tennyson imagines that the hero is now aging and weary of his inactive life. Penelope is old, his homeland seems sterile, his people brutish:

> It little profits that an idle king,
> By this still hearth, among these barren crags,
> Match'd with an aged wife, I mete and dole
> Unequal laws[222] unto a savage race,
> That hoard, and sleep, and feed, and know not me.

Ulysses becomes restless and longs to sail away in search of one final adventure:

> I cannot rest from travel; I will drink
> Life to the lees[223]....

With his customary but expected hubris, the legendary hero rehearses his mighty deeds:

> ...I am become a name...
> Much have I seen and known....
> I am a part of all that I have met....

Then he muses,

> Yet all experience is an arch wherethrough
> Gleams that untravell'd world whose margin fades
> Forever and forever when I move. ...

These lines are challenging. Tennyson suggests that we never come to the end of life's opportunities; there are always more to embrace. The poet emphasizes the need to strive rather than to give up. Ulysses repudiates a life without purpose and longs to experience more adventure:

---

[221] Tennyson uses the hero's Latin name not the Greek name, Odysseus.

[222] Tennyson suggests that Ulysses measured out rewards and punishments.

[223] dregs

> and vile it were
> For some three suns[224] to store and hoard myself,
> And this grey spirit yearning in desire
> To follow knowledge like a sinking star,
> Beyond the utmost bound of human thought....

Tennyson imagines that the aging hero yearns to experience one more quest, but more importantly, Ulysses is determined, old though he is, to engage in intellectual questing before it eludes him at death— "To follow knowledge like a sinking star." That idea is surely the poem's greatest value for the young, for all of us. And that's why it is one of my favorite poems for the high school classroom. It stresses intellectual curiosity. A teacher can teach many things but rarely that. A desire to learn comes from within. I encourage my freshman class to pray that God will increase in them the desire for knowledge.[225]

Ulysses leaves Telemachus to rule Ithaca confident that his son will be a fine administrator and rule the kingdom well. He urges his mariners to sail off with him. He acknowledges that they are aging men

> but something ere the end,
> Some work of noble note, may yet be done,
> Not unbecoming men that strove with gods. ...

In spite of his ebbing strength, this mighty warrior is determined set off on one last adventure and

> To strive, to seek, to find, and not to yield.

Tennyson's celebrated poem conveys a significant message for us all.

After the epic unit, we complete the freshman year by studying a selection of lyric poetry.

---

[224] three years

[225] A banner in my classroom reads, "Learning is not a spectator sport." The expression is generally attributed to Arthur W. Chickering and Stephen C. Ehrmann, 1996.

Unit V

Lyric Poetry

Like drama and epic poetry, students do not read lyric poetry on their own. We read and discuss poetry during class. In order to keep track of poems or sections of poems that we discuss, I print them all and distribute a poetry package in a ring binder with an attractive cover suitably titled "Poetry for Teens." This avoids wasted time distributing individual poems or stanzas that students promptly lose, and I can conveniently ask them to turn to a particular poem in their packet. There are countless fine books one can refer to when teaching poetry. Among others, I recommend the chapter on lyric poetry in *Realms of Gold: The Classics in Christian Perspective* by Leland Ryken and *The New Oxford Book of Christian Verse*.[226]

What is poetry?

We first talk about lyric poetry as opposed to epics. Whereas an epic is a lengthy narrative poem that recounts the adventures of a hero, a lyric is brief; it should be read in a single sitting, and it appeals to the heart or the mind. Freshmen students should be aware of three basic genres of poetry: epic, lyric, narrative, and a sub-genre of narrative poetry, the ballad. During the poetry unit, they study lyrics and one or two ballads. We define each type of poem:

- **An epic** is a long poem about the exploits of a hero who was placed somewhere between the gods and ordinary mortals and who achieved impossible feats. In addition to Homer's epics, other famous epics include the anonymous *Epic of Gilgamesh*, Virgil's *Aeneid*, the Old English *Beowulf*, Dante's *Divine Comedy*, and Milton's *Paradise Lost*.

- **A lyric** was once sung to the accompaniment of a lyre; hence the name. It is a short poem that expresses an emotion—fear, anger, love, nostalgia, patriotism—or it conveys an insight about life or human nature.

- **A narrative poem** tells a story. Famous examples include Tennyson's "Idylls of the King" and Keats's "Eve of St. Agnes."

- **A ballad** is a special type of narrative poem and an ancient form of poetry; most ballads are anonymous, and scholars don't know exactly when people began composing them. These ancient ballads were probably composed by uneducated folks in order to communicate ideas that were important to a particular society. They were originally sung and passed on by word of mouth for generations and eventually written down.

The class should understand that poetry is the last genre we study because it is so concentrated. A poem says a great deal in a few words; almost every word adds to the poem's overall meaning.

---

[226] *The New Oxford Book of Christian Verse* is edited by Donald Davie (New York: Oxford University Press, 2003).

Thus, poetry makes special demands on the reader; for instance, one must be familiar with the devices a poet uses to convey meaning. Poetry tells us a great deal about life and human nature. Boys object that poetry is about love and mushy stuff. I tell them they are misinformed. Poetry deals with war and patriotism and teenage boys. They'll like a lot of it.

Procedure for teaching poetry

I adopt a different approach for middle school classes, but this is my procedure for teaching poetry to high school students.[227] Rather than taking students through lists of poetic devices, we study the way these devices convey meaning in a particular poem. As expressively as possible, I read aloud a poem or a passage from a poem, occasionally to the accompaniment of appropriate music; I ask questions that guide students towards an understanding of the poet's meaning. When I question the class, a student sometimes responds, "I don't know"; I don't let him (or her) off the hook but assure the student I'll return to him later—and I do. He'd better have an answer ready. Neither am I content with a response like this: "Well, that's my opinion." One's opinion is not a statement of proof. I ask follow-up questions such as, "What line or lines most clearly support your reaction?" I want to train young people to think critically and to acquire the intellectual maturity to admit a potentially flawed interpretation. I hope they learn to love poetry. To promote this goal, one could add that scientific data has proved that one's intelligence quotient is increased by studying and analyzing poetry. That fact, however, will not elicit much interest among young people. Instead, I bring editions of poetry for students to browse through by fun poets such as Edward Lear, Hilaire Belloc, Lewis Carroll.[228]

"Jabberwocky"

To begin a 9th grade study of poetry, I read to the class one of the oddest poems in the English language, "Jabberwocky" by Lewis Carroll (1832–1898) included in *Alice through the Looking-Glass*.[229] Before reading the poem to the class, I suggest that it tells a story and ask students to think about what it means. Here's the first stanza:

---

[227] During middle school literature classes, I require students to design a poetry notebook. They select a dozen poems they enjoy, copy them, and paste them into a colorful binder. They include an introduction that explains their reactions to poetry they have studied and a detailed explanation of each poem they select. The entire notebook should be colorful with appropriate illustrations. Middle school boys and girls enjoy the assignment.

[228] Popular editions of Edward Lear and Hilaire Belloc's nonsense poems are titled *A Book of Nonsense* and *The Bad Child's Book of Beasts* respectively; some of Lewis Carroll's well-known nonsense verse is included in both the *Alice* books.

[229] Lewis Carroll is a pseudonym for Charles Dodgson who made up the stories in both *Alice* books for a little girl named Alice Liddell.

'Twas brillig, and the slithy toves
Did gyre and gimble in the wabe:
All mimsy were the borogroves,
And the mome raths outgrabe....

What does the first stanza describe? At least one student objects that it doesn't make any sense. After all, many of the words are made up. Yes, they are, but don't you think "brillig" sounds like "brilliant" and "gyre" suggests "gyrate"? The class looks dubious. Someone tentatively proposes that the description sounds like a quiet forest where creatures are dancing. Excellent. Don't some of the phrases in the second stanza create disturbing images for you? Would you like to meet a "Jabberwock" or a "frumious Bandersnatch?" Someone else comments that a boy's father cautions his son to avoid monsters such as the Jabberwock. Exactly. Does the son obey his father? Hands go up. No, he grabs his sword and sets out in search of the "manxome foe." While he is resting, the beast suddenly appears:

One, two! One, two! And through and through
The vorpal blade went snicker-snack!
He left it dead, and with its head
He went galumphing back....

The boy bravely fulfills his quest and returns home to show the monster's head to his proud and jubilant father.[230] What happens in the last stanza? All hands go up. The forest returns to its former tranquility, released from the terror caused by the evil creature. Well done.

The mood in the classroom has lightened. At this point, most freshmen students decide that poetry may not be too bad after all.

Understanding poetry

Here are some ways to aid one's understanding of poetry:

- Read the poem more than once.
- Look up unfamiliar words in a dictionary.
- Look at punctuation and note where a sentence ends.
- Read the poem aloud.
- Hear the sounds of the words in your mind.

---

[230] The boy's trophy reminds one of the anonymous Old English epic *Beowulf.* When the hero kills the monster, he tears off its arm and triumphantly returns with it to the Danish king's castle.

It's also helpful to ask specific questions about a poem:

- Who is the *speaker*?
- Who is the *audience* or to whom is he or she speaking?
- What is the *occasion* or why is the speaker impelled to convey his or her message?

Since every word counts in poetry, one should define unfamiliar words for the class, or students could look up unfamiliar words in the dictionary—if they can be trained to do so. Grammar too is important when studying poetry; one may need to work out the *syntax*—subject, verb, complement—in order to grasp the meaning. Studying poetry is hard work, but the teacher should strive to make it enjoyable.

Reading poetry aloud

I tell the class that in order to understand a poem, one has to read it aloud and listen to the way it sounds. From their study of *Romeo and Juliet*, students should remember the difference between *end-stopped* and *run-on* lines. We talk about the correct way to recite poetry. Young people tend to pause at the end of every line. One can't read a poem aloud like that. Instead, one must pause if there is punctuation at the end of the line or continue to the next line if there's none. I generally read to the class all poems studied—after all, I'm familiar with them, but young people are not.

Students must understand that their enjoyment of poetry will depend on their understanding poetic devices—metaphors, similes, images, for instance. We study these devices starting with the sounds of poetry.[231]

---

[231] Throughout the poetry unit, I quote from poems in the public domain or restrict quotations to a very few lines.

Sound Devices:
Rhyme

Rhyme is, of course, a type of sound device. In order to help the class understand how rhyme contributes to the meaning of a poem, we read some lines from another poem by Lewis Carroll included in *Through the Looking-Glass.*

"The Walrus and the Carpenter"
Here are a few stanzas:

> The sun was shining on the sea,
> Shining with all his might:
> He did his very best to make
> The billows smooth and bright—
> And this was odd, because it was
> The middle of the night….
>
> The Walrus and the Carpenter
> Were walking close at hand;
> They wept like anything to see
> Such quantities of sand:
> "If this were only cleared away,"
> They said, "it would be grand!" ….

You may remember that the Walrus and the Carpenter persuade some young oysters to join them on their walk, the youngsters being most "eager for the treat." Weeping profusely and profoundly sympathizing with them, the Walrus sorts out the plumpest oysters. As for the Carpenter—

> "O Oysters," said the Carpenter
> "You've had a pleasant run!
> Shall we be trotting home again?"
> But answer came there none—
> And this was scarcely odd, because
> They'd eaten every one.

I love this poem. It's fun to read to teenagers or students of any age. The fact that it's a nonsense poem is conveyed primarily via *rhyme.* In addition to the musical rhythm, the poem's rhyme scheme creates an amusingly hypnotic effect.[232]

---

[232] It may be of interest to note that both Lewis Carroll and Edward Lear built their reputations by writing nonsense verse.

Internal rhyme

We talk about *internal rhyme* that occurs when a mid-line word or syllable rhymes with a word or syllable at the end of a line. We notice the internal rhyme throughout a folk song that is generally attributed to Percy Montrose who wrote it in 1884.[233] Here is the first stanza:

"Oh My Darling Clementine"

> In a cavern, in a canyon, excavating for a line,
>
> Dwelt a *miner*, forty-*niner*, and his daughter, Clemen*tine*....
>
> How I *missed* her, how I *missed* her, how I *missed* my Clementine,
>
> But I *kissed* her little *sister* and forgot my Clementine. [Italics added.]

The internal rhyme enhances the humorous tone of a poem that parodies sentimental love songs.

"The Raven"

There's internal rhyme in many lines of this celebrated poem by Edgar Allan Poe (1809–1849):

> Once upon a midnight *dreary*, while I pondered, weak and *weary*,
>
> Over many a quaint and curious volume of forgotten lore—
>
> While I nodded, nearly *napping*, suddenly there came a *tapping*,
>
> As of someone gently *rapping*, *rapping* at my chamber door.
>
> "'Tis some visitor," I muttered, "*tapping* at my chamber door—
>
> > Only this and nothing more." [Italics added.]

The internal rhyme here enhances the mesmerizing effect the poet wishes to create. Here's the final stanza:

> And the Raven, never *flitting*, still is *sitting*, still is *sitting*
>
> On the pallid bust of Pallas just above my chamber door;
>
> And his eyes have all the *seeming* of a demon's that is *dreaming*,
>
> And the lamplight o'er him *streaming* throws his shadow on the floor;
>
> And my soul from out that shadow that lies floating on the floor
>
> > Shall be lifted—nevermore! [Italics added.]

The internal rhyme increases our sense of the raven's relentless presence. The speaker is thrown into the depths of despair: He will never again see his beloved Lenore or achieve relief from his sorrow. Students often ask about the bust or head-and-shoulders statue of Pallas. From reading the *Odyssey*, they will remember that Pallas Athena was the Greek goddess of wisdom;

---

[233] I have not been able to obtain dates or other information about this writer.

the raven, a symbol of death, perches on her head; the detail implies that the speaker's mental state is deteriorating into madness.

Approximate rhyme

Approximate rhyme or slant rhyme is the use of words that don't rhyme exactly, as in these single word lines from a poem written in his diary by a British World War I poet, Wilfred Owen (1893–1918). The end words rhyme exactly.

"From My Diary, July 1914"

    Leaves
      Murmuring by myriads in the shimmering trees.
    Lives
      Wakening with wonder in the Pyrenees....
    Flashes
      Of swimmers carving through the sparkling cold.
    Fleshes
      Gleaming with wetness to the morning gold.... [Italics added.]

The *approximate rhyme* throughout Owen's poem emphasizes the single word lines and gives those words a singular beauty.

Emily Dickinson (1830–1886) is famous for her use of approximate rhyme. In the following poem, every other line contains an approximate rhyme:

"As imperceptibly as Grief"

> As imperceptibly as Grief
> The Summer lapsed *away*—
> Too imperceptible at last
> To seem like *Perfidy*—
> A Quietness distilled
> As Twilight long *begun*,
> Or Nature spending with herself
> Sequestered *Afternoon*....   [Italics added.]

Who is the speaker and what is the occasion? I suggest to the class that the speaker, presumably the poet, has sustained the loss of a beloved person and that the poem conveys Dickinson's dealing with grief, although we don't know whom she is grieving.[234] Someone objects. Isn't the poem talking about summer? Well no. The poem's subject is grief. Dickinson is comparing grief that gradually diminishes to the summer season that ends almost without our noticing. She equates summer with happiness, but just as the summer season steadily ends without our discerning that fall is approaching, so grief lessens as time goes by. In other words, the poet explores the way grief gradually becomes less devastating with the passage of time. Just as summer passes on "imperceptibly," so we are unaware, as time goes by, that our sorrow is becoming less shattering. The *approximate rhyme* emphasizes the idea that grief over a devastating loss becomes gradually less severe. Many students reject what to them is convoluted literary analysis, but some, a few, may appreciate Dickinson's poem. It ends with summer escaping into "the Beautiful"; by this Dickinson implies that she longs to be happy but can never again achieve that supreme happiness because of her loss, presumably of a man she loved.

---

[234] Dickinson may have been grieving the death of one of the married men she fell in love with—possibly her father's friend Judge Otis Lord or a family friend and newspaper editor Samuel Bowles or Reverend Charles Wadsworth whom the poet heard preach in Philadelphia.

Sound Devices:
Alliteration and Onomatopoeia

We talk about other sound devices such as alliteration and onomatopoeia. *Alliteration* refers to repeated initial consonant sounds such as these: "clatter-clash, finger-forget, flung-flutter, morn-mean, step-stately." *Onomatopoeia* refers to words that sound like their meaning, words such as "hiss, buzz, murmur." We return to a poem in which Poe uses alliteration to great effect.

"The Raven"
Once upon a midnight dreary, while I pondered *w*eak and *w*eary,

Over many a quaint and curious volume of forgotten lore—
While I *n*odded, *n*early *n*apping, suddenly there came a tapping,
As of some one gentle *r*apping, *r*apping at my chamber door....

And the *s*ilken, *s*ad, un*c*ertain ru*s*tling of each purple *c*urtain....

.... this *g*rim, ungainly, *g*hastly, *g*aunt, and ominous bird of yore.... [Italics added.]

The *alliteration* in nearly every line (note italics) and particularly the alliterated *g*'s in the last line quoted enhance the effect of utter despair. Both alliteration and *onomatopoeic* words— "dreary, weary, rapping, rustling, gaunt"—throughout the poem suggest the speaker's despondency.

"The Bells"
In this poem, Poe shakes off his habitual gloom and uses *onomatopoeia* to create a musical effect. Note the italicized words in the following lines:

Hear the sledges[235] with the bells—
  Silver bells!
What a world of merriment their melody foretells!
  How they *tinkle, tinkle, tinkle,*
    In the icy air of night!
  While the stars that *oversprinkle*
  All the heavens, seem to *twinkle*
    With a *crystalline delight*;
  Keeping time, time, time...
To the *tintinnabulation*[236] that so *musically* wells...
  From the *jingling* and the *tinkling* of the bells.... [Italics added.]

---

235 sleighs

236 tinkling

Every line throughout the four sections of this lengthy poem suggests the charming jingling of bells.

"Come unto these yellow sands"

The canonical poet for all things poetic is, of course, Shakespeare. We read one of Ariel's songs in *The Tempest*, Shakespeare's last play. Ariel is a sprite or spirit who serves a magician, Prospero. Prospero has Ariel take the form of a nymph as the sprite sings. Via his lighthearted singing, Ariel, who is temporarily invisible, lures the shipwrecked Prince Ferdinand to meet Prospero, the ousted Duke of Milan:

> Come unto these yellow sands,
> And then take hands.
> Curtsied when you have and kissed,
> The wild waves whist:[237]
> Foot it featly[238] here and there,
> And, sweet sprites, the burden[239] bear.
> *Hark, hark*!
> *Bow-wow.*
> The watch-dogs *bark*!
> *Bow-wow.*
> *Hark, hark*, I hear
> The strain of *strutting* chanticleer. ...[240] [Italics added.]

---

[237] hushed

[238] nimbly

[239] refrain

[240] *The Tempest*, I.ii.375–86.

Students should note that the italicized words are *onomatopoeic*. The lines with their onomatopoeic diction create a playful, magical mood.

"Elegy Written in a Country Churchyard"

The Elegy by Thomas Gray (1716–1771) is one of the most celebrated poems in the English language. Here's the opening stanza:

> The curfew *tolls* the *knell* of parting day,
> The *lowing* herd wind slowly o'er the lea,
> The plowman homeward *plods* his *weary* way,
> And leaves the world to darkness and to me. [Italics added.]

Gray wrote the poem in 1751 when he was living near a village church in the south of England. I identify the *speaker* and the *occasion*: The speaker is the poet who stands in the church graveyard; the occasion consists of Gray's reflections on the lives of unknown local peasants who now lie in their graves.[241] *Onomatopoeic language* throughout the Elegy powerfully conveys the somber mood of this highly reflective poem—note the italicized words quoted above and the italicized diction in the following stanza:

> Now fades the *glimmering* landscape on the sight,
> And all the air a solemn stillness holds,
> Save where the beetle wheels his *droning* flight,
> And *drowsy tinklings lull* the distant folds. [Italics added.]

Alliteration— "*l*owing, *l*ea...*pl*owman *pl*ods...*l*andscape...*s*ight...*s*olemn *s*tillne*ss*"—further emphasizes the gravity of the poet's thoughts in the lines quoted above as well as elsewhere throughout this lovely poem:

> Save that from yonder ivy-*m*antled tower
> The *m*oping owl does to the *m*oon co*m*plain.... [Italics added.]

Gray's Elegy is a fine example of the way a great poet conveys meaning via sound devices.

---

[241] The poet is standing in the graveyard of a church in Stoke Poges, a small village in Buckinghamshire where he probably wrote most of his Elegy.

STOKE POGIS CHURCH.

Church and churchyard at
Stoke Poges, Buckinghamshire

Sound devices:
Refrain

"The Three Ravens"

A refrain consists of a repeated line or lines of poetry and is most common in a ballad.[242] The class reads these lines from an anonymous ancient ballad:

> There were three ravens sat on a tree,
> *Down-a-down, Hey! Down-a-down,*
> And they were black as they might be,
>   *With a down,*
> There were three ravens sat on a tree,
>   *With a down,*
> There were three ravens sat on a tree,
> They were black as they might be
>   *With a down derry, derry, derry, down, down.…* [Italics added.]

The *refrain* here creates a light-hearted and musical, even hypnotic effect throughout the poem.

"Edward"

Another anonymous ballad that intrigues freshmen students relates a heinous crime. I define archaic diction throughout the poem then two students read the mother and the son's lines.

---

[242] Ballads were originally sung not written down and passed on from generation to generation. The refrain made the words easier for the speaker to remember.

(They should notice the quotation marks so that they know who's speaking.) The first lines are spoken by Edward's mother:

> *"Why does your brand[243] so drip with bluid,[244]*
> Edward, Edward?
> *Why does your brand so drip with bluid,*
> And why so sad gang[245] ye, O?" ...

The son replies:

> *"O I have killed my hawk so guid,[246]*
> Mither, mither,
> *O I have killed my hawk so guid,*
> And I had nae mair[247] but he, O." ... [Italics added.]

After telling his mother he killed his hawk, the son then tells her he killed his horse before we learn his most appalling deed of all and arrive at the shocking conclusion. It's an intriguing ballad as students discover when they recognize the real villain in this macabre situation. Much of the suspense is achieved via the *refrains* spoken by both mother and son (note italics in lines quoted above) that operate throughout this bizarre tale.[248]

"When icicles hang by the wall"

We turn again to Shakespeare for a charming refrain from a song included in *Love's Labor's Lost*:

> When icicles hang by the wall,
> And Dick the shepherd blows his nail,
> And Tom bears logs into the hall,
> And milk comes frozen home in pail,
> When blood is nipped and ways be foul,
> *Then nightly sings the staring owl,*
> *"Tu-whit, tu-who!"A merry note,*
> *While greasy Joan doth keel the pot.[249]* [Italics added.]

---

[243] sword

[244] blood

[245] go

[246] good

[247] no more

[248] As an interesting parenthesis, I call students' attention to the *foreshadowing* that occurs in the second stanza when the mother objects that the color of the blood is not that of a hawk's blood.

[249] skim off the fat

The *refrain* in the last four lines quoted above (see italics) is repeated in the second stanza of this song; it interjects a cheerful note that softens details contained in the previous five lines suggesting a bitterly cold English winter.[250]

"The Highwayman"

This fascinating narrative poem by Alfred Noyes (1880–1958) is set in eighteenth-century England when highwaymen or outlaws lurked along dark roads to rob wealthy stagecoach passengers of their money. When caught, highwaymen were usually hanged. The unnamed highwayman of this poem loves Bess, a landlord's daughter, but a jealous stableman betrays him to the authorities with tragic results for the lovers. *Refrain* creates a romantic and suspenseful mood throughout in the poem; note the italicized lines in the first stanza:

> The wind was a torrent of darkness among the gusty trees,
> The moon was a ghostly galleon tossed upon cloudy seas,
> *The road was a ribbon of moonlight over the purple moor,*
> *And the highwayman came riding—*
> > *Riding—riding—*
> *The highwayman came riding*, up to the old inn door.... [Italics added.]

As the poem continues, we learn of the ultimate sacrifice made by the innkeeper's daughter for the man she loves, the handsome highwayman. Young people enjoy this highly romantic poem.

"Annabel Lee"

Sometimes a refrain consists of single lines as in this next example from one of Poe's best-known poems:

> It was many and many a year ago
> *In a kingdom by the sea,*
> That a maiden there lived whom you may know
> *By the name of Annabel Lee....*
>
> I was a child and she was a child,
> *In this kingdom by the sea,*
> But we loved with a love that was more than love,
> *I and my Annabel Lee....*

---

[250] English winters feel excessively cold partly because English people see fit to heat their houses with one coal fire downstairs in the living room but have no heat upstairs in the bedrooms.

For the moon never beams, without bring me dreams
Of the beautiful Annabel lee;
And the stars never rise, but I feel the bright eyes
Of the beautiful Annabel Lee....
(from "Annabel Lee," Edgar Allan Poe) [Italics added.]

Like other examples quoted above, the *refrain* throughout the poem creates a melodious, captivating mood.

Robert Frost (1874–1963) includes a one-line refrain at the end of his celebrated poem, "Stopping by Woods on a Snowy Evening." Fleetingly mesmerized by the beautiful woodland scene before him as snow drifts onto the trees transforming the landscape, the speaker stirs himself and becomes aware of responsibilities that await him. The *refrain* conveys the speaker's reluctance to turn homeward in order to fulfill those tasks.

A refrain creates interest as well as emphasis and enhances the pleasure of reading poetry.

Sound Devices:
Meter

Poetry resembles music in that it has a musical quality primarily attained via its rhythm or *meter*. In fact, much ancient poetry was written to be sung to the accompaniment of a musical instrument such as a harp. Students should know that meter refers to the regular beat of poetry as opposed to prose that lacks a regular beat. Meter is the regular pattern of stressed and unstressed syllables in a line of poetry, and poetry written before the modern age is composed with a regular meter or rhythm. Some modern poetry is written in *free verse*, poetry without a regular meter, much of which sounds like prose rather than poetry. I touch on *iambic pentameter* when studying *Romeo and Juliet*, but, with a couple of exceptions, I avoid discussion of other meters with 9th grade students.

"The Owl and the Pussy-Cat"
I read aloud lines from this nonsense poem by Edward Lear (1812–1888) so that the class appreciates the *insistent meter*:

> The Owl and the Pussy-Cat went to sea
> In a beautiful pea-green boat;
>> They took some honey, and plenty of money
> Wrapped up in a five-pound note.[251]
> The Owl looked up to the stars above,
> And sang to a small guitar,
> O lovely Pussy, O Pussy, my love,
> What a beautiful Pussy you are,
>> You are,
>> You are!
> What a beautiful Pussy you are....

The relentless rhythm strikes a light-hearted tone and creates in the reader or listener a sense of fun.

"The Destruction of Sennacherib"
One of the best poems to discuss in terms of its rhythm is a lyric by Lord Byron (1788–1824) that is based on a biblical incident.[252] The mighty Assyrian army attempts to invade Jerusalem:

> The Assyrian came down like the wolf on the fold,

---

[251] Five pounds sterling is equivalent to $7.70.

[252] II Kings 18—19.

And his cohorts were gleaming in silver and gold;
And the sheen of their spears was like stars on the sea,
When the blue wave rolls nightly on deep Galilee....

Byron's poem is written in *anapestic rhythm* that consists of two unaccented syllables followed by one accented syllable in each poetic foot. The rhythm echoes swiftly galloping horses' hoofs as the Assyrians bear down on the Israelites. I write some lines on the board to demonstrate the anapestic meter. The capitalized words are emphasized, and the slash indicates the end of each foot:

And their CO / horts were GLEAM / ing in SIL / ver and GOLD;
And the SHEEN / of their SPEARS / was like STARS / on the SEA....

However, in spite of the Assyrian King Sennacherib's vastly superior numbers, the Lord allowed the Israelites to win the battle. The *fast-paced rhythm* throughout the poem, especially in the last stanza, suggests that the miraculous victory was won because of the Lord's intervention:

And the widows of Ashur[253] are loud in their wail,
And the idols are broke in the temple of Baal;
And the might of the Gentile,[254] unsmote by the sword,
Hath melted like snow in the glance of the Lord!

Byron's last line compellingly suggests God's omnipotence.

King Sennacherib

---

[253] the Assyrian widows

[254] the Assyrians

"The Charge of the Light Brigade"

This poem by Alfred, Lord Tennyson (1809–1892) is based on an historical incident.[255] It is useful to study Byron and Tennyson's poems together because in each case the specific meter the poets select conveys the situation. Tennyson chose a *dactylic meter* throughout his poem. Dactylic meter consists of poetic feet that contain one accented syllable followed by two unaccented syllables, the reverse of anapestic meter. The meter creates a sense of urgency. I read the first stanza placing emphasis on the first syllable of each poetic foot:

> Half a league, half a league,
> Half a league onward,
>> All in the valley of Death
> Rode the six hundred.
> "Forward the Light Brigade!
> Charge for the guns!" he said:
> Into the valley of Death
>> Rode the six hundred....

An officer gave a poor command, but the British soldiers, obeying instantly and unquestioningly, charged into Russian gunfire. At the final stanza, Tennyson rephrased some key lines to lend weight to the soldiers' obedience and courage:

> When can their glory fade?
> Oh, the wild charge they made!
> All the world wondered.
> Honor the charge they made!
> Honor the Light Brigade!
> Noble Six Hundred!

I write a few lines on the board to demonstrate the dactylic meter. The capitalized words are emphasized, and the slash indicates the end of each foot:

> HALF a league / HALF a league
> HALF a league / onward...
> CHARGE for the / GUNS he said...
>
> THEIRS not to /MAKE reply,
> THEIRS not to / REA son why

---

[255] The incident took place during the Crimean War at the Battle of Balaclava in 1854. An officer issued a command, and 600 cavalry soldiers bravely charged into the heavily defended Russian position. Approximately 278 British soldiers were killed or wounded during the charge.

THEIRS but to / DO and die...
RODE the six / HUN dred....

Students write out other lines and scan them in order to gain a better grasp of dactylic meter. The meter emphasizes the soldiers' instant reaction to the officer's command. After some discussion, the class realizes that Tennyson chose just the right meter to convey the men's courage and their unquestioning obedience.

"Woman Work"

This poem by Maya Angelou (1928–2014) is a fine example of *free verse*. We look at the *staccato rhythm* of the first stanza that contrasts with the *relaxed rhythm* of subsequent stanzas. The speaker is an African-American, impoverished sharecropper. The contrasting rhythms carry the burden of meaning. Inside her hut, the woman feels overwhelmed with work; outside, she feels momentarily free to lift her face to the changing sky. As she catalogs her endless chores during the first long stanza, the staccato rhythm conveys her exhaustion. As she stands outside her hut in all kinds of weather, the tranquil rhythm of the following four stanzas suggests a sense of release from her responsibilities. The relaxed, gentle rhythm of the quatrains allows us to picture the woman during the changing seasons lifting her eyes to the sky for a brief moment of rest. Meaning is conveyed via the opposing rhythms.

"Tarantella"[256]

This poem by a prolific poet, Hilaire Belloc (1870–1953), is fun to read to young people because of the *fast-paced rhythm* that operates throughout much of the poem. The speaker addresses a woman and reminisces about an inn they once knew well. He remembers the wild clapping

> Of the hands to the twirl and the swirl...
> Snapping of the clapper to the spin
> Out and in—
> And the Ting, Tong, Tang of the guitar! ...

Belloc's powerful rhythm puts us right there with the dancing girl and the raucous cheers and excitement. At the final stanza, the rhythm becomes slow and heavy as the speaker remembers the past and confronts the grim reality of the present. Like many other poems, this is a fine poem to read to 9th grade students.[257]

---

[256] The tarantella is a dance.

[257] I read some of Hilaire Belloc's poems that are included in *Cautionary Tales for Children* to middle school students who find them most entertaining.

"America for Me"

A final poem we look at in term of its meter is a well-loved lyric by Henry Van Dyke (1852–1933). The *powerful rhythm*, particularly in the second stanza quoted below, creates a stirring patriotic mood:

'Tis fine to see the Old World, and travel up and down
Among the famous palaces and cities of renown,
To admire the crumbly castles and the statues of the kings, —
But now I think I've had enough of antiquated things.
So it's home again, and home again, America for me!

My heart is turning home again, and there I long to be,
In the land of youth and freedom beyond the ocean bars,
Where the air is full of sunlight and the flag is full of stars! …

I enjoy the opportunity to have students read an overtly patriotic poem.[258]

---

[258] Another of Henry Van Dyke's fine patriotic poems is titled "Peace-Hymn of the Republic."

Review of sound devices

I break the class into small groups for review assignments. They enjoy the activity and learn from one another. Students record in their notebooks the sound devices used in a selection of lines.[259] Here are some examples with responses in brackets:

1–2: Identify the type of rhyme used in the following two sets of lines:

1.   Deep into that darkness peering, long I stood there wondering, fearing,

         Doubting, dreaming dreams no mortal ever dared to dream before;

         But the silence was unbroken, and the stillness gave no token,

         And the only word there spoken was the whispered word, "Lenore?"

         (from "The Raven," Edgar Allan Poe)   [internal rhyme]

2.   Unmoved—she notes the Chariots pausing—

         At her low Gate—

         Unmoved—an Emperor be kneeling

         Upon her Mat—

         (from "The Soul selects her own Society," Emily Dickinson)   [approximate rhyme]

3–8: Name the sound device or devices used in these lines:

3.   Little lamb who made thee?

         Dost thou know who made thee?

         Little lamb I'll tell thee.

         Little lamb I'll tell thee.

         (from "The Lamb," William Blake)   [refrain]

4.   The curfew tolls the knell of parting day,

         The lowing herd wind slowly o'er the lea,

         The plowman homeward plods his weary way,

         And leaves the world to darkness and to me…

         (from "Elegy Written in a Country Churchyard,"

         Thomas Gray)   [alliteration, onomatopoeia]

5.   The wind was a torrent of darkness among the gusty trees,

         The moon was a ghostly galleon tossed upon cloudy seas,

         The road was a ribbon of moonlight over the purple moor,

         And the highwayman came riding—

             Riding—riding—

---

[259] During group work, one has to move around the classroom to ensure that everyone is indeed discussing and taking notes on the poetry.

The highwayman came riding, up to the old inn door....
(from "The Highwayman," Alfred Noyes)   [refrain]

6.   O wild West Wind, thou breath of Autumn's being....
        (from "Ode to the West Wind," Percy Bysshe Shelley)   [alliteration; apostrophe]

7.   When icicles hang by the wall....
        Then nightly sings the staring owl,
        "Tu-whit, tu-who!"
        A merry note,
        While greasy Joan doth keel [skim] the pot....

        When roasted crabs [crab apples] hiss in the bowl,
        Then nightly sings the staring owl,
        "Tu-whit, tu-who!"
        A merry note,
        While greasy Joan doth keel the pot.
        (from *Love's Labor's Lost*, Shakespeare)   [refrain; onomatopoeia]

8.   Why so pale and wan [listless], fond lover?
        Prithee, why so pale?
        Will, when looking well can't move her,
        Looking ill prevail?
        Prithee, why so pale?
        (from "Why so pale and wan, fond lover?"
        Sir John Suckling)   [refrain]

Imagery

Young people should realize that poets have an inward eye as Wordsworth called it. Poets see things in their imaginations in order to convey their ideas. Leland Ryken comments that poets think in terms of images.[260] I list the five main types of imagery—*visual, auditory, olfactory, gustatory, tactile*, define each one—sense of sight, hearing, smell, taste, touch—and distribute examples of each type:

"The Eagle"

visual: He clasps the crag with crooked hands;
Close to the sun in lonely lands,
Ringed with the azure[261] world, he stands....
(from "The Eagle," Alfred, Lord Tennyson)

Tennyson's imagery allows us to visualize that most majestic of birds perched high on a mountain top silhouetted against the sky observing fish in the distant sea. In our mind's eye, we plainly see the mighty eagle on its cliff with the sea far below. We have no doubt that this powerful bird will catch its prey.[262]

---

[260] Ryken, *Realms of Gold,* 109.

[261] blue

[262] The poem affords an opportunity to point out alliteration (lines 1 and 2), hyperbole (line 2), and as the poem continues, personification (line 4), and simile (line 6).

"When all aloud the wind doth blow"

auditory: When all aloud the wind doth blow,

And coughing drowns the parson's saw[263]....

When roasted crabs[264] hiss in the bowl,

Then nightly sings the staring owl,

"Tu-whit, tu-who!"

A merry note....

(from *Love's Labor's Lost*, Shakespeare)

When we return to these lines, the reader can hear the wind, the congregation coughing throughout the sermon, crab apples hissing in warm cider, and an owl's hooting.

"This Is Just to Say"

gustatory: The last lines of a modern poem describe fruit as

"delicious / so sweet / and so cold"

(from "This Is Just to Say," William Carlos Williams, 1883–1963)

"Season at the Shore"

tactile: many lines in "Season at the Shore"

(Phyllis McGinley, 1905–1978)

It's fun to read McGinley's poem to the class. Students enjoy the poet's amusing and extended description of the irritating pervasiveness of sand.[265]

"Out, out—"

olfactory: The buzz-saw...

made dust and dropped stove-length sticks of wood,

Sweet-scented stuff when the breeze drew across it....

(from "Out, out—," Robert Frost)

We discuss "Out, out—" in some detail partly in order to emphasize various types of imagery. The *auditory, olfactory*, and *visual* images in this powerful poem allow us to vicariously experience the tragedy. As the poem opens, we repeatedly hear the loud buzzing of the saw and smell the freshly cut wood. We see the mountain ranges of Vermont, the sister in her apron,

---

[263] voice; alternatively, "saw" could mean the parson's maxim or proverb. In any case, coughing renders the preacher's voice inaudible.

[264] crab apples

[265] McGinley's poem is also a fine source of other poetic devices such as alliteration, onomatopocia, repetition, and personification, not to mention ragged line endings that suggest the omnipresence of sand at the seashore.

and the ghastly jagged cut. We see the boy lying semi-conscious then completely drugged and family members leaning over him anxiously listening for the final heartbeat.

Students question the reason for the tragedy. We make certain assumptions. When his sister comes to tell him it's supper time, the hungry young boy hastily stops his chore; the saw slips and cuts his hand; the doctor amputates the mangled hand but cannot staunch the blood. The class is puzzled by the two last lines. A family member's reaction— "No more to build on there"—suggests the family realizes that the boy's sudden death will prevent his growing to manhood. So the family members "turn to their affairs." Frost implies a *theme* explored by other poets and writers. When tragedy occurs, people tend to become indifferent and react by returning to their own concerns. That appears to be everyone's reaction to the boy's death. The family is too busy with chores to spend time mourning the loss of a son who can no longer help with those endless tasks.[266]

"Richard Cory"

Death is a familiar theme in poetry and other literary genres. It is the subject of a well-known poem by E. A. Robinson (1869–1935). Compelling *visual imagery* conveys the man's appearance and personality:

> He was a gentleman from sole to crown,
> Clean favored, and imperially slim.
>
> And he was always quietly arrayed...
> and he glittered when he walked....

We can distinctly picture this aristocratic gentleman. We assume he enjoys everything life has to offer. He is wealthy and attractive. The hard-working townsfolk envy him. But our initial assumption is incorrect. One summer night, Richard Cory returned home and shot himself. Students always question why he committed suicide. Robinson does not disclose the cause of the man's misery. That is not the poet's concern. This powerful poem conveys a common *theme*: People who appear to enjoy all of life's pleasures sometimes present to the world a façade of comfort and contentment, but they are, in fact, deeply unhappy. However, I ask 9th graders to reread the poem in order to appreciate the specific *visual* imagery that describes the man—slim build, elegant attire, courteous demeanor.

---

[266] Frost's poem was based on an actual tragedy recorded in a local newspaper. The boy who died lived in New Hampshire and was one of Frost's teenage friends.

"Those Winter Sundays"

This poem by Robert Hayden (1913–1980) is a reminiscence. Who is the *speaker* and what is the *occasion*? The speaker remembers his childhood and his self-sacrificing father who unsparingly attempted to create a warm environment for his family during cold weather in spite of hostile feelings among family members. *Visual images* allow us to see, as it were, the bitter cold readily apparent throughout the first and second verses. We can clearly visualize the father's calloused hands, the warm fire he rekindled each day, and the boy's shiny Sunday shoes. We consider the rest of the poem. Later in life, the speaker remembers his father's selfless acts; more importantly, he remembers his own lack of gratitude. Now that he's a man, he realizes that he took his father's loving actions for granted and regrets his ingratitude. I suggest to students that they have probably regretted some past words or actions that hurt a loved one, and I assure them that we all experience similar moments of remorse. I urge the young people before me to do their best to correct the wrong.

The packet of poetry distributed to the class includes two poems set in woods that contain stunning imagery: "The Way through the Woods" by Rudyard Kipling (1865–1936) and "The Listeners" by Walter de La Mare (1873–1956). I read both poems accompanied by appropriate music such as Beethoven's *Moonlight Sonata*.

"The Way through the Woods"
Here are the first lines of Kipling's poem:

> They shut the road through the woods
> Seventy years ago.
> Weather and rain have undone it again,
> And now you would never know
> There was once a road through the woods....

The class identifies the *visual images* in the lines that follow and the tranquil mood they evoke— the trees, the dove, badgers, and anemones.[267] We note lines from the second and last stanza:

> Yet, if you enter the woods
> Of a summer evening late,
> When the night-air cools on the trout-ringed pools
> *Where the otter whistles his mate....*

---

[267] Anemones are delicate flowers that grow in a variety of colors.

You will hear the beat of a horse's feet,
And the swish of a skirt in the dew,
Steadily cantering through
The misty solitudes.... [Italics added.]

Students should appreciate the *auditory images* in the italicized lines that suggest otters at play as well as the sounds of horses' pounding hoofs and ladies' long skirts rustling in the grass. The rhythm makes this a lovely poem to read aloud. Young people are sensitive to its beauty. It has no theme, no moral to point out. It is simply beautiful. It's also mysterious. The poet evinces a tingling sense of mystery as he suggests that years ago there was a road through those particular woods along which horsemen galloped and ladies walked, their long dresses trailing along the dew-covered grass. I reread the entire poem to the class so that everyone appreciates its beauty. Freshman students are not going to volunteer enthusiasm for the poem, but it's good for them to listen to beautiful poetry.

"The Listeners"

Here's the first stanza of Walter de La Mare's poem:

"Is there anybody there?" said the Traveller,
Knocking on the moonlit door;
And his horse in the silence champed the grasses
Of the forest's ferny floor....

We can picture the scene—the man on his horse, the door in the moonlight, the forest. The man strikes the door again; no one responds. He stands in the moonlight feeling perturbed; inside the house, ghostly creatures hover on the stairs listening to his knocking. He is somehow aware of their presence while his horse becomes restless. *Auditory imagery* and *onomatopoeia* create a deliciously mysterious ending. Note the onomatopoeic words in the lines that end the poem:

> Ay, they heard his foot upon the stirrup,
> And the sound of *iron on stone,*
> And how the *silence surged softly* backward,
> When the *plunging* hoofs were gone. [Italics added.]

It would be sacrilege, wouldn't it, to dissect the lines any further? You just want to read the poem and say "Ah!" ignoring the person in the back row who breaks the mood by announcing, "I don't get it."

Review of imagery

I distribute a sheet of lines from various poems that convey distinct images. Students write down in their notebooks the predominant type of imagery and the feeling each image evokes. Again, students break into small groups for this assignment. Here are a few examples with responses in brackets:

1.   I will arise and go now, and go to Innisfree…
        And live alone in the bee-loud glade….

        I will arise and go now, for always night and day
        I hear lake water lapping with low sounds by the shore….
        (from "The Lake Isle of Innisfree," W. B. Yeats)   [auditory imagery; nostalgia]

2.   Break, break, break
        On thy cold grey stones, O Sea! …
        (from "Break, break, break," Alfred, Lord Tennyson)   [auditory and visual imagery; grief]

3.   When icicles hang by the wall,
        And Dick the shepherd blows his nail,
        And Tom bears logs into the hall,
        And milk comes frozen home in pail….
        (from *Love's Labor's Lost,* William Shakespeare)   [visual imagery; extreme cold]

4.   Who hath not seen thee [autumn] oft amid thy store? ….
        Drows'd with the fume of poppies….
        Or by a cider press, with patient look,
        Thou watchest the last oozings hours by hours….
        (from "To Autumn," John Keats)   [olfactory imagery; lethargy]

5.   As I bit into a crisp apple, its juiciness trickled
        down my chin.   [gustatory; pleasure]

6.   I must go down to the seas again, to the lonely sea
                        and the sky,
        And all I ask is a tall ship and a star to steer her by,
        And the wheel's kick and the wind's song and the
                        white sail's shaking….
        (from "Sea Fever," John Masefield)   [visual and auditory imagery;
                        urgent desire]

7.   Then a mile of warm sea-scented beach….
        (from "Meeting at Night," Robert Browning)   [olfactory imagery; pleasure]

8.   Hark, where my blossomed pear-tree in the hedge
        Leans to the field and scatters on the clover
        Blossoms and dewdrops—at the bent spray's edge….
        (from "Home-Thoughts from Abroad,"
        Robert Browning)   [visual imagery; nostalgia]

9.   John tore downstairs into the kitchen and could almost
        taste Mom's freshly baked pie with its sugary,
        spicy sweetness.   [gustatory; pleasure]

Figurative Language:
Simile and Metaphor

The class should be able to differentiate between *literal* and *figurative* language. When we speak literally, we mean exactly what our words express: I wish it were lunch time because I'm starving. When we speak figuratively, we don't mean to be taken literally: I'm so hungry I could eat a horse. Poets use figurative language in order to compress their meaning into a few words, and in doing so they convey more meaning than is possible when using literal language.

The most common figurative language poets use is comparisons. Poets constantly make comparisons in order to help us see or understand a particular emotion or insight. I remind the class that similes and metaphors are comparisons. What's the difference? Similes compare two items using comparatives words such as "like," "as," or "than." Metaphors compare two things without the use of comparative words.

"A narrow Fellow in the Grass"
In this poem, Emily Dickinson employs *metaphors* and *similes* to describe a snake slithering through tall grass:

> A narrow Fellow in the Grass
> Occasionally rides....
>
> The Grass divides as with a Comb
> A spotted Shaft is seen....
>
> Have passed I thought a Whip Lash....

Dickinson's description is so vivid that we are unaware the word "snake" is not mentioned; most freshman students don't figure out the subject until we've discussed the poem. Dickinson refers *metaphorically* to the snake as a "spotted Shaft" and a "Whip Lash" and via a *simile*— "The Grass divides as with a Comb"; the class should understand that all three comparisons precisely describe a snake's rapid movement.

"The Meadow Mouse"
Young people like this poem by Theodore Roethke (1908–1963) because it charmingly describes a baby mouse that the speaker has caught to keep it safe. In the first stanza, the poet's description of the tiny, vulnerable animal is conveyed via striking *similes* that allow us to appreciate its defenselessness in a world of predators.

"Dream Deferred"

Langston Hughes (1902–1967), a celebrated African-American poet, was a driving force during the Harlem Renaissance.[268] In one of Hughes's most well-known poems, "Dream Deferred," the poet explores the question of equality for African Americans via five *similes* and an *implied metaphor* in the last line. Also noteworthy are Hughes's *rhetorical questions* that suggest the dreams of his people are suppressed but never forgotten until those dreams explode into devastating riots like a detonated bomb. Hughes conveys his concern about racial tension with powerful questions and comparisons.

Extended metaphor

"Mother to Son"

In this poem by the same poet, Langston Hughes uses an *extended metaphor* of a crystal staircase to explore and commend a brave woman's victory over adversity. This mother has led a hard life full of trials, but she has endured. She has overcome hardship. We look closely at the metaphor that extends throughout the poem. The mother compares her life to a flight of stairs that is dilapidated and shabby—a far cry from a crystal staircase. Students realize that the defects in the stairs represent the woman's trials, whereas its turns and landings represent easier times in her life. She has persevered and endured ordeals "in the dark," that is, without anyone, anything to guide her. But one thing she's never done is to turn back down the stairs—in other words, to succumb to pity and defeat. Why is she giving this advice to her son? She has apparently noticed his depression and is encouraging him to meet life's difficulties with courage and endurance as she continues to do in spite of adversity she must face. It's fine advice. I take the opportunity to suggest to the young people before me that they listen to and obey their parents' counsel.

"She dwelt among the untrodden ways"

One cannot teach poetry without including William Wordsworth (1770–1850), so we look at the comparisons in one of this English Romantic's short lyrics:

> She dwelt among the untrodden ways
> Beside the springs of Dove....[269]

---

[268] The Harlem Renaissance refers to a burgeoning of African-American culture in the 1920s. During this decade, many African-American writers, musicians, and artists arrived in Harlem and produced fine works in various artistic genres.

[269] The Dove is a river in the Midlands in central England.

A violet by the mossy stone
Half hidden from the eye!
Fair as a star, when only one
Is shining in the sky....

Wordsworth's *speaker* is drawn to a maid or young woman called Lucy.[270] The first line tells us she lived in a remote area near the source or springs of a remote river. A *metaphor* compares the girl to a violet, and a *simile* compares her to a star. Violets are pretty flowers that hide away in mossy areas, and a lone star is beautiful but remote; these comparisons therefore suggest that the girl was attractive, but she was lonely. Wordsworth's comparisons convey important information about this unidentified girl. In the third and final stanza, we learn that Lucy died with few people to notice her passing; Wordsworth, however, is deeply distressed by her death.

Implied metaphors

Students should understand that metaphors can also be *implied* rather than stated. We return to Dickinson's "snake" poem. In the following lines, the poet's metaphors of a "spotted Shaft" and a "Whip Lash" are implied:

The Grass divides as with a Comb
A spotted Shaft is seen....

Have passed I thought a Whip Lash
Unbraiding in the Sun....

---

[270] Wordsworth wrote five "Lucy" poems. Scholars have not determined the identity of this young woman who may have been a figment of the poet's imagination rather than a real person.

Why are the metaphors implied? Well, Dickinson doesn't state that the snake *is* "a spotted shaft" or that it *is* "a whip lash"; she implies these comparisons so that the reader can imagine a snake's rapid movements. In the final stanzas, the speaker admits a liking for all other creatures, but another *implied metaphor* in the last line tells us something very different about his reaction to snakes. Students don't recognize the metaphor in this stanza. Where's the comparison? Dickinson compares the speaker's reaction when meeting a snake to "tighter breathing, / And Zero at the Bone." What do these lines mean? Snakes fill the speaker with terrifying, bone-chilling fear.

We have noted that it's useful to ask specific questions about poetry: Who's the *audience*? What's the *occasion*? Who is the *speaker*? Not every question can be helpfully applied to every poem; the audience in Dickinson's poem is undefined, whereas the occasion is obvious—the speaker encounters a snake. The female poet employs an unusual speaker. (But what is usual about Dickinson?) By the time we get to the third stanza, we realize the speaker is a barefoot boy who's doing what all young boys like to do—chasing a snake.

"It sifts from leaden sieves"

The subject of another cryptic poem of Dickinson's is developed via a series of *implied metaphors*:

> It sifts from leaden sieves,
> It powders all the wood.
> It fills with alabaster wool
> The wrinkles of the road....

Students will need help with Dickinson's metaphors. The implied metaphors throughout the poem refer to snow that fills the cracks and valleys in the landscape and covers the fenceposts during a snow storm transforming the scene into a white wonderland. In the first stanza quoted above, for instance, the poet implicitly compares falling snow to flour that sifts from dark clouds; in the next two lines, snow is implicitly compared to white wool that covers cracks in the road. In the third stanza, Dickinson implicitly compares the snow to a bride's veil, and in the last stanza, she compares the softly falling flakes to ruffles on a queen's garment. Why are the metaphors implied? Dickinson never names the thing described, falling snow.

"Bereft"

The speaker of an intriguing poem by Robert Frost feels bereft because of some tragedy or loss. Every line fills us with a sense of desolation. The occasion? A man is standing outside his house contemplating a grim landscape. It is fall. The wind sounds like a wild beast. Clouds gather in a dark sky. With a graphic *implied metaphor*, the poet suggests that dead leaves on his porch rise up and attempt to strike him like a snake. The figurative language conveys the speaker's bleak mood far more effectively that a mere statement of despair would have done.

Extended metaphors

"All the world's a stage"

Poets sometimes extend or continue a metaphor throughout several lines or an entire poem. One of the most famous passages in Shakespeare contains an *extended metaphor* that compares life to a stage. We examine the passage in some detail. The lines from *As You Like It* are spoken by a melancholy man called Jacques that begin with these iconic lines:

> All the world's a stage,
> And all the men and women merely players;
> They have their exits and their entrances,
> And one man in his time plays many parts,
> His acts begin seven ages....

Jacques cynically enumerates the seven stages of life, starting with a baby "mewling and puking in the nurse's arms," followed by

> ... the whining schoolboy, with his satchel
> And shining morning face, creeping like snail
> Unwillingly to school....

Students learn that a dictionary is indispensable when studying poetry; they discover that a satchel is the sixteenth-century English equivalent of a backpack. Young people recognize Jacques's morose attitude to life when they recall that babies are usually described not as "mewling and puking" but as sweet and lovable. They certainly agree with the speaker about the second stage and readily relate to the *simile* that defines the reluctant schoolboy. Jacques moves on to adulthood:

> And then the lover,
> Sighing like furnace, with a woeful ballad
> Made to his mistress' eyebrow....

Here Shakespeare is mocking Elizabethan love poetry, including his own. The furnace *simile* suggests a lover's passion (one thinks of Romeo). The boys are loud in their protests about writing a poem to a girl's eyebrow—but that, of course, is Shakespeare's point. Here's the fourth stage:

> Then a soldier
> Full of strange oaths, and bearded like the pard,[271]
> Jealous in honor, sudden and quick in quarrel,
> Seeking the bubble reputation
> Even in the cannon's mouth....

These lines remind the class of fiery Tybalt. Shakespeare suggests that the soldier's consuming desire is to protect his warlike reputation even when facing death via a cannon ball; but why "bubble"? A person's reputation is fragile and once ruined cannot easily be restored in men's eyes.[272] The remaining stages of life recounted in Jacques's cynical catalogue become increasingly ludicrous. The mature man is a well-fed judge who likes to display his erudition. Adopting a severe demeanor, he pronounces judgments tediously repeated from law books. In old age, a man deteriorates physically to such a degree that his hose doesn't fit, and his voice becomes weak. Finally, he loses all his faculties and everything that gives life meaning and worth:

> Last scene of all
> That ends this strange eventful history,
> Is second childishness and mere oblivion,
> Sans[273] teeth, sans eyes, sans taste, sans everything.

---

[271] whiskered like the leopard

[272] Elsewhere, another character from Shakespeare comments, "Good name in man and woman... / Is the immediate jewel of their souls. / Who steals my purse steals trash; 'tis something, nothing; / 'Twas mine, 'tis his, and has been slave to thousands; / But he that filches from me my good name / Robs me of that which not enriches him, / And makes me poor indeed." *Othello* III.3.155–61.

[273] without, Fr.

Jacques suggests that at no time in a man's life does one deserve accolades or exude dignity; on the contrary, Jacques has nothing but disdain for every stage of life. Shakespeare's *extended metaphor* conveys a decidedly cynical view of human nature. I include a memorization project as part of the poetry unit and suggest that Jacques's speech would be an excellent choice.

Certain *similes* have become as familiar as household words:

> O, my Luve is like a red, red rose.
> (from "A Red, Red Rose," Robert Burns, 1759–1796)

> Cool as a cucumber.
> (from "A New Song," John Gay, 1685–1732)

And many similes have become trite and should be avoided at all costs: I am as free as a bird and as happy as a lark, but I'm as poor as dirt and dumb as an ox.

Review of simile and metaphor

In order to review similes and metaphors, I circulate a sheet of quotations from poems that contain these devices. Students break into small groups to identify the comparisons and suggest their effectiveness. Here are some examples with bracketed responses:

1.   I wandered lonely as a cloud
That floats on high o'er vales and hills....
(from "I wandered lonely as a cloud,"
William Wordsworth)

[simile; the speaker's loneliness is compared to a cloud high in the sky. The lines suggest a forlorn mood]

2.   She walks in beauty, like the night
Of cloudless climes and starry skies....
(from "She walks in beauty, like the night,"
Lord Byron)

[simile; a woman is compared to a night sky studded with stars. The comparison suggests the woman's beauty.]

3.   My heart is like a singing bird
Whose nest is in a watered shoot:
My heart is like an apple-tree
Whose boughs are bent with thickset fruit;
My heart is like a rainbow shell
That paddles in a halcyon [tranquil] sea
My heat is gladder than all these
Because my love is come to me....
(from "My heart is like a singing bird,"
Christina Rossetti)

[similes; the speaker extravagantly compares her emotions at a lover's return to a bird that sings, an apple tree thick with fruit, and a fanciful rainbow gliding on the sea. The comparisons suggest the speaker's joy.]

4.   That time of year thou may'st in me behold
When yellow leaves, or none, or few, do hang
Upon those boughs which shake against the cold,
Bare ruined choirs where late the sweet birds sang.
(from Sonnet 73, Shakespeare)

[metaphor; the process of growing old is compared to bare tree limbs of winter. The comparison is appropriate because the winter season suggests the barrenness of aging. Shakespeare compares an aging man's increasing feebleness to dying leaves and stark tree limbs.]

5.   Out, out, brief candle!
Life's but a walking shadow, a poor player
That struts and frets his hour upon the stage
And then is heard no more.
(from *Macbeth,* Shakespeare)

[metaphor; the first metaphor compares one's life span to a flickering candle, a comparison that indicates life's brevity; the second and third metaphors compare life to a shadow then to an indifferent actor on a stage. These comparisons suggest that life is meaningless.]

6.   How sharper than a serpent's tooth it is
To have a thankless child.
(from *King Lear,* Shakespeare)

[implied metaphor; a parent's reaction to a child's ingratitude is compared to the bite of a venomous snake. The comparison conveys the anguish a parent feels about a son or daughter's thanklessness.]

7.   Fame is a bee
It has song—
It has a sting—
Ah, too, it has a wing.
("Fame is a bee,"
Emily Dickinson)

[metaphor; fame is compared to a bee in three ways. It creates feelings of exhilaration as well as bitterness; it is also fleeting. The comparison is effective because it conveys both positive and negative aspects of fame.]

I ask students to *paraphrase* the last poem quoted above. Here's a suggested paraphrase: Fame brings both happiness and sorrow but, sadly, it is short-lived. (The exclamation in the last line implies the speaker's regret at the brevity of fame.)

Wordsworth famously defined poetry as "the spontaneous overflow of powerful feelings." Poets employ ingenious comparisons to help us grasp setting, character, ideas, and keenly felt emotion.

Figurative Language:
Personification

We move on to another type of figurative language, *personification*, or language that describes inanimate objects or ideas or animals as if they were human. Students get confused between personification and metaphor. Here's the difference:

- **Personification** refers to or describes something inanimate as if it were living.
- **Metaphor** compares two objects without using comparing words such as "like" or "as."

"I wandered lonely as a cloud"

One of the best-loved poems in literature is Wordsworth's piece that describes daffodils growing in some woods beside a lake. The poem provides an example of a great poet's use of personification. The speaker is the poet himself. In a downcast mood, Wordsworth walks through a wooded area in the Lake District in Northwest England where he lived. Suddenly, "a crowd / A host, of golden daffodils" catches his eye. Wordsworth uses stunning *hyperbole* throughout the poem (for instance, note line 3 quoted below), but *personification* brings the scene vividly before us. Note the italicized wording here:

> Beside the lake, beneath the trees,
> *Fluttering and dancing* in the breeze....
> Ten thousand saw I at a glance
> *Tossing their heads in sprightly dance.*
>
> *The waves beside them danced*; but *they*
> *Out-did the sparkling waves in glee....* [Italics added.]

Both daffodils and lake are personified, and it is the poet's use of personification that brings the sight of bright spring flowers strikingly to life. I use artwork to enhance literature. Before we read this poem, I show the class photographs of daffodils growing in abundance.[274]

---

[274] You can find beautiful images of daffodils at www.gardenphotos.com.

"The world is too much with us"

In this sonnet, Wordsworth personifies the sea (note italicized line):

> The world is too much with us; late and soon,
> Getting and spending, we lay waste our powers;
> Little we see in Nature that is ours. . .
> *This Sea that bares her bosom to the to the moon…*
> For this, for everything, we are out of tune. . .. [Italics added.]

Wordsworth's *personification* intensifies the vision of a moonlit sea.

"I like to see it lap the Miles"

Here is a livelier instance of personification. In a widely anthologized poem, Emily Dickinson personifies a train:

> I like to see it lap the Miles—
> And lick the Valleys up—
> And stop to feed itself at Tanks—
> And then—prodigious step. . ..
>
> And neigh like Boanerges—[275]
> Then—prompter than a Star
> Stop—docile and omnipotent
> At its own stable door—

The class appreciates this witty example of *extended personification* that never names its subject as it implicitly and cleverly compares a train to a horse. The class should note that Dickinson achieves the comparison in part by run-on lines that suggest the continual motion of a train hurtling through mountain ranges, past country shacks, down hillsides, gliding smoothly along the tracks until it suddenly stops at its destination.

---

[275] Boanerges or "Sons of thunder" was the surname Jesus gave His disciples James and John. See Mark 3:17.

"Scholars"

Students will need help identifying the five types of students *personified* in this poem by Walter de La Mare. The poet lists the strictly logical student; the one who reasons accurately; the student who learns by rote; the cheat; and the inherently wise, nonconforming student who learns by his or her own methods. Ironically, the nonconformist is thought to be foolish by both the teacher and the other students.[276]

"Death, be not proud"

A seventeenth-century poet, John Donne (1572–1631), *personifies* death throughout this sonnet. He refers to death as if it were a prideful person. Here are the opening lines:

> Death, be not proud, though some have called thee
> Mighty and dreadful, for thou are not so;
> For those whom thou think'st thou dost overthrow
> Die not, poor Death….
> (from Holy Sonnet 10, John Donne)

Donne's purpose is to disparage the power that death wields over people. Donne argues that death should not be arrogant because it has no power over mankind; death simply ceases to be when men die. The poet argues that we need not fear death because when life is over we do not die eternally; rather, we go to God.

"Fifteen"

A final poem we read in order to appreciate a poet's use of personification is by William Stafford (1914–1993). The speaker is a young man who comes across a motorbike with its engine running at the side of a road. The poet personifies the bike as the boy admires it and thinks of it in terms of a favorite horse. (Note the diction in the second stanza.) Students name words in the poem that personify the bike. Any fifteen-year-old boy would love to jump on it and take off into the wild blue yonder. As the boy imagines the bike's seconding his notion to ride it, he almost succumbs to the mounting desire to steal it. But common-sense and integrity bring the boy to his senses. He looks for the owner, helps him onto the bike, and the man roars away. The class should realize that it is mainly via *personification* that we appreciate the impact of the experience on this young boy. By personifying the bike as if it were alive—more than

---

[276] The teacher in this poem insists that the nonconforming student must sit on a dunce's stool, which was once an ignominious place of punishment in the corner of a classroom for lazy or backward students. This student, however, is wise beyond his years.

that, a close friend—the poet emphasizes the boy's strong urge to ride away on it. Students always ask why the boy states his age four times. The first time is a factual statement; the second conveys the boy's excitement; the third implies a strong desire to steal the bike; the fourth conveys the importance of the incident—the boy has been strongly tempted but overcomes a major temptation and matures as a result. Boys in particular relate well to the poem.

Great poets employ personification in order to convey a specific emotion or mood or idea. Personification significantly enhances meaning for the reader.

Figurative Language:
Apostrophe

Apostrophe is another type of figurative language in which the speaker addresses an inanimate object or idea or someone who has died as if it or he could understand the speaker. Students often confuse apostrophe with personification. Here's the difference:

- **apostrophe**: a figure of speech in which a character addresses a non-living person or an inanimate object as if he or it were living.
- **personification**: something inanimate is referred to or described as if it were living.

I tell the class not to confuse this type of apostrophe with the punctuation mark one uses for contractions, and I provide one or two brief examples of figurative apostrophe. One can quote the nursery rhyme "Twinkle, twinkle, little star" and cite lines from "Holy Night." ("O holy night…O night divine.…") The strained looks begin to fade. You may want to take the class back to *Romeo and Juliet*. Juliet wakes up from her drug-induced coma, finds Romeo dead beside her, and commits suicide. She apostrophizes his dagger: "O happy dagger! / This is thy sheath; there rust, and let me die."[277] Why does she call it a "happy dagger"? It is the means by which she will join Romeo in death. (Yes, 9th grade students will look incredulous.)

"Death, be not proud"
Seventeenth and eighteenth-century poets frequently used apostrophe. We return to Donne's sonnet, which is an example of *extended apostrophe*. In addition to personifying death as if it were animate or living, the poet also apostrophizes death throughout the poem. In other words, he addresses or talks to death as one would speak to a person:

> Death, be not proud, though some have called thee
> Mighty and dreadful, for thou are not so.…

Donne wishes to denigrate people's dread of dying, a goal that he achieves far more effectively than he would have done if he had merely referred to death in an impersonal way. Instead, the poet apostrophizes death as if it were a person with whom he is arguing and conclusively points out that he—death—is not to be feared because it is death itself, not mankind, that will ultimately die.

---

[277] *Romeo and* Juliet, V.3.169–70.

"The Lamb"

William Blake (1757–1827) was a pre-Romantic poet. In this charming lyric, Blake *apostrophizes* a gentle lamb in order to ask a rhetorical question regarding the Creator of the universe:

> Little Lamb, who made thee?
> Dost thou know who made thee?
> Gave thee life and bid thee feed.
> By the stream and o'er the mead[278]….
>
> Little Lamb, I'll tell thee,
> Little Lamb, I'll tell thee….
> (from "The Lamb, William Blake)

Here are examples from poems by great English Romantics. John Keats (1795–1821) *apostrophizes* a bird throughout a famous ode; Percy Bysshe Shelley (1792–1822) *apostrophizes* a bird and the wind respectively in two of his odes:

> Thou wast not born for death, immortal Bird!
> No hungry generations tread thee down….
> (from "Ode to a Nightingale,"[279] John Keats)
>
> Hail to thee, blithe Spirit!
> Bird thou never wert….
>
> Higher still and higher
> From the earth thou springest
> Like a cloud of fire;
> The blue deep thou wingest,
> And singing still dost soar, and soaring ever singest.
> (from "Ode to a Sky-Lark,"[280] Percy Bysshe Shelley)
>
> O wild West Wind, thou breath of Autumn's being,
> Thou, from whose unseen presence the leaves dead
> Are driven, like ghosts from an enchanter fleeing….
> (from "Ode to the West Wind," Percy Bysshe Shelley)

Poets employ apostrophe to convey deeply felt emotion. The two Romantics quoted above use apostrophe to express intense joy.

---

[278] meadow

[279] The nightingale is a bird noted for its sweet nocturnal singing.

[280] A skylark is a small bird that sings only when it flies and when it is too high to be seen.

"Blow, blow thou winter wind"

Here's another instance when a great poet *apostrophizes* both wind and sky:

> Blow, blow thou winter wind.
> Thou art no so unkind[281]
> As man's ingratitude;
> Thy tooth is not so keen,[282]
> Because thou art not seen,
> Although thy breath be rude[283]....
>
> Freeze, freeze, thou bitter sky,
> That dost not bite so nigh[284]
> As benefits[285] forgot;
> Though thou the waters warp,[286]
> Thy sting is not so sharp
> As friend remembered not....
> (from *As You Like It*, Shakespeare)[287]

Via apostrophe, Shakespeare reminds us that winter weather, harsh though it may be, is not as devastating as people's thoughtlessness or neglect.[288] Poets as well as prose writers use apostrophe to convey powerful emotion.

---

[281] harsh

[282] sharp

[283] stinging

[284] so painfully

[285] good deeds

[286] even though you can freeze water

[287] *As You Like It*, II.vii.174–89.

[288] These lines remind one of more wisdom from Shakespeare: "How sharper than a serpent's tooth it is / To have a thankless child!" *King Lear* I.4.289–90.

Review of personification and apostrophe

I assign review of personification and apostrophe by compiling a sheet of quotations from poems that contain one of the two devices. Each student identifies the device and the object personified or apostrophized. Here are a few examples with bracketed responses:

1.   Bright star, would I were steadfast as thou art—
    Not in lone splendor hung aloft the night
    And watching, with eternal lids apart,
    Like nature's patient, sleepless Eremite[289]. . .
    (from "Bright Star," John Keats)   [apostrophe; a star]

2.   When the stars threw down their spears,
    And watered heaven with their tears,
    Did he smile his work to see? . . .
    (from "The Tyger," William Blake)   [personification; stars]

3.   Slowly, silently, now the moon
    Walks the night in her silver shoon.[290]
    This way, and that, she peers, and sees
    Silver fruit upon silver trees....
    (from "Silver," Walter de La Mare)   [personification; the moon]

4.   With how sad steps, O Moon, thou climb'st the skies,
    How silently, and with how wan[291] a face! …
    (from "With how sad steps, O Moon, thou climb'st the skies,"
    Sir Philip Sidney)   [apostrophe; the moon]

5.   The Wind—tapped like a tired Man—
          …entered then
    My Residence within

    A Rapid—footless Guest….
    (from "The Wind—tapped like a tired Man,"
    Emily Dickinson)   [personification; the wind]

---

[289] hermit

[290] shoes

[291] pale

Tone

As already mentioned, *tone* is the most difficult aspect of literature for students to grasp. They need a great deal of help and many examples. I frequently remind them that tone is the writer's attitude to his or her subject. The tone of poetry and all literature corresponds to the tone of one's voice when speaking. The best way to distinguish a writer's tone is to carefully read a piece in order to discern the writer's attitude to the subject matter. The modern American poet Theodore Roethke has suggested that we must actively listen to poetry because it is written to be heard.[292]

"The Lake Isle of Innisfree"

Before we read this lyric by William Butler Yeats (1865–1939), I ask students how they would feel if they had to leave home to live far away in another land. The consensus is predictable: They'd be appalled. Innisfree is a small island near Sligo in the northwest of Ireland where Yeats spent childhood vacations; it held many happy memories for the poet. When he wrote the poem, he was living in London and longed to return to his tranquil, uninhabited island:

> I will arise and go now, and go to Innisfree,
> And a small cabin build there, of clay and wattles[293] made
> Nine bean-rows will I have there, a hive for the honeybee,
> And live alone in the bee-loud glade

Here's the last stanza:

> I will arise and go now, for always night and day
> I hear lake water lapping with low sounds by the shore;
> While I stand on the roadway, or on the pavements gray,
> I hear it in the deep heart's core.

How does the poet feel about Innisfree? Most students recognize the poet's love for Innisfree and his tone of *longing* and *nostalgia*.

---

[292] Roethke gave this advice in a volume of his poetry entitled *Praise to the End!* that was first published in 1951. His wise words are quoted in *A Book of Poetry* 1, 2nd ed. (New York: Harcourt Brace Jovanovich, 1983), 32.

[293] twigs woven together

The coastline of
Sligo, Northern Ireland

"La Belle Dame sans Mercy"[294]

We read some lines from John Keats's ballad that tells the tale of a forlorn knight who falls under the fatal spell of a beautiful woman:

> O, what can ail thee, knight-at-arms,
> Alone and palely loitering?
> The sedge[295] has withered from the lake,
> And no birds sing....
>
> I met a Lady in the Meads,[296]
> Full beautiful, a faery's child,
> Her hair was long, her foot was light
> And her eyes were wild....

"A Birthday"

Then we read lines from this lyric by Christina Rossetti (1830–1894):

> My heart is like a singing bird
> Whose nest is in a water'd shoot;
> My heart is like an apple tree
> Whose boughs are bent with thickset fruit....
> My heart is gladder than all these
> Because my love is come to me....[297]

---

[294] The title means "The Beautiful Lady without Pity." This is another fine poem to read aloud.

[295] grass

[296] meadows

[297] These lines have already been quoted in the review section for similes and metaphors.

The tone of these poems is fairly well defined: The first is *haunting*; the second is *joyful*. Keats's tone is conveyed via his enigmatic attitude to the medieval knight and the lady. We know nothing about knight or lady other than the knight's tragic fascination with a lady, if she is indeed mortal, and the spell she casts upon him.[298] Rossetti's tone is self-explanatory: Someone the speaker dearly loves has returned to her.

"Does It Matter?"

Here is the first stanza of this poem by a World War I poet, Siegfried Sassoon (1886–1967):

> Does it matter? —losing your leg?
> For people will always be kind,
> And you need not show that you mind
> When the others come in after hunting
> To gobble their muffins and eggs....

The tone here carries the weight of meaning. It is *bitterly ironic*. How do we know that? Well, the interrogatives in the first line of every stanza are followed by answers that indicate the vast discrepancy between each response and the stark reality of the soldier's wounds. Sassoon fought in "the war to end all wars"[299] and wrote poems that convey the horror of trench warfare and the appalling conflict that took the lives of an entire generation of British men. The speaker in this scathing poem represents soldiers who have been horribly mutilated. Others attempt to comfort them and lift their spirits, but these brave warriors will carry with them mental and physical scars that will last the rest of their lives.

The great Victorian poet Alfred, Lord Tennyson was devastated when he lost a close friend.[300] In addition to a book-length poem, *In Memoriam,* Tennyson wrote a short poem that expresses his anguish at his friend's death:

"Break, break, break"

> Break, break, break
> On thy cold grey stones, O sea!
> And I would that my tongue could utter
> The thoughts that arise in me....

---

[298] Scholars have noted parallels between the ballad and Keats's life. Like the knight in his poem, Keats loved a lady, Fanny Brawne, and like the knight, he was aware of impending tragedy, which in Keats's case was an early death.

[299] World War I was first given this designation by H. G. Wells. It was also known as the Great War.

[300] The friend was Arthur Hallam who died of a stroke at twenty-two.

Break, break, break
At the foot of thy crags, O sea!
But the tender grace of a day that is dead
Will never come back to me.
(from "Break, break, break")

Tennyson's tone is *sorrowful*. Diction such as "break, grey, crags, dead" conveys his grief. The poet's sorrow is so intense that he cannot assemble his thoughts in a rational manner. The repeated word "break" in particular suggests heartbreak.

"Apparently with no surprise"

We resort again to America's most enigmatic poet. Dickinson's tone is *cynical*. The speaker is not only cynical but shocked by an ordinary event in the world of nature. Here are the first lines:

Apparently with no surprise
To any happy flower,
The frost beheads it at its play
In accidental power....

How do we know that the speaker is skeptical about a perfectly natural event? The description is not straightforward or nonchalant. On the contrary, Dickinson's words connote appalling injustice. An innocent flower is inadvertently beheaded and dies during a frosty day, the frost is an indifferent killer, and the sun lacks concern over the flower's death. We react with something close to horror. The cynical tone operates throughout the poem but is most evident in the last line. The sun is merely fulfilling the role assigned to it by a seemingly hardhearted Creator.[301]

"You are old, Father William"

We end discussion of tone with another amusing poem by Lewis Carroll. Here are the first two stanzas:

> "You are old, Father William," the young man said,
> "And your hair has become very white;
> And yet you incessantly stand on your head—
> Do you think, at your age, it is right?
>
> "In my youth," Father William replied to his son,
> "I feared it might injure the brain;
> But, now that I'm perfectly sure I have none,
> Why, I do it again and again." …
> (from "You are old, Father William," *Alice in Wonderland*, Lewis Carroll)

The writer's tone is undoubtedly *light-hearted*. I suspect that these lines are not entirely nonsensical but contain some wisdom about young people's attitudes to anyone over thirty.

Studying many examples, students gradually learn to identify a writer's approach or attitude to his subject matter, in other words, his or her tone.

Review of tone

I distribute lines from various poems where tone is important. Again, students break into small groups to define the tone of each poem. Responses are bracketed:

1.   Now it is the time of night,
        That the graves, all gaping wide,
        Every one lets forth his sprite,
        In the churchway paths to glide:
        And we fairies, that do run
        By the triple Hecate's team,[302]

---

[301] The class should know that Dickinson struggled with belief in the Christian religion all her life. She apparently never accepted Jesus as her Savior. In several of her poems, she depicts Almighty God as harsh and vindictive.

[302] Shakespeare's reference to "the triple Hecate's team" signifies that the goddess Hecate had three names: Phoebe, Diana, and Hecate.

In the presence of the sun,
Following darkness like a dream,
Now are frolic: not a mouse
Shall disturb this hallowed house:
I am sent, with broom, before,
To sweep the dust behind the door.
(from *A Midsummer Night's Dream,* William Shakespeare)   [tone: light-hearted]

2.   Come live with me and be my love
And we will all the pleasures prove,
That hills and valleys, dales and fields,
And all the craggy mountains yields. …
(from "The Passionate Shepherd to his Love,"
Christopher Marlowe)   [tone: ardent]

3.   Golden slumbers kiss your eyes,
Smiles awake you when you rise.
Sleep, pretty wantons, do not cry,
And I will sing a lullaby:
Rock them, rock them, lullaby. …
(from "A Cradle Song," Thomas Dekker)   [tone: soothing]

4.   Softly along the road of evening,
In a twilight dim with rose,
Wrinkled with age, and drenched with dew,
Old Nod, the shepherd, goes.

His drowsy flock streams on before him,
Their fleeces charged with gold,
To where the sun's last beam leans low
On Nod the shepherd's fold.
(from "Nod," Walter de La Mare)   [tone: peaceful]

5.   O Captain! my Captain! our fearful trip is done;
The ship has weather'd every rack, the prize we sought is won;
The port is near, the bells I hear, the people all exulting,
While follow eyes the steady keel, the vessel grim and daring:
                    But O heart! heart! heart!
                    O the bleeding drops of red,
                    Where on the deck my Captain lies,
                    Fallen cold and dead. …
(from "O Captain! My Captain!"
Walt Whitman)   [tone: mournful]

6.   Sunset and evening star,

And one clear call for me!

And may there be no moaning of the bar

When I put out to sea [die]….

Twilight and evening bell,

And after that the dark! [death]

And may there be no sadness of farewell

When I embark…

(from "Crossing the Bar," Alfred Lord Tennyson)   [tone: somber]

7.   There is no frigate [ship] like a book

To take us lands away,

Nor any coursers [horses] like a page

Of prancing poetry….

(from "There is no frigate like a book,"

Emily Dickinson   [tone: reflective]

8.   It little profits that an idle king,

By this still hearth, among these barren crags,

Matched with an agèd wife, I mete and dole

Unequal laws unto a savage race,

That hoard, and sleep, and feed, and know not me….

(from "Ulysses," Alfred, Lord Tennyson)   [tone: restless]

9.   Nymph, nymph, what are your beads? ….

Give me them. Give me them….

They are better than stars or water,

Better than voices of winds that sing,

Better than any man's fair daughter,

Your green glass beads on a silver ring….

(from "Overheard on a Saltmarsh,"

Harold Munro)   [tone: covetous]

10.   When the green woods laugh with the voice of joy,

And the dimpling stream runs laughing by;

When the air does laugh with our merry wit,

And the green hill laughs with the noise of it….

Come live and be merry, and join with me,

To sing the sweet chorus of "Ha, Ha, He!"

(from "Laughing Song," William Blake)   [tone: happy]

Theme

We read other poems in order to explore the *theme* or main idea of the poem rather than its relevant poetic techniques. When studying these poems, we talk about thematic concerns rather than subjecting them to further study.

"The Fool's Prayer"

This poem by Edward Sill (1841–1887) centers on the crucial need for heartfelt repentance. It tells the story of a prideful king who learns from his jester or fool that he should repent of his sins and beg God for mercy. Seeking some new diversion, the king casually asks his fool to pray:

> The royal feast was done; the King
> Sought some new sport to banish care,
> And to his jester cried: "Sir Fool,
> Kneel now, and make for us a prayer!"

The court is contemptuous of the fool, unaware that he bitterly resents the king's careless attitude to prayer:

> He bowed his head, and bent his knee
> Upon the monarch's silken stool;
> His pleading voice arose: "O, Lord,
> Be merciful to me, a fool!"

Far from diverting the king and his court, the fool's prayer is a heart-felt prayer of repentance and a plea for God's mercy. In the stanzas that follow, the sorrowful jester rehearses his many faults and freely admits he should expect censure rather than mercy. Like all mankind, he needs to be rebuked because he has been thoughtless and unfeeling. All he can do is to plead for the Lord's forgiveness.

The sovereign's reaction to the prayer is recorded in the final stanza. Realizing that the prayer describes his own attitude to wrongdoing, the king sadly leaves the court to plead, like his fool, for God's mercy:

> The room was hushed; in silence rose
> The King, and sought his gardens cool,
> And walked apart, and murmured low,
> "Be merciful to me, a fool!"

Like Shakespeare's fools, this fool is wiser than his master. However, the king's attitude changes from a careless desire for distraction to abject shame. A matter of tone. The poet's *theme* is timeless: Sometimes humility and sincere repentance in others create in the proudest man a sense of humiliation for his own shortcomings.

"A Poison Tree"

This poem by William Blake explores the dangers of harbored resentment towards others:

> I was angry with my friend:
> I told my wrath, my wrath did end.
> I was angry with my foe:
> I told it not, my wrath did grow.

The speaker's concealed anger towards his enemy grows like a cancer within him. The unacknowledged animosity between the two men eventually causes great harm to the speaker's enemy:

> And into my garden stole,
> When the night had veil'd the pole;
> In the morning glad I see
> My foe outstretched beneath the tree.

Blake figuratively explores another universal *theme*: It is wise to reveal resentment towards another person but harmful to suppress it. If we talk over real or imagined insults inflicted on us by others, healing can eventually take place, but if we hide those insults within us, our resentment towards the other person increases until real suffering occurs. Blake develops his theme with an *implied extended metaphor*. The speaker's anger is like a tree that bears bitter fruit, and the apple symbolizes his resentment that grows until it injures the person against whom he holds a grudge. Although we are not told the form of the harm inflicted, we infer that the speaker's enemy suffers greatly.[303]

"The Chimney Sweeper"

One could choose many other poems that address a specific *theme*.[304] As a final example of thematic poetry, we turn to another lyric by William Blake in which the poet bitterly

---

[303] The poem sometimes reminds teenagers of Poe's short story, "The Cask of Amontillado."

[304] Other fine thematic poems include Langston Hughes's "Dream Deferred," Robert Frost's "Stopping by Woods on a Snowy Evening," Thomas Hardy's "The Man He Killed," and Robert Hayden's "Those Winter Sundays."

protests the exploitation of children who used to be employed as chimney sweeps. During the nineteenth century in Britain, the wealthy lived in luxury while the poor lived in squalor. Houses were built with convoluted chimneys that had to be regularly swept free of grime. Poor people's children as young as four or five years old were sold to chimney sweepers to be sent up narrow, crooked chimneys to clean out soot. The little sweeps often suffocated and died or contracted incurable diseases. The speaker in this poem is one of the little chimney sweeps:

> When my mother died I was very young,
> And my father sold me while yet my tongue
> Could scarcely cry "'weep! 'weep! 'weep! 'weep!"
> So your chimneys I sweep, and in soot I sleep.

The following stanzas describe another child, Tom Dacre, whose head is shaved so that he can more easily climb up the tortuous chimneys; the speaker attempts to comfort Tom unaware of the heartbreaking discrepancy between his meager words and the lack of comfort these children, in fact, receive. That night, Tom dreams about thousands of little chimney sweeps who have died and lie in their coffins until an angel frees them from their caskets and sends them to heaven with a blithe assurance:

> And the Angel told Tom, if he'd be a good boy,
> He'd have God for his father, and never want joy.

After the dream, Tom wakes up, gathers his brushes, and sets off happily to do his day's work. The platitudes in the lines quoted above and in the final line most clearly convey Blake's bitterly ironic tone:

> So if all do their duty they need not fear harm.

Like other poems that convey a single idea, this poem conveys a powerful concept—the pitiful plight of little nineteenth-century chimney sweeps.[305]

****

At the end of the poetry unit, I remind students to choose and memorize a poem of approximately twenty-five lines. I used the same procedure as I do for other memorization projects. On an assigned day, students hand in the poem they have memorized then write it

---

[305] Poems such as "The Chimney Sweeper" created outrage over the plight of the poor in eighteenth-century England. The British Parliament eventually passed laws that eliminated the use of young boys as chimney sweeps.

out and submit it for grading. This procedure obviates my having to spend time finding the poem each student has memorized.

I hope freshman students acquire a good understanding of basic poetic conventions so that they can more readily appreciate poetry. Much poetry conveys emotion of some sort; in fact, one could probably find a poem for every emotion or situation it is possible for human beings to feel or experience. Countless other poems convey insights about life or human nature. We may or may not agree with those insights, but reflective poetry provides us with unique opportunities to think about difficult issues or situations we've never previously considered. In the highly technical, instant gratification world in which contemporary young people are growing up, poetry helps them to understand what nostalgia or regret or jealousy feels like. Connotations of words and images and the other elements poets use powerfully convey the human experience in all its variety. Poetry offers the young an opportunity to put aside their smart phones and vicariously experience the full gamut of emotions, experiences, and ideas conveyed in great poetry.

****

Thou wast not born for death, immortal Bird!
No hungry generations tread thee down;
The voice I hear this passing night was heard
In ancient days by emperor and clown:
Perhaps that self-same song that found a path
Through the sad heart of Ruth, when, sick for home,
She stood in tears amid the alien corn…

(from "Ode to a Nightingale" by John Keats)

A nightingale

Test

Throughout the poetry unit, freshman students have studied a vast amount of material from numerous poets who use different poetic devices. This is a lot of information to digest, so I schedule a thorough review before a unit test. A test on the poetry unit is included in the handouts.

Review questions on the poetry unit[306]

1 – 10: Name the poetic device or devices used in the following lines.

> You may choose from these devices. You will need to use some terms more than once: **simile metaphor onomatopoeia alliteration apostrophe personification**

1. He clasps the crag with crooked hands
   [alliteration]

2. The wrinkled sea beneath him crawls
   [personification]

3. And like a thunderbolt he falls
   [simile]

4. O wild West Wind, thou breath of Autumn's being....
   [alliteration, apostrophe]

5. She dwelt among the untrodden ways....
   A violet by the mossy stone
   Half hidden from the eye!
   [metaphor]

6. Thou wast not born for death, immortal Bird!
   [apostrophe]

7. Fair as a star, when only one
   Is shining in the sky.
   [simile]

---

[306] A student booklet that accompanies this teaching guide contains all 9th grade review questions and tests with answers omitted.

Any of these questions could be used for a graded discussion of the poetry unit.

8. Blow, blow thou winter wind.

   Thou art no so unkind

   As man's ingratitude.

   [apostrophe]

9. Tossing their heads in sprightly dance.

   [personification]

10. Hear the sledges [sleighs] with the bells—

    Silver bells!

    What a world of merriment their melody foretells!

    How they tinkle, tinkle, tinkle,

    In the icy air of night!

    While the stars that oversprinkle

    All the heavens, seem to twinkle

    With a crystalline delight….

    [onomatopoeia]

11. Mention two or three questions to ask of any poem.

    [speaker, audience, occasion]

12 – 14: Identify the poetic device or devices that is/are used in these lines:

12. Once upon a midnight dreary, while I pondered, weak and weary…

    While I nodded, nearly napping, suddenly there came a tapping,

    As of someone gently rapping, rapping at my chamber door….

    [mid-line rhyme]

13. Hark, hark!

    Bow-wow.

    The watch-dogs bark!

    [Onomatopoeia]

14. For the moon never beams, without bring me dreams

    Of the beautiful Annabel lee;

    And the stars never rise, but I feel the bright eyes

    Of the beautiful Annabel Lee….

    [internal rhyme; refrain]

15 – 21: Define these terms:

15. onomatopoeia
[words that sound like their meaning]

16. personification
[language that describes or refers to inanimate objects, ideas, or animals as if they were human]

17. meter
[the regular pattern of stressed and unstressed syllables in poetry]

18. free verse
[poetry without a regular meter or rhyme scheme]

19. internal rhyme
[a word in the middle of a poetic line rhymes with a word at the end of the line]

20. tone
[a writer's attitude or approach to his or her subject]

21. apostrophe
[the speaker addresses an inanimate object or a dead person]

22 – 26: Identify the type of imagery in the following lines:

22. I will arise and go now, and go to Innisfree,
   And a small cabin build there, of clay and wattles [twigs] made:
   Nine bean-rows will I have there, a hive for the honeybee….
   [visual]

23. While I nodded, nearly napping, suddenly there came a tapping,
   As of someone gently rapping, rapping at my chamber door….
   [auditory]

24. Little Lamb, who made thee? …
   Gave thee life, and bid thee feed…
   Gave thee clothing of delight,
   Softest clothing, woolly, bright….
   [tactile]

25. When roasted crabs hiss in the bowl,
    Then nightly sings the staring owl,
    "Tu-whit, tu-who"
    A merry note….
    [auditory]

26. Couched in his kennel, like a log,
    With paws of silver sleeps the dog;
    From their shadowy cote [shelter] the white breasts peep
    Of doves in a silver-feathered sleep….
    [visual]

Unit VI

Final Class Activities

In order to prepare for semester exams, I review with students elements of fiction and poetry we studied during the year, defining each element and discussing its contribution to the overall meaning of a piece of literature. Here is a list of literary elements they should by now be familiar with. I distribute the following list that we review during the last days of class:

I. Elements of fiction

1. Plot

    Parts of a plot's structure: exposition, rising action, turning point, climax, falling action, dénouement

2. Conflict

    external conflicts:

    a character's struggle with some aspect of the natural world

    a character's struggle with another character or antagonist

    a character's struggle with a community or society at large

    internal conflict: a character's struggle with himself/herself

3. Characterization

    direct characterization is stated

    indirect characterization is implied

    A character's personality is implied via speech, actions, thoughts, appearance, or other characters' reactions to him or her.

4. Purposes of setting

    to provide background for a story

    to provide conflict

    to reveal a person's character

    to evoke a specific atmosphere or mood

5. Point of view

    Three basic points of view:

    third-person omniscient: Events are related by an all-knowing narrator who is outside the story and knows the thoughts and feelings of all or several characters.

third-person limited: Events are related by a narrator who is outside the story but limits the perspective to one character.

first-person: Events are related from one person's perspective, the "I" narrator who participates in the events; a first-person perspective raises the question of the narrator's reliability.

6. Theme: the main idea the story reveals, usually an insight about human behavior. A story's theme should not be confused with its plot.

>   Two types of theme:
>
>   **explicit** or stated
>
>   **implicit** or inferred, which is more common in literature

7. Tone

>   Three types of irony:
>
>   **verbal irony** is spoken
>
>   **dramatic irony** occurs when the reader or audience knows something of which at least one character is unaware
>
>   **situational irony** occurs when events occur that are unexpected, or our expectations are reversed

II. Elements of poetry

1. Imagery: visual, auditory, olfactory, gustatory, and tactile
2. Similes and metaphors

>   Similes use comparative words; metaphors do not.
>
>   **implied metaphors** are not stated.
>
>   **extended metaphors** last for several lines of a story or poem.

3. Personification: something inanimate is referred to or described as if it were living.
4. Apostrophe: someone addresses an inanimate object or a dead person.
5. Rhythm: the regular beat of stressed and unstressed syllables in poetry

>   Free verse: poetry that has no regular meter or rhyme scheme

6. Rhyme:

>   **approximate rhyme:** slant or inexact rhyme
>
>   **internal rhyme:** words in the middle and the end of a poetic line rhyme

7. Onomatopoeia: words that sound like their meaning
8. Alliteration: repeated consonant sounds
9. Tone: the writer's attitude or approach to his or his subject

In addition to a comprehensive review, I distribute a study guide several days before exams. It lists all literary works studied during the semester as well as main aspects of each piece that we discussed, and literary terms students should know. A detailed study guide ensures that each student is aware of the content that may be covered on the exam, and it gives students a methodology for exam preparation.

****

Before the end of the course, I remind students to select two books to read from the summer reading list. They write reports on two novels during the first week of the next academic year.

As they shuffle out of the classroom with final exams approaching, I hear a few of them furtively wondering who's taken notes all year!

We all passed!

Glossary of Literary Terms

ALLEGORY A story in which the characters, settings, and places have a secondary meaning. e.g. Bunyan's *Pilgrim's Progress,* Orwell's *Animal Farm.*

ALLITERATION Repeated consonant sounds. e. g. *die distant dawn.* See consonance.

ALLUSION A reference to a something or someone that is historical, literary, biblical, mythological, or scientific and that is recognized by the reader.

AMBIGUITY The expression of an idea in such a way that the writer deliberately suggests several meanings.

ANALOGY A comparison.

ANAPEST A poetic foot that consists of two unaccented syllables followed by one accented syllable.

ANAPESTIC METER Meter that consists of feet that have two unaccented syllables followed by one accented syllable.
e.g. "The Assyrian came down like the wolf on the fold," Lord Byron.

ANECDOTE A brief story.

ANTAGONIST A person or force that opposes the protagonist.

ANTITHESIS A contrast.

APOSTROPHE A figure of speech in which a character addresses an inanimate object or a non-living person.
e.g. "Bright star, would I were steadfast as thou art!" John Keats.

APPROXIMATE RHYME Inexact or slant rhyme.

ASIDE An actor's brief, private comments intended for the audience that other characters do not hear.

ASSONANCE Repeated vowel sounds.

ATMOSPHERE Mood.

BALLAD A narrative poem written to be sung that includes a refrain. It has a strong rhythm and often includes supernatural or mysterious elements.

BLANK VERSE Unrhymed iambic pentameter or meter that has five feet that consist of one unstressed syllable followed by one stressed syllable.

CADENCE The rhythmical flow of sounds in poetry or prose.

CAESURA A mid-line pause in a line of poetry.

CATALOG A list included in a literary work.

CHARACTER
A dynamic character: a person who changes during the course of the story.
A flat character: a person who has one distinguishing personality trait.
A foil character: a minor character who contrasts with the protagonist.
A round character: a person who has many personality traits.
A static character: a person who does not change during the course of a story.

CHARACTERIZATION The methods used to develop a character.
Direct characterization occurs when the writer tells the reader a person's character traits.
Indirect characterization occurs when the reader is allowed to infer those traits via a character's speech, actions, thoughts, appearance, or other characters' reactions to him or her.

CLICHÉ An expression that is overused and stale.

CLIMAX See plot.

CONFLICT A struggle between opposing forces in a literary work.

CONNOTATION The suggested or associated meaning of a word.

COUPLET Two lines of poetry that rhyme.

DACTYL A poetic foot that contains one accented syllable followed by two unaccented syllables.

DACTYLIC METER Meter that consists of feet that have one accented syllable followed by two unaccented syllables.

> e.g. "Half a league, half a league, half a league onward," Alfred, Lord Tennyson.

DECORUM PRINCIPLE In drama, all violence should occur off stage and should be reported to the audience by a messenger.

DENOTATION The literal or dictionary definition of a word.

DÉNOUEMENT See plot.

DEUS EX MACHINA (god from the machine) An improbable ending to a story.

> e.g. "The Pit and the Pendulum," Edgar Allan Poe. *War of the Worlds,* H. G. Wells.

DIALECT Speech that is characteristic of a certain region of a country.

DIALOGUE Conversation between two or more characters in a literary work.

DICTION An author's choice of words. Diction can be formal or informal, ornate or plain, abstract or concrete. It can also be colloquial.

DIDACTIC WRITING Writing that is designed to teach.

DIRECT CHARACTERIZATION See characterization.

DRAMATIC IRONY See irony.

DYNAMIC CHARACTER See character.

ELEGY A poem that mourns the death of someone.

> e.g. "Elegy Written in a Country Churchyard," Thomas Gray

ELIZABETHAN (Shakespearean) SONNET A fourteen-line poem that consists of three quatrains and a couplet.

> e.g. That time of year thou may'st in me behold, William Shakespeare.

END RHYME Rhyme that occurs at the ends of lines of poetry.

END-STOPPED LINE A line of poetry that ends with a mark of punctuation

ENJAMBMENT (run-on line) A line of poetry that ends with no punctuation.

EPIC A lengthy narrative poem that describes the deeds of a hero who embodies the values of his culture.
> e.g. the *Iliad* and the *Odyssey*, Homer.

EPIC SIMILE A lengthy simile.

EPIGRAM A brief, witty saying that is often critical of someone or something.
> e.g. "I am not young enough to know everything," Oscar Wilde.

EPITHET A descriptive phrase used in place of a name in order to characterize someone or something.
> e.g. "That man skilled in all ways of contending," Homer referring to Odysseus.

EUPHONY Pleasant sounding words.

EXPOSITION See plot.

EXTENDED (sustained) APOSTROPHE An apostrophe that lasts throughout several lines.

EXTENDED (sustained) METAPHOR A metaphor that lasts throughout several lines.

EXTENDED (sustained) SIMILE A simile that lasts throughout several lines.

FABLE A short story usually involving animals with a moral.
> e.g. Aesop's *Fables*.

FALLING ACTION See plot.

FIGURATIVE LANGUAGE Language that uses figures of speech or non-literal language.

FIGURE OF SPEECH Non-literal language.

FLASHBACK Prose that describes events that occurred in the past.

FLAT CHARACTER See character.

FOIL CHARACTER See character.

FOOT A metrical unit of poetry that contains one or more accented syllables and usually one or more unaccented syllables. There are several different types of feet in poetry:

Anapest Two unstressed syllables followed by one stressed syllable.
Dactyl One stressed syllable followed by two unstressed syllables.
Iamb One unstressed syllable followed by one stressed syllable.
Spondee Two stressed syllables.
Trochee One stressed syllable followed by one unstressed syllable.

FORESHADOWING Hints about what will happen later in the story.

FRAME NARRATIVE An outer framework within which characters tell stories.
e.g. "The Story-Teller," Saki.

FREE VERSE Poetry without regular meter or rhyme scheme.

GENRE A type of literature such as poetry, novel, or drama.

HAIKU A three-line poem containing lines of five, seven, and five syllables respectively.

HYPERBOLE (Overstatement) A figure of speech that uses exaggeration.

IAMB One unstressed syllable followed by one stressed syllable.

IAMBIC PENTAMETER (blank verse) A line of poetry that has five feet that consist of one unaccented syllable followed by one accented syllable.
e.g. "Shall I compare thee to a summer's day?" William Shakespeare.

IMAGE / IMAGERY A word or words that appeal to the senses; can be visual (sight), auditory (hearing), gustatory (taste), olfactory (smell), tactile (touch), or kinesthetic (movement).

IMPERATIVE A command.

INDIRECT CHARACTERIZATION See characterization.

INEXACT RHYME Approximate or slant rhyme.

IN MEDIAS RES (in the middle of things) A story that begins in the middle of critical events and uses flashback to tell what happened earlier.

e.g. the *Iliad* and the *Odyssey*, Homer.

INTERNAL RHYME A word in the middle of a poetic line that rhymes with a word at the end of the line.

INVERSION The normal word order of a sentence (subject, verb, and object) is inverted.

INVOCATION An appeal to a muse to inspire the writer.
e.g. the *Iliad* and the *Odyssey*, Homer.

IRONY A discrepancy between what is said and what is meant.

Dramatic irony: A discrepancy between what a character says and what the reader knows to be true.
Situational irony: A discrepancy between what the reader expects to happen and what actually happens.
Verbal irony: A discrepancy between what a character says and what he or she means.

ITALIAN (Petrarchan) SONNET A fourteen-line poem that consists of an octave (8 lines) and a sestet (6 lines).
e.g. "On First Looking into Chapman's Homer," John Keats.

LIMERICK A nonsense poem consisting of five lines of anapestic meter that rhymes *aabba*.

LYRIC A short poem that expresses an emotion or emotions.

METAPHOR A comparison that does not use the comparative words *like* or *as*.
Direct metaphor: The comparison is explicitly stated.
Implied metaphor: The comparison is not explicitly stated.
Extended metaphor: A comparison that is developed throughout several lines.

METER A regular pattern of stressed and unstressed syllables in poetry.

MONOLOGUE A lengthy speech given by one character.

MONOMETER A line of poetry consisting of one foot.

MOOD Atmosphere; the feeling one gets from reading a passage.

MOTIF A recurring idea in a literary work.

NARRATOR The speaker or the person who tells a story.

OCTAVE An eight-line section of an Italian or Petrarchan sonnet; an eight-line stanza.

ODE A formal poem on a serious subject.
> e.g. "Ode to a Nightingale" by John Keats.

ONOMATOPOEIA Words that sound like their meaning. e.g. *swish, hum, hiss.*

ORAL TRADITION The passing of literature or songs from one generation to the next by word of mouth.

OVERSTATEMENT (Hyperbole) A figure of speech that uses exaggeration.

PARADOX A seemingly contradictory statement that is, in fact, true.
> e.g. "For to me, to live *is* Christ, and to die *is* gain." Phil. 1:21.

PARALLELISM Repetition of words, phrases, or clauses using the same syntax.

PARAPHRASE To rewrite a sentence or passage in one's own words.

PATTERN POEM An emblematic poem or a poem with a shape that suggests its subject.
> e.g. "A Christmas Tree," William Burford. "Swan and Shadow," John Hollander.

PENTAMETER A line of poetry that consists of five feet.

PERSONA The role or character a writer assumes; synonymous with the speaker.

PERSONIFICATION A writer describes or refers to something inanimate as if it were living.
> e.g. "Slowly, silently, now the moon / Walks the night in her silver shoon [shoes]," Walter de La Mare.

PERSPECTIVE See point of view.

PETRARCHAN SONNET A fourteen-line poem that consists of an octave (eight lines) and a sestet (six lines).
> e.g. "On First Looking into Chapman's Homer," John Keats.

PLOT The sequence of events in a literary work that consists of several parts:

exposition: The basic situation.

rising action: Complications develop.

turning point: The hero or heroine's reversal of fortune. In comedy, his or her fortunes begin to be happy; in tragedy, his or her fortunes begin to worsen irrevocably.

climax Moment of most intense emotion

falling action Resolution of conflicts begins to occur.

dénouement All conflicts are resolved happily or unhappily.

POINT OF VIEW The perspective from which a story is written. There are several basic perspectives:

1st person: An author tells the story from the perspective of one character who is a character in the story and uses the first person. The narrator may or may not be reliable.

3rd person limited: An author limits the reader to knowing the thoughts and feelings of one character who tells the story using the third person.

3rd person omniscient: The story is told by an all-knowing author who allows us to know the thoughts and feelings of several characters who use the third person.

PROTAGONIST The main character in a literary work.

PUN A play on words.

e.g. ...*all* that I live by is with the *awl*.

Now is it *Rome* indeed, and *room* enough. (*Julius Caesar*, I.ii.24,156.)

QUATRAIN A four-line section of an Elizabethan or Shakespearean sonnet; a four-line stanza.

REFRAIN A repeated line or group of lines within a poem.

RHETORICAL QUESTION A question that does not require an answer.

RHYME The repetition of sounds in poetry at the end of the line or mid-line. See approximate rhyme and internal rhyme.

RHYTHM The regular beat of stressed and unstressed syllables in poetry or prose.

RISING ACTION See plot.

RITE OF PASSAGE A ceremony or event that marks a significant transition or maturing experience in someone's life.
"Through the Tunnel, Doris Lessing. "The Bridge," Nicolai Chukovski.

ROUND CHARACTER See character.

RUN-ON LINE (enjambment) A line of poetry that ends with no punctuation.

SARCASM Speech that is belittling or mean.

SATIRE Writing that uses humor or wit to expose folly or vice in order to effect reform or change.
e.g. Orwell's *Animal Farm*.

SESTET A six-line section of an Italian or Petrarchan sonnet; a six-line stanza.

SETTING The time and place of a literary work.

SHAKESPEAREAN (Elizabethan) SONNET A fourteen-line poem that consists of three quatrains and a couplet.
e.g. "That time of year thou may'st in me behold," William Shakespeare.

SIMILE A comparison that uses comparative words such as *like* or *as*.

SITUATIONAL IRONY See irony.

SLANT RHYME Inexact or approximate rhyme.

SOLILOQUY A long speech delivered by the protagonist, who is usually alone on stage, which reveals his thoughts and feelings.

SONNET A fourteen-line poem. See Elizabethan (Shakespearean) sonnet and Italian (Petrarchan) sonnet.

STANZA A group of lines in a poem that form a single unit.

STATIC CHARACTER See character.

STEREOTYPE A fixed concept of a person or idea.

      e.g. Clover, the motherly type; Benjamin, the hardened cynic in *Animal Farm*.

STRUCTURE Organization of a piece of writing.

STYLE The particular way a writer uses words to convey ideas.

SUMMARY A brief but comprehensive version of a longer work.

SURPRISE ENDING An ending that is unexpected.

SYMBOL A person, place, thing, or event that represents an abstract idea.

SYNTAX Sentence structure.

TALL TALE An extremely exaggerated, amusing story.

      e.g. American legends about Paul Bunyan.

THEME(S) The main idea or ideas conveyed by a literary work.

TONE A writer's attitude to his or her subject.

TURNING POINT See plot.

VERBAL IRONY See irony.

Index

Selected bibliography

Many fine editions of literary works are available. This bibliography includes editions of the *Odyssey, Romeo and Juliet*, and the novels discussed in this teaching guide although I do not always cite from a specific edition of a work due to copyright law. It does not include short stories or short poems since both genres can be readily accessed via the internet or literature anthologies. I also include works that have most profoundly impacted my studies as well as books that may be of interest to literature teachers.

Bloom, Allan. *The Closing of the American Mind.* New York: Simon & Schuster, 1987.

Bloom, Harold. *Shakespeare: The Invention of the Human.* New York: Penguin Putnam, 1998.

——, *The Western Canon: The Books and School of the Ages.* New York: Harcourt Brace, 1994.

Bradbury, Malcolm, General Editor. *The Atlas of Literature.* New York: Stewart, Tabori & Chang, 1998.

Bradbury, Ray. *Fahrenheit 451.* New York: Ballantine, 1991.

Cowan, Louise and Os Guinness. *Invitation to the Classics.* Grand Rapids, MI: Baker Books, 1998.

Highet, Gilbert. *The Art of Teaching.* New York: Vintage Books, 1958.

Homer. *Odyssey.* Translated by Robert Fitzgerald. New York: Anchor Press, 1963.

Leithart, Peter J. *Heroes of the City of Man: A Christian Guide to Select Ancient Literature.* Moscow, ID: Canon Press, 1999.

McCallum, Elizabeth and Jane Scott. Second edition. *The Book Tree: A Christian Reference for Children's Literature.* Moscow, ID: Canon Press, 2008.

Orwell, George. *Animal Farm.* New York: Signet, 1996.

Ryken, Leland. *Homer's The Odyssey.* Wheaton, IL: Crossway, 2013.

——, *Realms of Gold: The Classics in Christian Perspective.* Wheaton, IL: Harold Shaw, 1991.

Shakespeare, William. *Romeo and Juliet.* Folger Shakespeare Library. Edited by Barbara A. Mowat and Paul Werstine. New York: Washington Square Press, 1992.

Veith, Gene Edward, Jr. *Reading Between the Lines: A Christian Guide to Literature.* Wheaton, IL: Crossway, 1990.

Specific class assignments

Essays

Book reports throughout the year

Account for the tragic ending of "To Build a Fire"

Irony in "The Necklace"

Topics in *Fahrenheit 451*

Topics in *Animal Farm*

Aspects of Shakespeare's life based on the A & E video

Human error versus coincidence in *Romeo and Juliet*

Topics in the *Odyssey*

Book report posters

Plot diagram

Plot diagram of "Through the Tunnel"

Plot diagram of *Romeo and Juliet*

Memorization

Soliloquy in *Romeo and Juliet*

Poem of twenty-five lines

List of general teaching techniques

- Write major discussion points on the board before class.
- Use humor in the classroom.
- Vary teaching methods. Do not become predictable but strive to achieve variety when planning instruction.
- Repeat, repeat, repeat important information throughout the school year.
- Seize the teachable moment: Depart from your lesson plan to discuss a relevant subject or assign a brief writing task that arises from students' comments.
- Write and define unfamiliar literary terms on the board.
- After giving an essay assignment, discuss the topic and write students' ideas on the board as the class takes notes.
- Ensure that everyone is taking notes by checking students' notebooks as you lecture.
- Periodically, collect and grade notebooks.
- In order to engage everyone's attention, ask questions of an entire class not an individual student. Then ask one person to respond.
- Train students to ask questions about all literature you teach.
- Train students to make inferences about literature.
- Train students to realize that literature does not always answer questions. It raises them.
- In general, students should read short stories and novels before class discussion. Read epics, lyric poetry, and plays with the class.
- Ensure that students have the same edition of a novel or play in order to facilitate discussion.
- When reading a play, allow students to act a key scene in front of the rest of the class.
- Do not sit as you lecture. Move around the classroom.
- Divide the class into small groups to discuss and take notes on a topic.
- Occasionally, ask students to silently read a poem or prose passage then write a short personal reaction to it.
- Ask a student to read a key passage from a literary work.
- Place interesting material related to literature on the classroom walls.
- Challenge students to work to their best ability.
- Make literature enjoyable and never lose control of the class!

9th grade Reading List[307]

- Choose books you have not previously read.
- Choose books by different authors.
- With the teacher's approval, you may choose different books by an author on this list.

Aldrich, Bess Streeter, *A Lantern in Her Hand*

—, *A White Bird Flying*

Bunyan, John, *The Pilgrim's Progress*

Colson, Charles, *Gideon's Torch*

Conrad, Joseph, *Lord Jim*

Crane, Stephen, *The Red Badge of Courage*

Defoe, Daniel, *The Adventures of Robinson Crusoe*

Dickens, Charles, *A Christmas Carol*

Douglas, Lloyd, *The Robe*

Doyle, Sir Arthur Conan, *The Memoirs of Sherlock Holmes* or any other short story collection

Dumas, Alexandre, *The Count of Monte-Cristo*

—, *The Three Musketeers*

du Maurier, Daphne, *Frenchman's Creek*

—, *Jamaica Inn*

—, *My Cousin Rachel*

—, *Rebecca*

Forester, C. S., *Hornblower and the Atropos*

—, *The Last Nine Days of the Bismarck*

—, *Lieutenant Hornblower*

Frank, Anne, *Anne Frank: The Diary of a Young Girl*

Hamilton, Edith. *Mythology: Timeless Tales of Gods and Heroes*

Henry, O. *The Best Short Stories of O. Henry*

Herriot, James, *All Creatures Great and Small*

Hickam, Homer H. Jr., *Rocket Boys*

Hilton, James, *Goodbye, Mr. Chips*

Kipling, Rudyard, *Captains Courageous*

Lewis, C. S., *Out of the Silent Planet*

---

[307] I have read and approve of these books for teenage readers. The reading list excludes biographies and works studied during the school year.

—, *Perelandra*

—, *That Hideous Strength*

London, Jack, *The Call of the Wild*

—, *White Fang*

MacDonald, George, *The Fisherman's Lady*

—, *The Marquis' Secret*

MacLean, Alistair, *The Guns of Navarone*

—, *Ice Station Zebra*

—, *Night Without End*

Marshall, Catherine, *Christy*

—, *Julie*

Musser, Elizabeth, *The Swan House*

—, *The Sweetest Thing*

—, *Words Unspoken*

Orczy, Baroness Emma, *The League of the Scarlet Pimpernel*

—, *The Scarlet Pimpernel*

Plaidy, Jean, *Meg Roper*

Poe, Edgar Allan, *Tales of Mystery and Imagination* or any other short story collection

Raymond, Grace, *How They Kept the Faith: A Tale of the Huguenots of Languedoc*

Sabatini, Rafael, *Captain Blood*

—, *Scaramouche*

Schaefer, Jack, *Shane*

Smith, Dodie, *I Capture the Castle*

Steinbeck, John. *The Pearl*

Stevenson, R. L. *The Strange Case of Dr. Jekyll and Mr. Hyde*

ten Boom, Corrie, *The Hiding Place*

Thurber, James, *My Life and Hard Times*

—, *The Thurber Carnival*

Tolkien, J. R.R., *The Hobbit*

—, *The Fellowship of the Ring*

—, *The Return of the Ring*

—, *The Two Towers*

Twain, Mark, *A Connecticut Yankee in King Arthur's Court*

—, *The Prince and the Pauper*

Verne, Jules, *Around the Earth in Eighty Days*

—, *A Journey to the Center of the Earth*

—, *Twenty Thousand Leagues Under the Sea*
Wallace, Lew, *Ben-Hur: A Tale of the Christ*
Weatherby, W. J., *Chariots of Fire*
Wells, H. G., *The Invisible Man*
—, *The Time Machine*
—, *The War of the Worlds*
West, Jessamyn, *Cress Delahanty*

*A classic is a book that has never exhausted all it has to say
to its readers.*

Italo Calvino

Basic writing rules

- Avoid self-reference.
- Use 3rd person pronouns. Avoid 1st and 2nd person pronouns
- Every pronoun should have a clear antecedent.
- Maintain verb tense consistency.
- Use concrete verbs and nouns.
- Use modifiers sparingly. Avoid *very, quite,* and *rather.*
- Adopt formal usage. Avoid slang, clichés, and abbreviations.
- Know your audience: Eliminate needless explanation and identification.
- Subordinate less important ideas using complex sentences.
- Emphasize with word placement: Place key words at the beginning or end of a sentence.
- Do not emphasize by underlining or using exclamation points.
- Vary the syntax: Do not start every sentence with its subject.
- Be succinct.

Each essay you write is a reflection of you; your writing reveals much about your personality and your attitude to your school work. Take pride in your work.

Outline of an essay

I. Organization

An essay must include the following sections:

- Introduction
    - one short paragraph that ends with a main idea or thesis that is developed throughout the essay
- Body
    - several long paragraphs each of which discusses an aspect of the thesis
    - paragraphs should begin with a topic sentence
- Conclusion
    - a brief paragraph that adds closure to the essay but does not repeat the thesis

II. Adequate development

Each body paragraph must develop or explore one aspect of the thesis at some length.

Length of essay: approximately 2 pages.

Diagram of a well-written essay

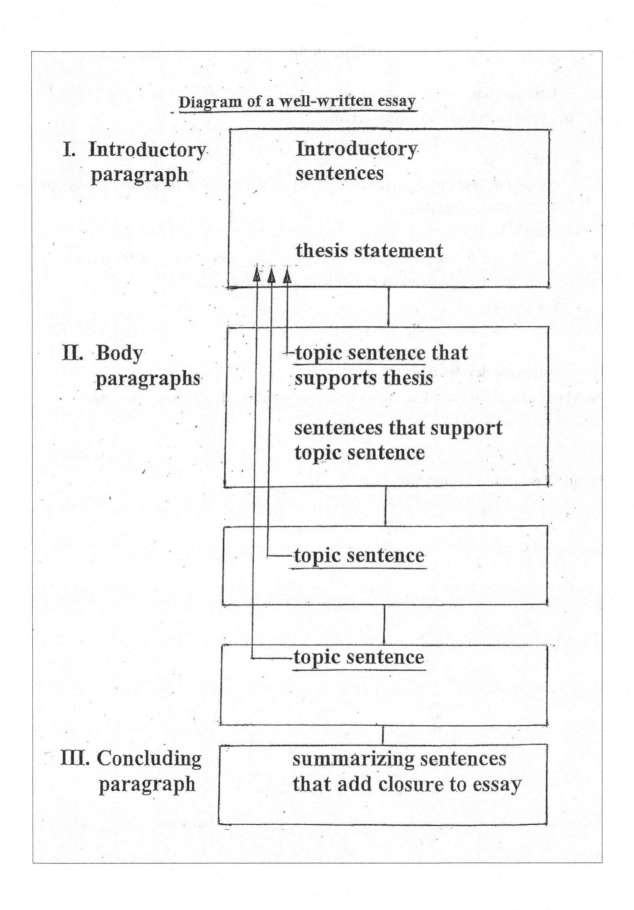

I. Introductory paragraph — Introductory sentences / thesis statement

II. Body paragraphs — topic sentence that supports thesis / sentences that support topic sentence / topic sentence / topic sentence

III. Concluding paragraph — summarizing sentences that add closure to essay

Guidelines for writing book reports

- A book report is well-organized, well-developed essay that expresses your opinions about a book.
- It discusses key aspects of the book but does not give away surprises or information that would spoil the book for another reader.
- It provides copious examples that support your comments.
- It helps the reader decide whether or not to read the book.

Take detailed notes and refer to them as you write the report.

Introduction: The introduction should include the title, author, and thesis; it should engage the reader's attention.

> Example: *Animal Farm* by George Orwell is an amusing allegory of early twentieth-century Russian history. More importantly, it is a warning about the dangers of all totalitarian governments.

Body: The body of your report should consist of three or four paragraphs that discuss different aspects of the thesis.

Conclusion: The last paragraph may be brief but should include a final statement about your opinion of the book's value. Do not repeat your thesis statement.

DO NOT PROVIDE A PLOT SUMMARY OF THE BOOK.

The man who does not read has no advantage over the man who cannot read.

Mark Twain

Book report topics to discuss

Here are some ideas designed to help you think about and organize your ideas about each topic listed:

- **Characterization**: You were able to relate well to either the main character or several characters. Although you did not necessarily agree with the characters, you could, to some extent, understand their situation, motivation, thoughts, and actions. You came to know them as you know people in real life.

- **Theme**: You were intrigued by the central idea the novel explored, which was something you had not previously thought about or knew anything about.

- **Conflict**: The conflicts among the characters were realistic and well-developed. You enjoyed following the main character's inner conflict.

- **Setting**: The time and place in which the book was set were believable and well described. You felt as if you were experiencing events with the characters.

- **Ending**: The ending was unpredictable and satisfying. It may have been sad or ambiguous, but it was the only possible ending for that particular book, given the characters and their circumstances. The ending was artistically prepared for so that you were not unduly surprised or shocked by it.

- **Knowledge or insights gained**: The book taught you something new about life, people, and/or unfamiliar places.

This is not a definitive list. You could discuss other topics that are meaningful to you after reading a particular book. A novel can transport you into a time period, culture, or situation different from any you have previously experienced. It can broaden your horizons and provide you with new information about other people and the ways they deal with situations, conflicts, or relationships that were previously unfamiliar to you.

This is how you prepare to write about a book you have read:

- Decide on your topic or topics.
- Take copious notes.
- Organize your notes into meaningful sections.
- Bring the book and your notes to class on the day you write your report.

Words and expressions to avoid when you write

stale qualifiers:

very

really

rather

nice

great

awesome

wonderful

interesting

slang and jargon:

cool or neat (as in "a cool or a neat idea")

far out

tight (as in a close relationship)

clichés or trite expressions:

old as the hills

strong as an ox

sharp as a tack

flat as a pancake

fat as a pig

dead as a doornail

soft as a kitten

sweet as honey

padding

in my opinion, I think

at this point in time

last but not least

due to the fact that

the reason why is that

because of the fact that

I call your attention to the fact that

I was unaware of the fact that

Dickens (or any other writer) did a good job of. . .. implies the writer is a better judge of good prose than Dickens (or any other writer)

Abbreviations for common errors

cs	comma splice
frag	fragment
r-on	run-on
s/vb agr	subject/verb agreement
pro/ant agr	pronoun/antecedent agreement
pro ref	pronoun reference
t	tense
sp	spelling
p	punctuation
cap	use a capital letter
lc	use lower case; no capital letter
ww	wrong word
awk	awkward wording
il	illegible
R	rewrite
X	wrong
ONW	omit needless words[307]

[308] *The Elements of Style* by William Strunk, Jr. and E. B. White (New York: Person, 2000), 23.

Short Story Unit topics

"Through the Tunnel"
- elements of the plot
- contrasted settings
- internal conflict
- rite of passage theme

"To Build a Fire"
- setting
- contrasts between man and dog
- reasons for the man's failure to survive

"Top Man"
- setting
- antagonist
- differences in characters of Nace and Osborn
- symbolism of the axe
- the "top man"

"Antaeus"
- significance of allusion in the title
- setting
- contrast between T.J. and city boys
- T.J.'s leadership ability
- antagonists

"A Christmas Memory"
- methods of characterization
- antagonists
- symbolism of the kites

"Thank you, M'am"
- methods of characterization

"The Storm"
- atmosphere
- clues that point to the murderer

"The Story-Teller"
- frame narrative
- respective merits of the two storytellers
- theme

"Young Ladies Don't Slay Dragons"
- reversals that contribute to the satire

"The Bridge"
- rite of passage
- methods of characterization
- explicit theme

"The Ransom of Red Chief"
- examples of irony

"The Necklace"
- characterization of M. and Mme. Loisel
- symbolism
- multiple ironies
- theme

"The Sniper"
- historical background
- situational irony

"The Open Window"
- point of view
- characterization

"The Cask of Amontillado"
- point of view/ unreliable narrator
- multiple ironies
- audience

"The Hat"
- point of view

Student essay on parallels between *Fahrenheit 451* and our contemporary world

In his dystopian novel *Fahrenheit 451*, Ray Bradbury depicts aspects of life that are alarmingly similar to the lives of contemporary Americans.

Lack of an intellectual life is one similarity that today's Americans share with the inhabitants of Bradbury's futuristic world. In the novel, books and reading are banned; people spend their leisure hours watching mindless interactive television programs. The addiction results in poor attention span, bad eyesight, and general apathy. Conversation revolves around the televised characters' antics, and viewers become brainwashed by four walls of television in every home that inform citizens of governmental regulations. We have similar conditions in America today. Few people read for pleasure any more but prefer to spend their evening hours watching television programs or surfing the net. Like the people in Bradbury's world, the destruction of intellectual life has destroyed the imaginations and mental ability of countless American citizens.

Education in this country shares ominous similarities with Bradbury's fictional world. Schools in Bradbury's book are controlled by government officials so that students' understanding of important issues such as past history or moral values is strictly monitored; rigorous discussion and the exchange of ideas, questions, opinions are non-existent. Many of our schools' methodologies have become increasingly similar to those referred to in *Fahrenheit 451*.

Most importantly, parenting in Bradbury's world bears a striking resemblance to family values in some contemporary American homes. Women in *Fahrenheit 451* regard children as an inconvenience to be avoided by subjecting their offspring to endless television watching and government sponsored schooling.

Fahrenheit 451 carries an ominous warning about the appalling dangers of subjecting the citizens of any country to totalitarian government control. America's teenagers need to be informed about this inherent danger so that they avoid indoctrination and instead become well-informed, intelligent citizens of this great country.

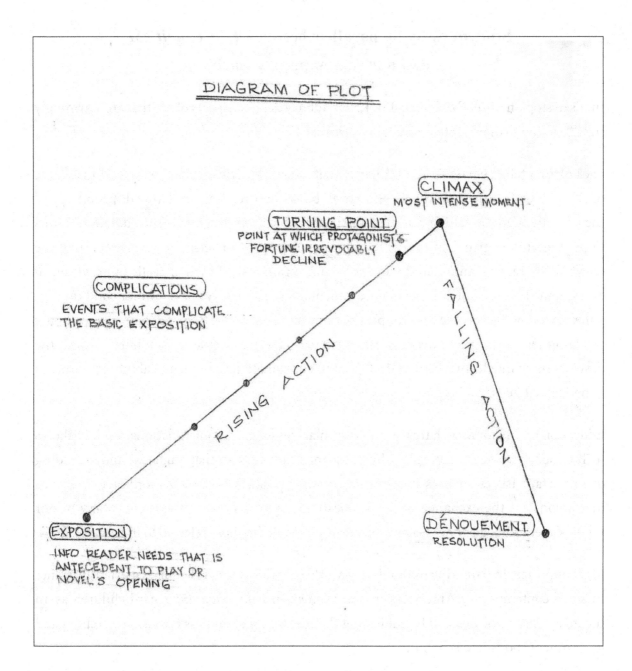

DIAGRAM OF PLOT

CLIMAX
MOST INTENSE MOMENT

TURNING POINT
POINT AT WHICH PROTAGONIST'S
FORTUNE IRREVOCABLY
DECLINE

COMPLICATIONS
EVENTS THAT COMPLICATE
THE BASIC EXPOSITION

RISING ACTION

FALLING ACTION

EXPOSITION
INFO READER NEEDS THAT IS
ANTECEDENT TO PLAY OR
NOVEL'S OPENING

DÉNOUEMENT
RESOLUTION

Student essay on human error in *Romeo and Juliet*

From the beginning of Shakespeare's play, it seems that the lovers' tragic destiny is fated. The feud between the Capulets and Montagues ends with their children's tragic deaths. Although the outcome is the result of both coincidence and human error, people's mistakes play the most significant role. Prince Escalus's irresponsibility, Romeo's rashness, Friar Laurence's dishonesty, and above all the two families' hateful feuding contribute to the deaths of the lovers.

For years, the Prince has ignored the feuding families. When arguments and fights break out, the Prince merely issues threats and warnings. In the end, he regrets not doing more to stop the feuding and realizes that he played a vital role in Romeo and Juliet's deaths.

Romeo's rash thinking and actions are continually seen throughout the play. It is Romeo's impatience that spurs him on to marry Juliet so rapidly. He fails to consider the consequences of killing Tybalt. Upon hearing of Juliet's supposed death, he immediately plans to take his own life. Finally, on seeing Juliet's body in the tomb, he does not delay before drinking the poison.

Friar Laurence certainly plays a major part in this tragedy. When Romeo and Juliet arrive at his cell to get married, he considers their union a good way to end the feud. In this sense, his intention is good, but his methods are deceptive. He does not encourage the young people to be honest with their parents. When Romeo is banished, it is the Friar's plan to fake Juliet's death that brings the play to its tragic climax.

More than any other factor however, the hatred that exists between the feuding families results in an outcome far costlier than any punishment that could be meted out by the Prince. Both families lose their most precious possession, their children.

In all four cases, the errors committed are fatal errors of judgment. If any of these people had acted with more wisdom and integrity, the outcome could have been averted. If Prince Escalus had punished the two families for their endless feuding, their quarreling would perhaps have ended. If Romeo had thought before he acted, he might have realized the consequences of his rash acts. If the Friar had encouraged the lovers to be honest, their marriage may have ended their parents' feud. Above all, Lord Montague and Lord Capulet should have taken effective steps to end the vicious feud. All these people had control over the choices they made, but they failed to prevent the tragic results. Their errors cost the lives of Shakespeare's "star-crossed" lovers.

Characters in the *Odyssey*

Ithaca
Penelope, Odysseus's wife

Telemachus, Odysseus's son

Laertes, Odysseus's father

Antinous, Penelope's leading suitor

Eurycleia, Odysseus's old nurse

Eumaeus, Odysseus's swineherd

Philoeteus, Odysseus's cowherd

Argo, Odysseus's dog

Telemachus's travels
Menelaus, king of Sparta and brother of Agamemnon

Helen, wife of Menelaus

Nestor, king of Pylos

Odysseus's travels
Alcinous, king of Phaeacia and Nausicaa's father

Nausicaa, Alcinous's daughter

Calypso, a goddess who lives on the island of Ogygia

Sirens, nymphs whose singing is irresistible

Cyclopes, a race of one-eyed monsters

Polyphemus, the one-eyed Cyclops blinded by Odysseus; the son of Poseidon

Charybdis, a female monster that forms a whirlpool

Scylla, a female monster with six serpent heads

Circe, a witch who turns men into pigs

Teiresias, the blind prophet of Thebes

The gods
Zeus, the most powerful god

Athena, Zeus's favorite daughter and goddess of wisdom, crafts, and warfare

Hermes, the messenger god

Poseidon, the god of the sea

Helios, the sun god

Aeolus, the wind god

Short Story Unit Test[309]   **Name** _____

Your responses should be as detailed as possible.

"Through the Tunnel"

1. Do you think Jerry acted wisely? Why or why not?

   [Students always fault Jerry for attempting a dangerous feat that could have killed him. In doing so, he risked his life.]

2. Explain why this is a rite of passage story.

   [The story dramatizes the way Jerry matures to a significant degree by preparing for his ordeal and overcoming his dependence on his overly nurturing mother, his physical limitations, and his fears about his self-imposed feat.]

3. How does the author use contrasted settings to convey boy's dilemma?

   [The author describes the crowded beach where the mother sits with warm colors that suggest safety. Lessing describes the bay where the French boys are swimming with ominous colors and diction that suggest wildness and danger. The two settings imply Jerry's need to overcome his mother's stifling influence and to achieve some measure of independence from her by accomplishing something dangerous.]

"A Christmas Memory"

4. Describe the personality of the boy's friend. Suggest both positive and negative traits.

   [The old woman's is old-fashioned, unmaterialistic, and somewhat senile. She is also generous, resourceful, and imaginative.]

5. What does the writer imply with the references to kites at the end of the story?

   [The kites symbolize the affection the old woman and Buddy felt for each other and the fun they shared throughout Buddy's childhood.]

"Thank you, M'am"

6. What is Roger's reaction to Mrs. Jones's kindness? Do you think the boy will change his behavior in future?

   [Roger has never met anyone who takes an interest in him as Mrs. Jones does. At some level, he realizes that this woman is attempting to instill in him decency and respect for others. Students are certain that Mrs. Jones teaches the boy lessons he will never forget.]

---

[309] Owing to the number of stories discussed in this teaching guide, I have included more questions than teachers will want to include on a unit test. They may want to select from the following questions.

Some questions on this test and subsequent tests could be included on semester exams.

There is a student booklet that accompanies this teaching guide. It contains all 9th grade review questions and tests with answers omitted.

7. Do you think Roger is a chronic thief? Why or why not?
    [Invariably, students do not think Roger is a habitual thief because he is naïve, obviously terrified of the woman as well as a possible jail sentence, and unfamiliar with the methods of hardened criminals. He is tempted to steal because he longs to own a particular type of shoe. He appears to be immediately sorry for trying to steal the woman's purse and terrified of Mrs. Jones. Apparently, he has never been taught the difference between right and wrong behavior.]

"Top Man"

8. Explain how the setting is the story's antagonist.
    [The author explicitly states that the mountain is the story's antagonist that pits itself, as it were, against the men who are attempting to reach its summit. It is a formidable opponent. The author describes it as an intimidating enemy that the men must conquer in order to reach the summit.]

9. What do you think Nace's axe symbolizes? Explain your opinion.
    [Some students decide that the axe symbolizes sacrifice, specifically Osborn's sacrificing the honor of getting to the top of K3 and giving that honor to Nace who made the ultimate sacrifice. Others think the axe symbolizes courage—the courage it took Nace to lead the expedition and Osborn to ascend to the top of K3. Still others state that the axe symbolizes selflessness, particularly Nace's exemplary selflessness.]

"Antaeus"

10. Explain the title's connection to this story.
    [The title alludes to the mythical giant who received his superhuman strength as long as he remained in contact with the earth. When Hercules learned the giant's secret, he lifted Antaeus off the ground and killed him. T. J. is a modern-day Antaeus because he too receives his emotional strength from the earth and is not content in an urban area.]

11. What is the role of the antagonist or antagonists in this story?
    [The businessmen who appear on the rooftop represent adult authority and the impossibility of T.J.'s dream of a roof garden. The men also clarify in our minds the hopelessness of T.J.'s dream of renewing his contact with the earth in an urban setting.]

"The Bridge"

12. Explain how this story conveys a rite of passage.
    [Kostya is excessively shy and immature. He dreads going far away to enroll in a technical school to train as a navigator. After he has rescued the girl, he acquires some self-confidence.]

13. Explain the connection between the title and the story that follows.
    [Kostya crosses a metaphorical bridge when he matures as a result of rescuing the girl. After that experience, he no longer feels insecure but achieves a new self-confidence.]

"The Cask of Amontillado"

14. As precisely as possible, state this story's setting.

    [Poe's story is set in the medieval period during the Spanish Inquisition in the vaults of an Italian city at carnival time.]

15. Explain what we can deduce about the person to whom the narrator is speaking? Name the narrator.

    [Montresor is probably speaking to a priest to whom he is confessing his crime having suffered decades of guilt for the grisly murder he committed.]

16. List at least four of the story's ironies.

    [Fortunato's name is obviously ironic.

    The murder ironically takes place during carnival time, a time of festivity and celebration.

    It is highly ironic that Fortunato walks to his death because of his pride in being a connoisseur of fine wine.

    Montresor tells Fortunato that he drinks to his victim's long life.

    When the murderer has shackled Fortunato to the wall, Montresor begs his victim to leave the crypt.

    The entire story is an extended example of dramatic irony because the reader knows, as the victim does not, that Fortunato is walking to his death.]

17. From what point of view is this story told? Why is this an effective perspective?

    [The perspective is first person. It is effective because the story is told by a madman, Montresor, who imagines that his friend Fortunato has offended him so severely that he murders his friend. This perspective allows Poe to create a bone-chilling horror story.]

"The Necklace"

18. Does the author appear to be critical only of Madame Loisel? Explain your opinion.

    [Most students realize that de Maupassant condemns the husband as well as the wife. Monsieur Loisel was overly indulgent and did nothing to curb his wife's selfishness and discontent. He corroborates in the deception over losing the necklace, and in part payment for a new diamond necklace, he sacrifices his honor and his reputation.]

19. Summarize some of the story's ironies.

    [Madame Loisel's discontent results in a lifestyle that is inferior to her previous lifestyle.

    Her discontent also leads to the deterioration of her husband's character.

    Because both husband and wife lack the integrity to tell Madame Forestier about the loss of the necklace, their lives are ruined.

    More than any other detail, the lost necklace is ironic. It represents prestige and luxury for Mme. Loisel but is, in fact, almost worthless.]

20. What do you think the necklace symbolizes?

    [Students invariably decide that the necklace symbolizes materialistic desires.]

"The Sniper"

21. Explain in as much detail as possible the setting of this story.

    [The story is set in Ireland in the 1920s during a civil war between Irish republicans who wanted Ireland to be free of British rule and become a republic and Irish nationalists who wanted only limited independence from Great Britain.]

22. How does the author gain our sympathy for the sniper?

    [The sniper is young and hungry; he is wounded, he painfully dresses his wound, and he attempts to ignore the pain.]

"The Open Window"

23. Supply two adjectives that define the personality of Mrs. Sappleton's niece.

    [Vera is self-possessed and imaginative.]

24. Why does the niece tell such an outrageous story to Mr. Nuttel?

    [She is bored by the visitor and tells the story to amuse herself.]

25. Why do we accept the fact that Mr. Nuttel believed the girl's inventive tale?

    [Mr. Nuttel is gullible.]

26. Identify the change in perspective at the end of the story. Why do you think the writer changes the perspective at this point?

    [The writer changes the perspective from third-person limited to third-person omniscient in order to allow the reader to know the reactions of other characters such as Mrs. Sappleton; the switch lets the reader fully appreciate the irony of the situation.]

"To Build a Fire"

27. What is the story's conflict?

    [The conflict involves man versus nature, in this case, the sub-zero temperature.]

28. Why does the author include a dog in this story?

    [He does so to indicate that animals have better instincts than men and are more likely to overcome danger and survive.]

29. List as many of the man's mistakes as possible.

    [Because he is a newcomer to the Yukon, he should not have traveled alone.

    He should have traveled on the main trail.

    He should have been far more aware of danger such as thin ice and frigid temperature.

    He should have built a fire in the open rather than under a snow-laden tree.]

"The Story-Teller"

30. What is the author criticizing in this story? What do you think about his criticism?

    [The author is criticizing conventional children's stories. Students realize that it is important to tell young children stories with a good moral; they also know that children dislike predictable moral tales, and they enjoy stories that are fun and unusual.]

31. Why do the children highly approve of the bachelor's story and disapprove of their aunt's ability as a storyteller?

    [The bachelor's story is entertaining and imaginative; the aunt's story is dull and predictable.]

32. What is the aunt's attitude to the bachelor's story?

    [The aunt is outraged by a story that she believes to be thoroughly inappropriate for young children.]

"The Ransom of Red Chief"

33. In some detail explain why this story is ironic.

    [The kidnappers are terrorized by their victim; they are "two desperate men" because they are only too anxious to get rid of him. Their victim doesn't want to return home, and nobody misses him. Mr. Dorset is reluctant to have his son returned to him; rather than receiving a ransom for the boy's return, the kidnappers must pay the father for his son's return.]

34. Describe the personality of "Red Chief."

    [The boy is fun-loving, mischievous, and imaginative.]

35. What moment do you think is the story's climax?

    [Students generally decide that the most climactic moment occurs when the kidnappers read Mr. Dorset's letter.]

36. How does O. Henry foreshadow the ending?

    [When the boy is first mentioned, he is throwing stones at a cat, behavior that indicates he is feisty and hardly a suitable kidnapping victim. He torments Bill with his Indian games and has the time of his life being kidnapped. When Sam reconnoiters the area, he realizes that no one is out looking for the boy. It quickly becomes apparent that "Red Chief" would much rather remain with his kidnappers than return home.]

"The Storm"

37. In your opinion, what probably happens after Janet runs out into the storm? Explain your opinion.

    [Students generally decide that the husband catches Janet and kills her because she realizes he is a murderer. He will be able to murder his wife without fear of spectators because there are no neighbors around during the storm and no passing cars or trains because the roads are flooded.]

38. In a short paragraph, explain how one of the stories we read has increased, to some degree, your understanding of life or human nature. Provide the title of the story in your response. Do not repeat information you have provided in your responses to other questions on this test.

    [Responses will vary. Students often discuss lessons they have learned in "Through the Tunnel," "To Build a Fire," "Top Man," or "The Bridge."]

Fahrenheit 451 Test   Name _____

Your responses should be specific and supported by details from the novel.

1. In as much detail as possible, explain why the firemen in Bradbury's fictitious world burn books.

   [The novel is science fiction. It is set at a future time in America when fire departments burn the property of book owners rather than saving burning homes and the people in them. Bradbury imagines that America is controlled by a totalitarian government. One way of accomplishing the agenda of such a government is to eradicate books and with them people's ability to think and evaluate. Bradbury infers that this is one way in which people can be subjected to the will of the state.]

2. What is the function of television screens in every home?

   [Television screens are placed in every home to function as entertainment in order to placate and control the masses and to broadcast government propaganda.]

3. When the fire department destroys a woman's books, the woman apparently quotes Bishop Latimer who is speaking to Bishop Ridley, both famous sixteenth-century English martyrs who wanted to spread the Protestant religion throughout England. Explain the significance of the quotation.

   [The woman undoubtedly hopes that her rejection of the government's determination to burn books will help to stop the destruction of knowledge in the world Bradbury describes.]

4. Clarisse is a foil for Mildred. In some detail, contrast the personalities and values of the two women.

   [Clarisse McClellan does not conform to the dictates of the despotic state; she enjoys life's simple pleasures. She is a thinker and a nonconformist, thus a treat to the totalitarian government that is attempting to eradicate intellectual life in this country. Montag's wife is Clarisse's foil because Mildred conforms to the dictates of the state. Unlike Clarisse, Mildred is deeply unhappy. She spends her time watching the mindless antics of her television family and swallowing drugs to induce a false sense of contentment.]

5. What does the fire chief attempt to tell Montag about books? Mention his name.

   [Captain Beatty attempts to persuade Montag that books are mere pieces of fiction that upset people. He suggests a false premise: It is best to remove books that create controversy and anxiety so that people will always be happy.]

6. What is Mildred's attitude to Montag's reading aloud to her?

   [Mildred is incapable of responding to the beauty of the books her husband reads to her. She has been indoctrinated by a totalitarian government. She cannot appreciate great literature or the value of absorbing the wisdom to be found in books.]

7. Faber tells Montag that books should have value and convey wisdom about life and that people should have the leisure to enjoy books. Identify Faber and his circumstances. Explain what you think about his criteria for books.

    [Faber is a retired English professor who went into exile many years earlier than the events described. Students understand that it's important that people read good books and that we have the opportunity to do so. Students realize that people should read rather than occupy their leisure hours watching mindless television shows and that books contain much wisdom that helps young people to mature into compassionate, knowledgeable adults.]

8. On the subway, Montag remembers being at the seaside as a child and trying to fill a sieve with sand. What is the point of this memory and why does he weep?

    [The futile attempt to fill a sieve with sand becomes Bradbury's metaphor for the loss of learning in the world he describes. Montag is overwhelmed with sadness at the loss of knowledge found in books.]

9. Why are Mildred's friends angry and distressed when Montag reads them Matthew Arnold's poem "Dover Beach"?

    [Because Mildred and her friends cannot relate to something beautiful, they cannot appreciate the poem and can only resort to anger and tears.]

10. Explain the point of Faber's allusion to the Antaeus myth.

    [According to the myth, the giant Antaeus retained his strength as long as his feet touched the earth. Learning the source of Antaeus's strength, Hercules lifted him from the ground and killed him. Alluding to the myth, Faber implies that books are indispensable to mankind's well-being just as the earth was indispensable to the well-being of Antaeus.]

11. Briefly describe Montag's last image of Mildred.

    [Montag imagines Mildred in a hotel room mindlessly watching the antics of her television family as he cries out to her to escape.]

12. Explain what Bradbury implies about censorship in this novel.

    [The novel alerts the reader to the dangers of censorship. Bradbury powerfully implies that everyone should have access to the free interchange of ideas, which is a constitutional right. The novel makes it clear that censorship, the lack of access to ideas and one's cultural roots, results in intellectual stagnation and incorrect notions about one's culture.]

Animal Farm **Test**   **Name** _____

Your responses should be specific and supported by details from the novel.

1. Explain how Orwell provides a version of society in miniature in the characters of farm animals such as Molly, Clover, and Boxer. Why does he do so?
   [The animals represent a cross-section of human nature. For instance, Mollie typifies the vain woman; Clover is the motherly type; and Boxer is the hard-working but dull-witted worker. In this way, Orwell conveys his concern that people in any community world-wide can be oppressed by tyrannical rulers.]

2. What is the function of Moses the raven? Why do the pigs allow the raven to remain at the farm?
   [The raven's talk of Sugarcandy Mountain gives the animals hope of happiness after they die, thus preventing their rebelling against the pigs; this is the reason why the pigs allow the raven to remain at the farm.]

3–7: In terms of Orwell's allegory of Russian history whom do the following characters represent?

3. Napoleon
   [Stalin, the Russian leader who replaced Lenin after Lenin's death]

4. Mr. Jones
   [Czar Nicholas II, the last emperor of Russia]

5. Old Major
   [Lenin, founder of the Communist Party who ruled Russia until his death]

6. Squealer
   [Stalin's propaganda agent]

7. the other farm animals
   [the proletariat or ordinary citizens]

8. Do you think the book has a hero or heroine? Explain.
   [Most students decide that the novel lacks a true hero because the reader feels little concern for any of the individual animals, and none of them stand out as particularly heroic, although we sympathize with hard-working Boxer more than the other characters. A few students decide that Boxer is the novel's hero because he constantly works hard and suffers an undeserved fate.]

9. How do the pigs control the other farm animals?

[The pigs remain in control by propaganda techniques. A revolutionary song, for instance, raises the farm animals' spirits and keeps them focused on their new life without human beings to subjugate them. Other propaganda techniques include the use of slogans, fear tactics, confessions extorted from alleged traitors, and the use of loaded diction.]

10. What is the significance of the pigs' decision to teach themselves, but not the other animals, to read and write?

[Orwell is suggesting that successful leaders must be literate, whereas the masses should remain illiterate and ignorant so that they can be kept in subjection.]

11. Why does Squealer tell the other animals that Boxer was driven to a hospitable?

[Squealer lies to the other animals about Boxer's being in hospital in order to allay the other animals' fears about Boxer's fate. If they had known the truth about Boxer, they may have realized that their situation was hopeless, and they may have rebelled against the pigs.]

12. At the banquet at the end of the novel, Napoleon announces several changes that will take place. Which is the most significant change and why it is so important?

[The most significant change occurs when the name of the farm is changed back to Manor Farm. This is most significant because it signifies that the animals' revolt against man was futile and their situation is ultimately unchanged.]

13. In the final scene, what transformation do the animals notice as they peer though the farmhouse windows? Why is this transformation significant?

[The animals realize that the neighboring farmers are indistinguishable from the pigs. The change conveys Orwell's fundamental irony because it signifies the fact that the animals' leaders have become identical to the tyrannical farmer they revolted against in the first place.]

14. This novel is filled with many instances of the animals' gullibility, and the pigs take advantage of this weakness in order to maintain control. What point is Orwell making about human behavior in the face of tyranny? What does Orwell suggest men should do in order to avoid becoming enslaved by tyrants?

[Orwell is pointing out that gullible men can become enslaved by tyrants because such men cannot evaluate their circumstances or resist tyranny. In avoid to avoid tyranny, people must be well-educated, able to think lucidly and assess their circumstances, so that they can live in a free society and enjoy the free interchange of ideas instead of becoming helpless victims of a totalitarian state.]

15. In your opinion, what is the novel's climax? Explain.

[Most students cite the ending when the neighboring farmers look and act just like the pigs. This final scene in which the farmers and the pigs socialize together brings into sharp focus Orwell's point that the animals have merely exchanged one despotic ruler for another.]

16. One film version changes the novel's ending to make it happy. Napoleon is expelled, and the animals live happily ever afterwards. Explain whether or not you think this is a better ending than the one Orwell provided.

[Students realize that a happy ending defeats Orwell's purpose. Orwell wrote the book to convey the evils of totalitarian governments that enslave people and make their lives miserable. To end with the animals living happily together would completely undermine this premise.]

Romeo and Juliet *Poetry Devices Test*   Name _____

Identify the poetry devices used in these passages. Choose from the following list, and use each term only ONCE:

**metaphor oxymoron allusion dramatic irony apostrophe
simile pun soliloquy personification foreshadowing**

1. When Juliet lies in a drug-induced coma, Lord Capulet describes his apparently dead daughter:

    Death lies on her like an untimely frost

    Upon the sweetest flower of all the field. _____ [simile]

2. When Mercutio suggests to his sad friend that Romeo should dance at the Capulets' party, Romeo replies,

    You have dancing shoes

    With nimble soles; I have a soul of lead

    So stakes me to the ground I cannot move. _____ [pun]

3. When the lovers say goodnight after their conversation in the Capulets' orchard, Juliet cries,

    Yet I should kill thee with much cherishing....

    Parting is such sweet sorrow.... _____ [oxymoron]

4. When a major character in a play makes a long speech that reveals his thoughts, that speech is called a/an _____ [soliloquy]

5. Juliet calls out to the night:

    Come, civil night.... _____   [apostrophe]

6. Having married Juliet, Romeo awakes at dawn and says,

    Night's candles are burnt out, and jocund day

    Stands tiptoe on the misty mountain tops. _____ [personification)]

7. After Romeo is banished from Verona, Lady Capulet finds Juliet crying and comments,

    Ever more weeping for your cousin's death? _____ [dramatic irony]

8. On his way to the Capulets' ball, Romeo comments,
    My mind misgives
    Some consequence yet hanging in the stars
    Shall bitterly begin his fearful date
    With this night's revels and expire the term
    Of a despisèd life, closed in my breast,
    By some vile forfeit of untimely death. _____ [foreshadowing]

9. After marrying Romeo, Juliet longs for the night so that she can be united with her
    husband:
    Gallop apace, you fiery-footed steeds,
    Towards Phoebus' lodging! Such a wagoner
    As Phaethon would whip you to the west
    And bring in cloudy night immediately. _____ [allusion]

10. Underneath Juliet's balcony, Romeo cries,
    What light through yonder window breaks?
    It is the East, and Juliet is the sun!   _____ [metaphor]

Romeo and Juliet Test   Name _____

Your responses should be as detailed as possible.

1. Occasionally, Shakespeare uses rhyming couplets or prose in his dramas, but what <u>main</u> poetic form does he use in this play and all his dramas?
   [blank verse or iambic pentameter]

2. What is meant by "the Wooden O"?
   ["The Wooden O" refers to the Globe Theater in London where Shakespeare's plays were performed.]

3. Why are Romeo and Juliet called "star-crossed lovers"?
   [Shakespeare's audience believed that the position of the stars at the lovers' births determined that both young people were fated to die tragically.]

4. Although Rosaline never appears, what purpose does she serve by being a character in the play?
   [At the beginning of the play, Romeo is deeply in love with Rosaline but falls in love with Juliet as soon as he meets her. The sudden shift in his affections conveys Romeo's immaturity.]

5. Why would you be glad to have a friend like Benvolio? Explain your response.
   [All students want a close friend like Benvolio whose very name means "good will." Benvolio is sensible and loyal. When Romeo is sunk in dejection over his unrequited love for Rosaline, Benvolio advises his friend to admire other girls. When Romeo kills Tybalt, Benvolio urges Romeo to escape from Verona in order to escape death. As he explains the tragedy to Prince Escalus, Benvolio attempts to lessen Romeo's involvement in the sword fight.]

6. Most of the time, the two lovers act impulsively and unwisely. Pretend you are Romeo (boys) or Juliet (girls). List several things you would have done differently if you were faced with his or her situation. Answer this question in one full paragraph.
   [Students make some of the following points:

   Romeo
   I would not have abandoned my love for another girl so hastily.
   I would have gotten to know Juliet over a lengthy period of time. I would certainly not have decided to marry her shortly after I had met her.
   I would have thought deeply about the consequences of marrying a Capulet, a family my parents hated.
   I would not have asked the Friar to marry us without informing my parents about my marriage plans.
   I would not have placed myself in grave danger by attempting to prevent the sword fight between Mercutio and Tybalt, an action that led to Mercutio's death.

I would have born the news about my exile with more forbearance, and I would not have attempted to kill myself.

When I arrived at Juliet's grave, I would have resisted my impulse to kill the Count.

I would not have drunk poison and killed myself.

Juliet

I would have gotten to know Romeo over a lengthy period of time. I would have attempted more diligently to postpone marriage to Romeo rather than agree to marriage shortly after I had met him.

I would have told my parents of my love for a member of the detested Montague family and my desire to marry Romeo.

I would not have agreed to Friar's Lawrence's plan that I should swallow a drug causing me to lose consciousness for several days.

I would have taken time to consider my parents' suggestion that I marry the Count.

I would not have stabbed myself when I saw Romeo lying dead beside me in my family's crypt.]

7. Explain why the Friar's reason for marrying the lovers is ironic.
[The Friar believes that he will end the respective parents' feud by marrying Romeo and Juliet. However, the feud is ended only with their beloved children's deaths.]

8. Mention one or two instances of comic relief in this tragic story.
[Students usually suggest that the following aspects of the play add brief humor:
Mercutio's amusing dialogue, the talkative Nurse, and servants frenziedly preparing for the Capulets' ball.]

9. Explain the difference between Romeo and Mercutio's attitudes to love.
[Romeo has a romantic attitude to love. At the beginning of the play, he pines for the affections of a lady who is indifferent to him, but on meeting Juliet, he immediately falls in love with her. Mercutio adopts a frivolous attitude to love; he is realistic and would not waste time courting a lady who is unresponsive to his advances. Mercutio thinks that lovers are foolish.]

10. Explain in detail why both lovers' closest confidants are, in fact, very poor friends.
[The Nurse conspires with Juliet in arranging to marry Romeo and does not inform Juliet's parents of their daughter's marriage plans. Knowing Juliet is already married, the Nurse encourages Juliet to commit bigamy by marrying the Count.
Neither does the Friar inform either set of parents about the young people's hastily arranged marriage plans. He agrees to marry the couple without their parents' knowledge or consent. When he finds that Juliet has woken up in the Capulets' crypt, he fails to persuade Juliet to accompany him and leaves her behind, although he probably suspects that she will commit suicide.]

11. List ways in which Romeo and Juliet's personalities differ radically.
[Romeo is a rash, impractical romantic.
He is also undisciplined.

He proposes marriage to Juliet just after meeting her in spite of Juliet's being a Capulet.
When he hears that he is exiled, he grovels on the ground and threatens to commit suicide.
Juliet is more sensible and practical.
She is concerned about Romeo's safety when he scales the wall to enter the Capulets' orchard.
She is hesitant to marry Romeo so soon after they have met.
She is reluctant to swallow the Friar's sleeping potion.]

12. Why do you think Shakespeare gave Juliet another suitor? Suggest a logical reason or reasons for his being a character in the play.

[Shakespeare includes Count Paris in the play mainly as a complication for the lovers. The Count's gaining the Capulets' consent to be Juliet's suitor also suggests that Juliet's parents truly care for their only child and want her to marry a responsible man whom she can love. Therefore, we realize that Juliet's parents are not stage villains but realistically portrayed human beings.]

13. Provide a reason why the following idea is a major theme in this play: A world that is full of hatred can ruin people's lives.

[The long-standing feud between the Capulets and Montagues results in Lady Montague's death caused by grief at her son's exile; the untimely deaths of Tybalt, Mercutio, and Paris; as well as the deaths by suicide of the parents' most precious possessions, their children.]

14. Do you think it was primarily coincidence OR human error that caused the lovers' deaths? Refer in detail to the play to support your opinion about <u>one</u> of these topics. Supply a detailed list of points.

[**coincidence**

Some students decide that coincidence primarily caused the tragedy and make the following points:

Romeo finds out by chance that Rosaline will attend the Capulets' party and meets Juliet there.
Lord Capulet decides to advance Juliet's wedding to Count Paris by one day. This change of date ensures that Juliet will still be in a coma in the Capulets' crypt; when he arrives there, Romeo will assume Juliet is dead.
Although Mantua is celebrating a holiday and the chemist's shop is closed, the chemist happens to pass by his shop just as Romeo arrives there.
Friar John happens to stay at a house in Mantua that is closed up because plague victims are housed there, so Friar John cannot get his letter regarding Friar Laurence's plan to Romeo.
Friar Laurence arrives just after Romeo drinks poison; the Count's servant arrives just after Juliet stabs herself. Were it not for both coincidences, both lovers' deaths may have been prevented.

human error

Other students think the lovers' tragic deaths were primarily caused by human error and make these points:

Prince Escalus fails to end the feud.
Tybalt does not control his emotions and kills Mercutio.

Foolishly avenging Mercutio's death, Romeo kills Tybalt.

Romeo is far too rash when he instantly abandons his love for Rosaline on meeting Juliet.

Having just met Juliet, he decides to marry her and carries out those plans without further reflection.

Although she is briefly hesitant, Juliet agrees to marry Romeo whom she has only just met.

Both lovers marry without their respective parents' knowledge or permission.

Neither the Nurse nor the Friar, the lovers' close friends, give the lovers wise counsel.

Both the Nurse and the Friar should have told the parents about their children's marriage plans instead of colluding in those plans and, in the Friar's case, performing the marriage.

On hearing that their daughter will not marry the Count, Juliet's father verbally abuses her, and both parents disown her.]

15–25: Identify the following passages as examples of these terms:

pun, allusion, metaphor, personification, simile

You will need to use each term <u>at least once</u> and, in some cases, <u>more than once</u>.

15. Romeo to Juliet's apparent corpse:

      Shall I believe

That unsubstantial Death is amorous,

And that the lean abhorrèd monster keeps

Thee here in dark to be his paramour? _____ [personification]

16. Romeo:

Love goes toward love as schoolboys from their books. _____ [simile]

17. Romeo:

Give me a torch. I am not for this ambling.

Being but heavy I will bear the light. _____ [pun]

18. Friar:

The gray-eyed morn smiles on the frowning night. _____ [personification]

19. Juliet:

I would tear the cave where Echo lies. _____ [allusion]

20. Juliet to Romeo:

This love

May prove a beauteous flower when next we meet. _____ [metaphor]

21. Mercutio:

Ask for me tomorrow, and you shall find me a grave man. _____

[pun]

22. Nurse (referring to the Count then Romeo):

I think it best you married with the county.

O, he's a lovely gentleman!

Romeo's a dishclout [dishcloth] to him. _____ [metaphor]

23. Romeo:

It seems she hangs upon the cheek of night

As a rich jewel in an Ethiopian's ear. _____ [simile]

24. Lord Capulet:

. . . well appareled April on the heel

Of limping winter treads. _____ [personification]

25. Romeo:

O, speak again, bright angel, for thou art

As glorious to this night…

As is a wingèd messenger of heaven. _____ [simile]

the Odyssey Test   Name _____

Your responses should be as detailed as possible.

1. What is Odysseus's most outstanding character trait? In a full paragraph, describe one occasion when this trait is particularly evident.
    [Odysseus is chiefly known for his resourcefulness. He demonstrates this trait when he escapes with his men from Polyphemus's cave. In answer to the Cyclops's questions, Odysseus tells him that his ship has been destroyed on the rocks and that his name is "Nobody." The hero gives the monstrous giant wine to drink, and while the Cyclops sleeps, he drives a red-hot pointed pole into the Cyclops's eye. When the blinded creature calls out to other Cyclopes that "Nobody" has hurt him; the Cyclopes who live nearby think that no one has wounded Polyphemus and fail to help him. Odysseus ties three rams together then ties each of his men under the belly of the middle ram. He himself hangs underneath the belly of the largest ram. In the morning, the hero and his men escape as Polyphemus drives his sheep out of the cave.]

2 – 8. Briefly identify these characters:

2. Menelaus
    [King of Sparta; husband of Helen and brother of Agamemnon]

3. Scylla
    [a female monster with six heads that devours sailors as they pass by her]

4. Hermes
    [the messenger god]

5. Nestor
    [the wise king of Pylos]

6. Anticleia
    [mother of Odysseus]

7. Charybdis
    [a female monster who creates a whirlpool that sucks men into her orbit so that they drown]

8. Circe
    [a witch-goddess who turns men into swine]

9. Complete this sentence by supplying two names:

_____ sends the hero to Hades in order to hear from _____ who will relate what will happen to him in the future.
[Circe; Teiresias]

10. Although Odysseus is an epic hero, he is prone to error. Mention one example of a serious mistake he makes and explain his error.
[After Odysseus escapes from Polyphemus's cave, his hubris gets the better of him. He brags to the Cyclops that it was Odysseus who blinded the giant before escaping from the creature's cave. Polyphemus is so enraged that he uproots the top of a hill and throws it at Odysseus's ship sending the ship back to shore. All the men could have drowned or they could have been devoured by the Cyclops.]

11. Disguise is a motif many writers employ. Mention <u>two</u> instances of disguise in the *Odyssey*.
[Athena is disguised as an old family friend called Mentor when she counsels Telemachus about finding his father. The king of Ithaca returns to his kingdom disguised as a beggar.]

12 – 13: Describe the following creatures that Odysseus meets during his voyage home:

12. the Lotus Eaters
[The Lotus Eaters live on an island covered in lotus flowers, which they eat. The delicious flower produces feelings of lethargy and absent-mindedness so that men who arrive on the island and eat the flower lose all desire to leave the Lotus Eaters and return home.]

13. the Sirens
[The Sirens are lovely sea nymphs who lure men to their deaths by their irresistible singing. Sailors steer their ships towards the Sirens and are shipwrecked on the rocks around the Sirens' island and drown.]

14. How does Odysseus satisfy his renowned curiosity about the Lotus Eaters and the Sirens, and how does he escape from both of those dangers?
[Odysseus satisfies his curiosity and learns about the Lotus Eaters by allowing three sailors to venture onto the Lotus Eaters' island and eat the lotus plant until he forces them to return to the ship and ties them to their rowing benches. Odysseus plugs his sailors' ears so that they won't be lured by the Sirens' singing, and he satisfies his own curiosity about their singing by having his men lash him to the ship's mast so that he can listen with impunity. He and his men are thus able to escape from the Sirens' enticing voices.]

15 – 17: Define the following words that are derived from the epic:

15. a mentor
[a wise counselor]

16. a muse

    [the person or power that inspires someone]

17. an odyssey

    [a long, difficult journey in search of something]

18. Summarize what you have learned about ancient Greeks' attitude to hospitality.

    [Ancient Greeks placed great value on hospitality. For instance, Nestor feeds his guests before inquiring into their business; Alcinous, king of Phaeacia, provides a feast for Odysseus and a ship for his journey home; Penelope is hospitable to the stranger who arrives at Ithaca and insists that he be allowed to compete in the test of the Great Bow.]

19. Give a valid reason for Homer's including the Argos incident. Identify Argos.

    [Odysseus's reunion with his mistreated dog Argos implies the wretched state of Ithaca at the king's return. During Odysseus's absence, the kingdom has become disorderly and neglected.]

20. What was the importance of the gods in Homer's time?

    [The ancient Greeks prayed to and obeyed their gods. They believed that no man could disobey the gods with impunity.]

21. How does Telemachus mature during the course of the *Odyssey*?

    [At the beginning of the epic, Telemachus is immature and insecure. He is unable to deal with the suitors that harass his mother. By the end of the epic, he is confident and helps his father secure order in Ithaca.]

22 – 23: Mention two examples of dramatic irony in this epic.

    [When Odysseus returns home, his servant the swineherd joyfully greets Telemachus like a long-lost son while Odysseus, the real father, watches the reunion.

    Penelope talks to the beggar and does not definitively recognize his being her husband until she orders Eurycleia to move their marriage bed.]

24. Summarize how Odysseus restores order to his kingdom.

    [Odysseus returns to Ithaca in disguise. He tells his son to remove the suitors' weapons from the great hall. After winning the contest of the Great Bow, he enlists the help of his son and kills the suitors' ringleader, Antinous, before killing the rest of the suitors. He then hangs the immoral maids after they have cleaned the hall.]

25. Works of literature are considered to be classic if they are relevant to all cultures and time periods. List some reasons why people throughout the world continue to read Homer's epic.

[Students usually make some of these points:

The *Odyssey* conveys significant lessons about courage and perseverance.

It also tells us what it means to be human—to be curious and to brag about our exploits, for instance.

It emphasizes the value of one's home and loved ones.

It stresses the importance of hospitality.

It emphasizes the need to be courteous to people in all classes of society.

Most important, Homer's epic is a great story.]

Poetry Unit Test   Name _____

Imagery

1 – 5: Images appeal to one or more of our senses. Identify the sense—hearing, sight, touch, taste, or smell—that the following passages appeal to:

1. A narrow Fellow in the Grass
    Occasionally rides
    You may have met Him—did you not
    His notice sudden is….
    (from "A narrow Fellow in the Grass," Emily Dickinson)
    [sight]

2. Beat! Beat! Drums! —blow! bugles! blow!
    Over the traffic of cities—over the rumble
    of wheels in the streets….
    (from "Beat! Beat! Drums!" Walt Whitman)
    [hearing]

3. The sun that brief December day
    Rose cheerless over hills of gray….
    (from *Snow-Bound*, John Greenleaf Whittier)
    [sight]

4. When all aloud the wind doth blow
    And coughing drowns the parson's saw [voice]
    When roasted crabs [crabapples] hiss in the bowl,
    Then nightly sings the staring owl….
    (from *Love's Labor's Lost*, Shakespeare)
    [hearing]

5. Upon her hearthstone a great fire blazing
    Scented the farthest shores with cedar smoke
    And smoke of thyme….
    (from the *Odyssey*, Homer)
    [smell]

Personification

6 – 9: Name who or what is personified in the following lines. Then underline the words that convey the personification:

6. A <u>wrinkled</u>, <u>crabbed man</u> they picture <u>thee</u>,
    <u>Old Winter</u>, with <u>a rugged beard</u> as gray
    As the long moss upon the apple tree;
    <u>Blue lipped</u>, an ice drop at <u>thy sharp blue nose</u>….
    (from "A wrinkled, crabbed man they picture thee," Robert Southey)
    [winter]

7. Blow, blow, <u>thou</u> winter <u>wind</u>.
    <u>Thou art not so unkind</u>
    As man's ingratitude.
    <u>Thy tooth</u> is not so keen [sharp]
    Because <u>thou</u> art not seen,
    Although <u>thy breath</u> be rude [biting]….
    (from *As You Like* It, William Shakespeare)
    [wind]

8. The buzz-saw <u>snarled</u> and rattled in the yard
    And made dust and dropped stove-length sticks of wood….
    (from "Out, out—," Robert Frost)
    [a saw]

9. Beside the lake, beneath the trees,
    <u>Fluttering</u> and <u>dancing</u> in the breeze….
    Ten thousand saw I at a glance
    <u>Tossing their heads in sprightly dance.</u>
    (from "I wandered lonely as a cloud," William Wordsworth)
    [daffodils]

Simile and metaphor

10 – 14: Indicate whether the following lines contain a simile or metaphor. Then underline the words that convey the comparison:

10. The <u>Lord</u> is my <u>Shepherd</u>; I shall not want [lack anything].

    (from Psalm 23)

    [metaphor]

11. Bent double, like <u>old beggars under sacks</u>,

    Knock-kneed, coughing like <u>hags</u>, <u>we</u> trudged through sludge. .

    (from "Dulce et decorum est," Wilfred Owen)

    [simile]

12. I think that I shall never see

    A <u>poem</u> lovely as a <u>tree</u>. . ..

    Poems are made by fools like me,

    But only God can make a tree.

    (from "Trees," Joyce Kilmer)

    [simile]

13. The <u>Lightning</u> is <u>a yellow fork</u>

    from tables in the sky. . ..

    (from "The Lightning is a yellow fork," Emily Dickinson)

    [metaphor]

14. The <u>wind</u> was <u>a torrent of darkness</u> among the gusty trees,

    The <u>moon</u> was <u>a ghostly galleon</u> tossed among cloudy seas.

    (from "The Highwayman," Alfred Noyes)

    [metaphors]

Tone

15 – 17: With one adjective, identify the tone of the following lines:

15. If I were fierce, and bald, and short of breath,

    I'd live with scarlet Majors at the Base. . ..

    And when the war is done and youth stone dead,

    I'd toddle safely home and die—in bed.

    (from "Base Details," Siegfried Sassoon)

    [bitter]

16. Break, break, break,

    At the foot of thy crags, O Sea!

But the tender grace of a day that is dead
Will never come back to me.
(from "Break, break, break," Alfred, Lord Tennyson)
[heartbroken]

17. My heart is like a singing bird
Whose nest is in a water'd shoot;
My heart is like an apple tree
Whose boughs are bent with thick-set fruit…
My heart is gladder than all these
Because my love is come to me.
(from "A Birthday," Christina Rossetti)
[joyful]

18. We read one of Robert Frost's poems entitled "Out, out—" Explain how the title adds
to the meaning of the poem.
[Frost's title is an abbreviated quotation from Shakespeare's *Macbeth*. Having just heard about his
wife's death, Macbeth decides that life lacks meaning. In his poem, Frost appears to imply a similar
attitude to a world in which a young, hard-working boy is needlessly killed in a tragic accident.]

19. In one adjective, identify the tone or attitude to life expressed in Jacques's speech in
Shakespeare's play *As You Like It* that opens with these lines:
All the world's a stage,
And all the men and women merely players.
They have their exits and their entrances,
And one man in his time plays many parts,
His acts being seven ages….
[cynical]

20. Read this stanza from "The Bells" by Edgar Allan Poe:
Hear the sledges with the bells—
        Silver bells!
What a world of merriment their melody foretells!
        How they tinkle, tinkle, tinkle,
        In the icy air of night!
        While the stars that oversprinkle
        All the heavens, seem to twinkle
        With a crystalline delight;

Keeping time, time, time,

In a sort of Runic [mysterious] Rhyme,

To the tintinnabulation that so musically wells

From the bells, bells, bells, bells

Bells, bells, bells—

From the jingling and the tinkling of the bells.

Write out the words in Poe's poem that are onomatopoeic. You should list at least five words.
[tinkle, oversprinkle, twinkle, crystalline, tintinnabulation, jingling, tinkling]

21. What is the mood of "The Bells"?
[joyful]

22. What is the implied metaphor in the following lines by Emily Dickinson?

Have passed, I thought, a Whip Lash

Unbraiding in the Sun—

When, stooping to secure it,

It wrinkled, and was gone....
[Dickinson implies a comparison between a snake's movement and the lash of a whip.]

23 – 27: Choose one lyric poem we have read this year that taught you a valuable lesson or provided you with a new insight on life or human nature. In a half-page paragraph, explain in detail what you have learned by studying that particular poem.

[Answers will vary. Students often choose "Fifteen" by William Stafford, "Those Winter Sundays" by Robert Hayden, or "A Poison Tree" by William Blake.]

****

Psalm 23 is the finest poem ever penned:

The Lord is my Shepherd; I shall not want.

He maketh me to lie down in green pastures:

He restoreth my soul;

He leadeth me in the paths of righteousness

for His name's sake.

Yea, though I walk through the valley of the shadow of death,

I will fear no evil,

for Thou art with me;

Thy rod and thy staff

they comfort me.

Thou preparest a table before me

in the presence of my enemies;

Thou anointest my head with oil;

my cup overflows.

Surely goodness and mercy shall follow me

all the days of my life,

and I shall dwell in the house of the LORD

forever.

About the Author

Elizabeth McCallum Marlow, M.A., taught high school and College English for thirty-five years. She developed approaches that she found were effective in teaching teenagers to enjoy literature. This is the fourth and last in a series of high school textbooks on teaching literature that provides teachers with an experienced teacher's methodology. Elizabeth is co-author of *The Book Tree*, a reference guide that helps young people find books they enjoy and that cultivates a life-long habit of reading.

Printed in the United States
By Bookmasters